Korean Business Law

ELGAR KOREAN LAW

IN ASSOCIATION WITH THE LAW RESEARCH INSTITUTE OF SEOUL NATIONAL UNIVERSITY

Series editor: In Seop Chung, *Law Research Institute, Seoul National University, Korea*

In the dramatic transformation Korean society has experienced for the past 40 years, law has played a pivotal role. However, not much information about Korean law and the Korean legal system is readily available in English. The *Elgar Korean Law* series fills this gap by providing authoritative and in-depth knowledge on trade law and regulation, litigation, and law and society in Korea. The series will be an indispensable source of legal information and insight on Korean law for academics, students and practitioners.

Titles in the series include:

Litigation in Korea
Edited by Kuk Cho

Trade Law and Regulation in Korea
Edited by Seung Wha Chang and Won-Mog Choi

Korean Business Law
Edited by Hwa-Jin Kim

Korean Business Law

Edited by

Hwa-Jin Kim

Professor of Law, Seoul National University School of Law, South Korea

ELGAR KOREAN LAW

Edward Elgar

Cheltenham, UK • Northampton, MA, USA

Published by
Edward Elgar Publishing Limited
The Lypiatts
15 Lansdown Road
Cheltenham
Glos GL50 2JA
UK

Edward Elgar Publishing, Inc.
William Pratt House
9 Dewey Court
Northampton
Massachusetts 01060
USA

A catalogue record for this book
is available from the British Library

Library of Congress Control Number: 2012935323

MIX
Paper from
responsible sources
FSC® C018575
FSC
www.fsc.org

ISBN 978 1 78100 339 8

Typeset by Servis Filmsetting Ltd, Stockport, Cheshire
Printed and bound by MPG Books Group, UK

Contents

Contributors

Bernard S. Black is the Nicholas D. Chabraja Professor at Northwestern University School of Law and Professor of Finance at Kellogg School of Management. He received a B.A. from Princeton University, an M.A. in Physics from the University of California, Berkeley, and a J.D. from Stanford Law School. He was Professor of Law at Stanford Law School from 1998 to 2004.

Brian R. Cheffins is the S.J. Berwin Professor of Corporate Law at University of Cambridge Faculty of Law. He received B.A. in History and LL.B. degrees from University of Victoria, British Columbia, Canada, and an LL.M. from Cambridge University. Professor Cheffins also taught at Harvard and Stanford Law Schools.

Alice Z. Chen is an incoming associate at Davis Polk & Wardwell LLP. She received her J.D. *cum laude* from the University of Michigan Law School, and her B.A. *cum laude* from Columbia University.

Joseph Cho is General Counsel at Samsung Thales Co., Ltd. He received a B.A. from the University of Toronto, a J.D. from Osgoode Hall Law School of York University, and an LL.M. from the University of London.

Hee Jeu Kang is a partner in the Capital Markets Practice Group of Lee & Ko. He primarily practices in the areas of private equity and venture capital funds, M&As and securities. He received his LL.B. from Yonsei University, Master's degree in Law from Seoul National University, and LL.M. from Santa Clara University Law School.

Tony DongWook Kang is a partner of Bae, Kim & Lee, LLC and deals with international litigation and control disputes, including hostile takeovers and M&As. Mr Kang served as a judge for the Korean judiciary for twelve years before he joined his law firm. He received his LL.M. from Harvard Law School, and LL.B. *cum laude* from Seoul National University.

Hwa-Jin Kim is a Professor of Law at Seoul National University School of Law. He also has taught at Stanford, Michigan, and Tel Aviv Law

Schools. He received his Dr. Jur. *magna cum laude* from University of Munich, where he was an Adenauer Scholar, and an LL.M. from Harvard Law School.

Hyun Kim is an associate in the Capital Markets Practice Group of Lee & Ko. He primarily practices in the areas of private equity and venture capital funds, M&As and securities. He received his B.A. in Economics from Seoul National University.

Sang Gon Kim is a partner at Lee & Ko. He has concentrated on general corporate and business laws, focusing on mergers and acquisitions. He has worked on a wide variety of merger and acquisition transactions. He received his LL.M degree in 2001 from University of Minnesota Law School and received his LL.B degree from the Seoul National University in 1992.

Michael Klausner is the Nancy and Charles Munger Professor of Business and Professor of Law at Stanford Law School. Before joining the Stanford Law School faculty in 1997, he was a professor of law at New York University School of Law. Professor Klausner received a B.A. from University of Pennsylvania and an M.A. in Economics and a J.D. from Yale University.

Kyung Hwa Moon is a partner at Shin & Kim. Her main area of practice is structured financing including asset-backed securitization, banking, and project financing. She has participated in various domestic and cross-border asset-backed securitization transactions in Korea. She received her LL.B. from Seoul National University and an LL.M. from Stanford Law School.

Hyunjoo Oh is a partner in the Capital Markets Group at Lee & Ko. Her main area of practice is securities and derivative transactions, and regulatory compliance. She received her B.A. in International Relations from Seoul National University and LL.M. from Columbia Law School.

Sung-Joon Park is a partner at Shin & Kim. He received his LL.B. from Seoul National University, Master's degree in Law from Korea University, and LL.M. from Columbia Law School. His areas of practice include corporate governance and M&A.

A.C. Pritchard is the Frances and George Skestos Professor of Law at the University of Michigan Law School. He received his J.D. from the University of Virginia and his M.P.P. from the University of Chicago.

Hyeok-Joon Rho is an Associate Professor at Seoul National University School of Law. He received his Ph.D. in law from Seoul National

University. Before he joined the law faculty, he had worked as a senior associate lawyer of the Yulchon Law Firm and as a judge of the Seoul Southern District Court.

Eun Young Shin is a senior associate at Lee & Ko. She received an LL.B. and LL.M. from Seoul National University. Her areas of practice include corporate governance and M&A.

Preface

The Korean business and financial sectors continue to evolve rapidly in a dynamic and sophisticated way. Accordingly, the corresponding laws and regulations of such continue to adapt by promulgating new laws and creating precedents in an attempt to provide a fair and effective governance and market environment.

This book describes corporate and financial laws of Korea and analyzes current issues from academic and practical perspectives, providing a unique tool for understanding law, business and finance in Korea. The book provides commentaries from the most renowned scholars and professionals engaged in business and financial laws. The content of the book largely covers three major practice areas: corporate law, financial law, and mergers and acquisitions. Each area is covered thoroughly and provides a practical perspective in addition to political implications. The chapters explore such standard issues of Korean corporate law as director liability and minority shareholder protection from a comparative perspective, paying special attention to the dynamic practice area of mergers and acquisitions. They also cover the cutting-edge topics of Korean financial law, including private equity, structured finance and foreign financial institutions. Finally, the book provides a grand picture of the Korean business and financial sector that allows readers to compare and understand Korea's position in connection with the global advancement of business and financial law.

Some of the chapters of this book are shortened and updated versions of the articles previously appeared in the *Journal of Korean Law*. I thank the *Journal* for graciously giving its permission to reprint the articles. I also thank Heewon Ghim, Jung Kyu Wang and Seungwon Yoo for excellent assistance.

Hwa-Jin Kim
April 2012

General notice

Since its promulgation in 1962, Korean corporate law, which is a chapter of the Korean Commercial Code (KCC) has been developed under the influence of Continental European corporate law statutes, cases, and scholarly works. Until 1962, Korea used Japanese corporate law, which was a chapter of the Japanese Commercial Code (JCC). (Japanese corporate law was promulgated in 1899 adapting to the German corporate law and was completely revised after the Second World War in 1950 modeled after the U.S. Illinois Business Corporation Act of 1933.) However, Korean corporate law is undergoing significant changes, strongly influenced by that of the United States since 1997. The KCC (which is within the domain of the Korean Ministry of Justice) has been generally revised in 1984, 1995, 1998, 1999, 2001, 2009 and 2011. The recent general revision in 2011 will greatly modify Korean corporate law, and it is scheduled to be enforced on April 15, 2012.

Practically, the more important source of Korean corporate law used to be the Korean Securities and Exchange Act (KSEA), which was within the domain of the Korean Ministry of Finance and Economy. The KSEA was promulgated in 1962 and has been revised numerous times especially after 1997. However, the KSEA was repealed and partially replaced by the KCC and the Korean Financial Investment Services and Capital Markets Act (KCMA) on February 4, 2009. The stock company in Korea can exist as a private or as a public company such as a "Korea Exchange-listed company" or "KOSDAQ-listed company." In addition to the requirements of the KCC related to the corporate governance of private companies, public companies are also partially subject to provisions of the KCC and the KCMA which are generally not applicable to private companies.

In Korea, certain companies engaged in a specialized business (such as banking, securities, or insurance) will be subject to additional regulations and requirements in terms of corporate governance under the relevant laws, i.e., the Korean Banking Act, etc. Directors of financial institutions may be subject to a stricter liability regime.

Disclaimer: No part of this book should be construed as legal advice or opinion of the professional organizations with which some contributors to this book work. The contributors, editor and publisher are not responsible for any action taken by the reader on the basis of this book.

1. Directors' duties and liabilities in Korean companies

Hwa-Jin Kim and Sung-Joon Park

I. INTRODUCTION[1]

In order for the directors of a company to effectively carry out their duties, they need clear guidance on the scope of their fiduciary duties and liabilities. This is particularly true for contests and shifts in corporate control, where conflict of interests is most likely to occur. Duties imposed on directors also tend to be stricter in corporate control and restructuring transactions because greater shareholder value is at stake. However, laws on the rules of the board room, either at peace or "at war," in particular, and corporate governance, in general, are only in the early stage of development in Korea because no strong need was felt for legal norms governing the conduct of corporate directors and managers before the financial crisis of 1997, prior to which no single derivative suit had been filed in Korea. It could be said that the Korean history of a market for corporate control started only in April 1997, when a previous ceiling of 10 percent share ownership for public companies was abolished. This chapter describes the most important recent court cases in Korea, with special reference to corporate control and restructuring cases, in which the directors' liabilities and business judgment rule were discussed.

In a country where civil law-based, sophisticated mandatory rules are interpreted by conservative judges, can we expect the business judgment rule to shape and develop the liability of corporate directors?[2] The answer may be a surprising "yes" as far as Korea is concerned. While the current

---

[1] This chapter is a shortened and updated version of Hwa-Jin Kim, *Directors' Duties and Liabilities in Corporate Control and Restructuring Transactions: Recent Developments in Korea*, 7 Oxford University Comparative Law Forum 2 (2006).

[2] *Cf.* Katharina Pistor & Chenggang Xu, Fiduciary Duty in Transitional Civil Law Jurisdictions: Lessons from the Incomplete Law Theory (Working Paper, 2002). On the role of the judges in the development of the corporate law, *see* Brian Cheffins, Company Law 308–63 (1997).

Korean law on corporate directors' fiduciary duties is characterized by a hybrid of case law and statute, there is a trend toward refinement of applicable rules and principles through a gradual recognition of the business judgment rule[3] as it was developed in the United States. Korean courts have begun to apply those rules to corporate control and restructuring transactions, which are filed more frequently as the mergers and acquisitions market is growing fast.

Taken from a comparative corporate law perspective, the Korean case also proves to be interesting. Korea, a German civil law country, has been influenced greatly by Continental Europe. Since its promulgation in 1962, Korean corporate law in particular has been developed under the influence of Continental European corporate law statutes, cases, and scholarly works.[4] However, the cases in this article will show that Korea's system of corporate governance and financial markets is undergoing significant changes, strongly influenced by that of the United States. Korea could be a test case for the convergence thesis and also may be a good starting point for studying whether civil and common law systems can converge with each other through a globalizing market.[5]

II. DIRECTORS' FIDUCIARY DUTIES AND LIABILITIES IN KOREA

A. Legal Sources

The primary corporate entity in Korea is the stock company, which can exist as a private or as a public company such as a "Korea Exchange-listed

---

[3] According to the rule directors should not be held liable for honest mistakes in judgment that are made in good faith, after exercising reasonable care and within the scope of their managerial authority. *See generally* Robert C. Clark, Corporate Law 123–40 (1986); Henry R. Horsey, *The Duty of Care Component of the Delaware Business Judgment Rule*, 19 Del. J. Corp. L. 971 (1994).

[4] Until 1962, Korea used the Japanese corporate law, which was a chapter of the Japanese Commercial Code. Japanese corporate law in 1950 was modeled after the U.S. Illinois Business Corporation Act of 1933. Corporate law experts within the U.S. military occupation authorities were from the State of Illinois. *See* Mark D. West, The Puzzling Divergence of Corporate Law: Evidence and Explanations from Japan and the United States (Working Paper, 2000) (arguing that a likely explanation for the divergence between the corporate laws of Japan and the United States is the tendency of the Japanese system to rely on exogenous shocks to stimulate statutory change).

[5] *Cf.* Philip R. Wood, Comparative Financial Law 51 (1995) (characterizing Korea as a mixed Roman/common law jurisdiction).

company" or "KOSDAQ-listed company." In addition to the requirements of the Korean Commercial Code (KCC) related to the corporate governance of companies, public companies were also subject to provisions of the Korean Securities and Exchange Act (KSEA) before it was repealed and was partially replaced by the KCC and Korean Financial Investment Services and Capital Markets Act (KCMA) on 4 February 2009. Certain companies engaged in a specialized business (such as banking, securities, or insurance business, etc.) will be subject to additional regulations and requirements under the relevant laws.

In September of 1999, the Korean Committee on Corporate Governance adopted the Code of Best Practice for Corporate Governance, which was revised in early 2003. The code, however, remains as an informal guideline for the corporate governance of public companies. There is no "comply-or-explain" obligation[6] imposed on public companies in Korea.

B. Basic Rules

With respect to general duties and liabilities of directors to the company, the KCC provides that where a director (1) has acted in violation of any laws and regulations, or of the company's articles of incorporation or (2) has neglected to perform his or her duties, such director shall be jointly and severally liable for damages to the company resulting from such acts or omissions.[7] If any such act has been done in accordance with a resolution of the board, the directors who have assented to such resolution shall take the same liability, and the directors who have participated in such resolution and whose dissenting opinion has not been entered in the minutes shall be presumed to have assented to such resolution.[8] In addition, a director may also be held liable for damages to the company resulting from the lack of supervision or oversight of employees.

---

6 *See, e.g.*, Art. 161 Aktiengesetz (Germany).

7 Art. 399 Para. 1 KCC. The director's basic duty of care is provided in Art. 382 Para. 2 KCC that refers to Art. 681 (fiduciary duty in the agency relationship) Korean Civil Code. In practice, the duty of care shall require the directors of the following actions: duty of attention on the activities of the company; duty to attend meetings; duty to review corporate information and documents; duty to thoroughly discuss major policies and business issues; and duty to review all major filings with the regulatory agencies. *Cf.* NACD, Governance Policy Workbook 24 (2003).

8 Art. 399 Paras 2 and 3 KCC.

With respect to general duties and liabilities of directors to third parties, the KCC provides that directors may be held jointly and severally liable to third parties for any damages incurred by failure of such directors to perform their duties, either willfully or by gross negligence.[9] The KCC provides that if a director has obtained, or made a third party obtain, any pecuniary benefit by acting in breach of his duty and has thereby inflicted loss on the company, he/she will be deemed to have committed crimes of special misappropriation, and may be punished by imprisonment or a monetary fine.[10]

As directors are obliged to use utmost care when discharging their fiduciary duties,[11] statutory liability enforces a rather high standard of duties regardless of the fact that this liability is negligence-based.

The role of outside directors, i.e., non-executive directors, of a public company is recognized by the KCC[12] and the KCC requires that public companies maintain a minimum number of outside directors on their board. The number of outside directors of a public company, with certain

---

9 Art. 401 Para. 1 KCC.

10 Art. 622 Para. 1 KCC.

11 *See* Art. 382-3 KCC. The October 1998 amendments to the KCC included, *inter alia*, the concept of corporate directors' duty of loyalty, as well as other concepts such as the *de facto* director, cumulative voting, and shareholder proposal right. Although the concept of corporate directors' duty of loyalty had long been recognized by the Korean Supreme Court, the KCC did not clearly introduce the concept into the statute until the October 1998 amendments. Although Korean corporate law scholars' opinions are split, many of them regard the newly-introduced concept as importation of the U.S. concept of duty of loyalty.

A director may effectuate a transaction with the company for his own account or for an account of a third person only if he has obtained the approval of the board and can prove the fairness of the transaction. Art. 398 KCC. The KCC provides that a public company with total assets of 2 trillion Korean won or more at the end of the immediately preceding business year must obtain approval from the board for certain transactions between the public company and its largest shareholders (quite often a director), affiliates of the largest shareholder or affiliates of the public company. The public company must report specific matters in connection with such transactions to the first regular general shareholders' meeting held after such board approval. Art. 542-9 Paras. 3 and 4 KCC. The KCC provides that no director shall, without the approval of the board, effectuate for his own account or for the account of a third person any transaction which falls within the class of businesses of the company or become a director of any other company whose business purposes are the same as those of the company. Art. 397 Para. 1 KCC. In addition, a director who has a special interest in a certain matter will not have a voting right in the board resolution concerning such matter. Art. 391 Para. 3 and Art. 368 Para. 4 KCC.

12 Art. 317 Para. 2, No. 8, Art. 382 Para. 3 KCC.

exceptions, must be not less than one-fourth of its total number of directors.[13] Outside directors are generally subject to the same duties and potential liabilities as executive directors.[14]

The December 1999 amendments to the KCC introduced an audit committee.[15] This internal committee is not mandatory, and Korean companies may instead opt for the conventional statutory auditor. However, if they introduce the audit committee by charter provision, such a committee must have at least three directors, of which the number of outside directors must exceed two-thirds.[16] The audit committee is mandatory for certain large listed companies, banking institutions and certain large securities companies, securities investment trust companies, insurance companies, and merchant banks. The KCC requires certain large public companies to have at least one expert on accounting or finance in their audit committees.[17]

According to the leading scholarly opinions, the legal effect of the resolution made by a sub-committee of the board of directors is equivalent to the same by the entire board unless revoked by the entire board afterwards. Therefore, the liability of a member of the audit committee can potentially arise from a resolution of that committee. Also, the audit committee members are liable for the breach of their fiduciary duties based on the KCC provisions on the statutory auditor.[18] As the non-audit committee member directors are obliged to monitor the resolutions of the audit committee[19] and call the entire board meeting to revoke the resolution of the audit committee if needed, they will be held liable if they do not discharge such obligation to monitor and rectify.

---

13 Art. 542-8 Para. 1 KCC.

14 *See generally* Bernard S. Black, *The Core Fiduciary Duties of Outside Directors*, Asia Bus. L. Rev. 3 (July 2001).

15 *See* Art. 415-2 KCC. It also introduced shareholders' resolution by written statements, i.e., vote by mail, board meeting by audio-visual instruments, and stock options.

16 Art. 415-2 Para. 2 KCC.

17 Art. 542-11 Para. 2 No. 1 KCC. *Cf.* Mark Defond et al., Does the Market Value Financial Expertise on Audit Committees of Board of Directors? (Working Paper, Feb. 2004) (finding significantly positive CARs around the appointment of accounting financial experts to the audit committee, but not around the appointment of non-accounting financial experts or directors without financial expertise).

18 Art. 414 KCC.

19 *See* Chul Song Lee, Corporate Law 553 (20th ed., 2012) (Korean).

C. Directors' Liabilities and the KCMA

With respect to public companies, the KCMA provides that a director of a public company may be held liable to any party for any damages incurred as a result of the false or misleading statements in or material omissions from any public disclosure documents.[20] They have a due diligence defense.

The controversial Securities Class Action Act (SCAA) was passed by Korea's National Assembly in December of 2003 with the aim of providing a more effective means of relief for small investors while at the same time enhancing the transparency of corporate management. The SCAA came into effect on 1 January 2005, but for companies whose total assets, as of the end of the fiscal year immediately prior to 1 January 2005, amount to less than 2 trillion Korean won, certain damage claims were allowed by the SCAA after 1 January 2007.[21] Claims for damages under the SCAA are limited to the recovery of loss arising from false statements in the registration statements, business prospectuses, annual, semiannual and quarterly reports, insider trading, stock price manipulation, and faulty auditing.[22]

Modeled after the U.S. Sarbanes–Oxley Act of 2002,[23] the KCMA has introduced the CEO/CFO certification. The representative director or other relevant officers are obliged to confirm and sign the disclosure documents, including registration statements, annual, semi-annual and quarterly reports.[24]

---

20 Art. 125 Para. 1 KCMA.

21 For damages arising out of stock price manipulation, the law applies from 1 January 2005 regardless of the value of the company's assets. The securities class action is allowed if the following requirements are met: (1) the number of members in the harmed class is 50 persons or more; (2) the class collectively holds one ten-thousandth of the total outstanding shares of the defendant corporation; (3) major questions of law or fact are common to all members of the class; and (4) the class action suit is an appropriate and efficient method for the members in the class to exercise their rights or protect their interests. Art. 12 Para. 1 SCAA. The SCAA mandates that both the plaintiff and defendant appoint a legal counsel to represent them in the suit. Art. 5 Para. 1 SCAA.

22 Art. 3 SCAA.

23 Currently, the Sarbanes–Oxley Act applies to ten Korean firms listed on the NYSE and NASDAQ. *See* Hwa-Jin Kim, *Cross-Listing of Korean Companies on Foreign Exchanges: Law and Policy*, 3 J. Korean L. 1. (2003).

24 Art. 119 Para. 5, Art. 125 Para. 1 No.2 KCMA.

III. TWO LANDMARK CASES

A. The Samsung Electronics Case[25]

On 27 December 2001, the Suwon District Court held nine former and current directors of Samsung Electronics, the largest company in Korea, jointly and severally liable for 90.28 billion Korean won (approximately 70 million US dollars) for having neglected their duties.[26] On 20 November 2003, however, the Seoul High Court rejected some of the alleged breaches of duty and at the same time reduced the amount of damages. These landmark decisions show how Korean courts engage with the business judgment rule, on which the defendants had relied.

This was not a Supreme Court case. The impact of the decisions, however, was significant because of the amount of damages as well as the fact that it was rendered against the largest solvent company in Korea. We will now look at the most important legal issues raised by this case.

1. Acquisition of majority stake in a financially troubled affiliate firm

In early 1997, the directors of Samsung Electronics decided that their company would acquire a majority stake in Lechon Electric by purchasing existing shares from the then controlling shareholder, and by subscribing to newly-issued shares. Lechon Electric was in serious financial difficulties at the time when Samsung Electronics acquired their shares. Lechon Electric's financial conditions deteriorated further, and when it was all but bankrupt by the end of 1998, Samsung Electronics sold its stake in Lechon at a huge loss. Samsung Electronics' total losses resulting from the acquisition, including subsequent cash injections, totaled almost 200 billion Korean won.

In defending their decision to acquire, the directors argued that the Lechon Electric takeover was at the time beneficial to Samsung Electronics in three ways. First, Lechon Electric had an abundance of skilled engineers which Samsung Electronics lacked in an industry into which it was trying to expand. Second, by acquiring Lechon Electric's base of expertise, Samsung Electronics could drastically reduce its product development time. Third, the Lechon Electric purchase would ultimately allow

---

25 Case No. 98-Gahap-22553.

26 For the background of the district court's judgment, see Hasung Jang & Joongi Kim, *Nascent Stages of Corporate Governance in an Emerging Market: Regulatory Change, Shareholder Activism and Samsung Electronics*, 10 Corporate Governance: An International Review 94 (2002).

Samsung Electronics to substantially increase its overall market share in the industry.

The Suwon District Court rejected these assertions and their business judgment defense. The court ruled that, although there may have been several compelling reasons in favor of acquiring Lechon Electric, the directors had failed to analyze the risks of the acquisition, and hence their decision-making process was not prudent. The directors had decided to acquire Lechon Electric after reviewing a poorly-prepared report that had not been made available in advance of the board meeting, which lasted no longer than one hour.[27]

The court found the directors liable for 27.62 billion Korean won (a proportion directly relating to the acquisition itself, out of the approximately 200 billion Korean won of total losses) for neglecting to exercise the level of care required to decide whether a takeover of Lechon Electric was truly beneficial for Samsung Electronics. The court stated that the Samsung directors should have analyzed Lechon Electric's financial position more thoroughly, and should also have considered other options available to Samsung Electronics.

Reversing the district court's decision, the Seoul High Court found that the directors were not negligent in performing their fiduciary duties owed to Samsung Electronics and, thus, were not liable to pay damages to the company. The court stated that the director of a company has the discretion to make a business judgment to the extent such judgment is made in compliance with the laws and regulations and the articles of incorporation of the company. Furthermore, the court stated that the management of a company necessarily involves taking a certain degree of risk, and therefore, as long as the directors have diligently and reasonably performed their duties, they should not be liable to the company for any adverse consequences of their business judgment, unless self-dealing was involved. The court found that when the directors decided on the acquisition of Lechon Electric or other related matters, they made a reasonable decision within the scope allowed for them to make a business judgment.

2. Losses for payment guarantee

In June of 1998, after Lechon Electric's financial position became increasingly serious, Samsung Electronics' directors decided to guarantee Lechon Electric's debt payments and provide Lechon Electric with 170.9 billion

---

[27] *Cf.* Smith v. Van Gorkom, 488 A. 2d 858 (Del. 1985); Lynn A. Stout, *In Praise of Procedure: An Economic and Behavioral Defense of* Smith v. Van Gorkom *and the Business Judgment Rule*, 96 Nw. U. L. Rev. 675 (2002).

Korean won in the form of a new share purchase in order to prevent Samsung Electronics' guarantee from being called in. The directors' decision was based on the fact that, had they not done so, Samsung Electronics would have been blacklisted by its own creditor banks as a dangerous credit risk, since it was the controlling shareholder of a subsidiary that would have defaulted in loan repayments.

The Suwon District Court absolved the directors of any liability for their subsequent decision to guarantee Lechon Electric's debt payments and purchase its new shares, despite the fact that this subsequent decision was the direct result of the initial decision, for which they were held liable. The court found that the directors had exercised reasonable care in making their subsequent decision to guarantee Lechon Electric's payments and purchase its new shares and thus, the directors' subsequent decision can be protected "as a business judgment."[28]

The Seoul High Court affirmed the district court's finding.

3. Sale of shares at below market price

On 17 December 1994 the directors decided to sell 20 million shares of Samsung General Chemicals (SGC) to two other Samsung Group affiliates. Although the selling price of the shares was 2600 Korean won per share, their market value was estimated to be around 5733 Korean won per share. In addition, Samsung Electronics had originally purchased the shares over the course of six years (between July of 1988 and April of 1994) at the price of 10000 Korean won per share.

The directors argued that the 2600 Korean won per share was justifiable, given that it was calculated on the basis of a reputable accounting firm's share appraisal report and in accordance with a formula prescribed by the Inheritance Tax and Gift Tax Act. The Suwon District Court noted that the formula prescribed by the Inheritance Tax and Gift Tax Act was one of several ways in which the directors could have calculated the share price and that a more accurate method should have been chosen after reviewing every available method.[29] The actual share price could not be readily quantified, since the shares were not listed on any exchange, but the court listed several other factors which, in totality, led to the directors' liability.

---

28 Note that the court does not use the term "business judgment rule" here. In another case, the Supreme Court talks about "business judgment" that could potentially release the bank managers from liabilities arising out of the bankruptcy of debtors. See 2001-Da-52407, 14 June 2002.

29 *Cf.* Weinberger v. UOP, Inc., 457 A. 2d 701 (Del. 1983); Note, *Using Capital Cash Flows to Value Dissenters' Shares in Appraisal Proceedings*, 111 Harv. L. Rev. 2099 (1998).

These factors were as follows: (1) the directors' decision to sell the shares was made in a very short time and it caused Samsung Electronics to lose its majority stake in SGC; (2) between July of 1988 and April of 1994 Samsung Electronics had consistently purchased the shares at the price of 10000 Korean won per share; and (3) in June of 1993, Hansol Paper, an affiliate in Samsung Group, sold its holding of SGC shares to another affiliate of Samsung Group at the price of 6600 Korean won per share and SGC's profitability had improved since then.

The directors submitted two other arguments in their defense, namely that the proceeds of sale were sorely needed for investment purposes and that they were protecting Samsung Electronics from possible anti-trust prosecution. The Suwon District Court rejected these arguments and held the directors to be jointly and severally liable for a total of 62.66 billion Korean won, as the difference between the price for which the court felt Samsung Electronics should have sold the shares less the price for which they were actually sold. The court stated again that the directors' decision cannot be protected as a business judgment, partly because the decision was made in a meeting that lasted for only one hour.

The Seoul High Court also stated that the directors failed to demonstrate any cause that might have justified the sale of the shares at such a low price. Consequently, the court found that the directors who had voted for the resolution to sell the shares had failed to perform their duties diligently.

Although the Seoul High Court agreed with the district court that Samsung Electronics suffered a loss of 62.66 billion Korean won from the sale of the shares, it opined that the directors' liability should be limited. According to the court it would be proper for the company and the directors to fairly apportion the loss suffered by the company in connection with the directors' performance of their duties, in light of such factors as the type and size of business in which the company was engaged, the performance of the directors, and other circumstances. In this case, under the circumstances, the court viewed that it would be proper to limit the liability of the directors to 12 billion Korean won, approximately 20 percent of the loss suffered by Samsung Electronics.[30]

4. Criminal act and the business judgment rule

Another issue considered by the Suwon District Court concerned a series of payments in the aggregate amount of 7.5 billion Korean won made

---

30 Since there was no statutory basis for this part of the decision, it almost looks like a judgment based upon equity, which represents a peculiarity of the Anglo-American judicial system.

between March of 1988 and August of 1992 to the then president of Korea. The chairman of Samsung Group, who was a director of Samsung Electronics, allegedly ordered them to be paid on behalf of Samsung Electronics.

In his defense, chairman of Samsung Group argued that the payments were made to enhance Samsung Electronics' business development and were well within the amounts normally allowed by Samsung Electronics' established internal accounting regulations. In addition, he argued that such amounts were approved by Samsung Electronics' shareholders as part of the financial statements presented to them at their annual general meetings.

The Suwon District Court noted that bribery is a crime, and that a director who commits criminal acts cannot be regarded as acting reasonably and in the best interests of any company. In other words, the court refused to protect a director's criminal act under the business judgment rule. Consequently, the defendant was ordered to repay the full amount. The Seoul High Court basically affirmed the district court's view and ordered the repayment of 7 billion Korean won, excluding the portion for which the statute of limitation had elapsed.

5. Implications

The court's ruling marks a potential turning point in the way in which corporate governance will be conducted in the future. The Seoul High Court's decision has been confirmed by the Supreme Court,[31] and directors are no longer safe to make blind decisions (often based solely on the whims of the chairman of a conglomerate) without exercising their reasonable judgment.

The courts discussed the directors' fiduciary duties and business judgment (rule) in this case. However, this case may have to be analyzed as a self-dealing case. In this case, transactions between affiliated companies essentially resulted in the transfer of value from a more successful affiliate to a less successful one, obviously to benefit the less successful company.[32] The District Court should then have focused its discussion on the directors' duty of care and negligence in an attempt to let the plaintiff prevail without having to prove all the elements of a wrongful self-dealing transaction as is quite often the case in the United States.[33] It should be noted,

---

31 Case No. 2003-Da-69638, 28 October 2005. Both parties appealed. However, it has been reported that the directors paid the damages in full to the company in December of 2003 and January of 2004.

32 *See* Black, *supra* note 14, at 4.

33 *See* Clark, *supra* note 3 at 126–8.

though, that the High Court stated that this was not a case of self-dealing, and then granted the defendant directors the protection afforded by the business judgment rule.

Another issue to be noted is that outside directors were not sued even where this would have been possible. Also, those directors who were absent in the relevant meeting were held not liable because they did not know, and were not able to know, of decisions the board would take at those meetings.[34]

B. The Korea First Bank Case[35]

On 15 March 2002, the Korean Supreme Court held four former directors of the Korea First Bank (KFB) jointly and severally liable for 1 billion Korean won (approximately 800 000 US dollars) for breaching their duties as directors. According to this landmark ruling, directors of banks and other financial institutions must conform to higher standards of fiduciary duties than directors of other companies. To the author's best knowledge, this was the first case of derivative litigation in Korea.[36] Although the KCC promulgated shareholders' derivative action in 1962, not a single derivative action had been filed until this case.[37]

1. Background

Between November of 1993 and January of 1997, the directors of KFB decided to grant several loans to Hanbo Steel without obtaining any collateral security. Hanbo Steel was already in serious financial difficulties when KFB provided its first loan, and in early 1997 it defaulted on the loans, which totaled approximately 1.08 trillion Korean won

---

34 It is said that many outside directors of Korean companies are tempted to avoid board meetings dealing with sensitive agenda. *Cf.* Barnes v. Andrews, 298 F. Suppl. 614 (S.D.N.Y. 1924).

35 Case No. 2000-Da-9086. *Cf.* Woo Yun Kang Jeong & Han, Courts Apply Higher Standards to Directors of Banks (International Law Office Newsletter, 29 April 2002).

36 On 22 August 2003, the Seoul High Court held that the shareholders of a corporation have standing to file a double derivative action on behalf of one of the corporation's subsidiaries against the subsidiary's directors even when they possess no shares therein. Case No. 2002-Na-13746. *Cf.* David W. Locascio, *The Dilemma of Double Derivative Suits*, 83 Nw. U. L. Rev. 729 (1989).

37 For a good description of the Japanese situation, see Shiro Kawashima & Susumu Sakurai, *Shareholder Derivative Litigation in Japan: Law, Practice, and Suggested Reforms*, 33 Stan. J. Int'l L. 9 (1997); (2001); Mark D. West, *Why Shareholders Sue: Evidence from Japan*, 30 J. Leg. Stud. 351 (2002).

(approximately 830 million US dollars). By the end of 1997, Hanbo Steel still had not repaid any of the outstanding amounts, prompting KFB to sell the non-performing loans to the Korea Asset Management Corporation at a heavily discounted price, resulting in losses of nearly 270 billion Korean won (approximately 208 million US dollars), excluding interest. After defaulting, Hanbo Steel underwent corporate restructuring.

In April 1998, the minority shareholders of KFB filed a derivative suit on KFB's behalf at the Seoul District Court. The shareholders claimed 40 billion Korean won (approximately 30 million US dollars) against the former directors of KFB for breaching their fiduciary duties under the KCC.

2. Decision

The directors argued that their decision to grant the unsecured loans fell within the scope of the business judgment (rule).

The Seoul District Court rejected this defense and ruled that the directors had breached their fiduciary duties in failing to: (1) properly analyze the risks of default; (2) secure the loans with adequate collateral; (3) properly manage the loans after granting them; (4) monitor changes in Hanbo Steel's business plans; and (5) prevent employees from forging inspection reports relating to Hanbo Steel's loan qualification (in fact, it turned out that some of the directors had ordered the employees to do this).

The court's focus was not on the correctness of the decision to grant the loans, but rather on the decision-making process occurring before, during and after the decision had been taken. Initially, the directors were held liable for the entire loss to KFB of 270 billion Korean won (approximately 208 million US dollars). However, the court went on to recognize only the extent of the minority shareholders' claim of 40 billion Korean won.

The Seoul High Court rejected the directors' appeal. However, KFB (by then the sole plaintiff) reduced its claim from 40 billion Korean won to 1 billion Korean won (approximately 800000 US dollars), which was awarded. The minority shareholders lost their status as KFB shareholders due to a capital reduction and were removed from the suit.

The Supreme Court upheld this ruling. The Supreme Court did not mention the business judgment rule directly but recognized the rule by stating that the failure of bank directors to get the loans repaid *per se* does not constitute a breach of their fiduciary duties. However, the role of banks differs from that of other companies. Banks are required to contribute to the stability of the financial markets and to the development of the national economy in the following ways: bank directors must fulfill their fiduciary duties with utmost (enhanced) care in (1) the protection of the properties of depositors; (2) the maintenance of credit systems; and (3) the promotion of efficiency in finance brokering.

The court set out the following criteria which the directors of the banks were to assess when they decided on whether to grant loans: (1) the terms and conditions of the loan; (2) the loan amount; (3) the repayment plan; (4) the existence of collateral and its substance; (5) the status of the debtor's assets and business operations; and (6) the debtor's future business prospects.

This ruling enhanced for the first time the standards of fiduciary duties of directors of financial institutions and established standards to which financial institutions must adhere when deciding whether to grant loans. The Korean courts have increasingly emphasized the fiduciary duties of directors since the Korean financial crisis of 1997,[38] and this case highlighted the trend.[39]

IV. RESTRICTIONS OF DIRECTORS' LIABILITIES

A. Indemnification and D&O Insurance[40]

The KCC provides that directors may be released from liability to their company by the unanimous consent of the shareholders of the company.[41]

---

[38] *See* generally Hwa-Jin Kim, *Toward the "Best Practice" Model in a Globalizing Market: Recent Developments in Korean Corporate Governance*, 2 J. Corp. L. Stud. 345 (2002); Hwa-Jin Kim, *Living with the IMF: A New Approach to Corporate Governance and Regulation of Financial Institutions in Korea*, 17 Berk. J. Int'l L. 61 (1999).

[39] In December of 1999, the Korea Deposit Insurance Corporation announced plans to commence legal actions against 764 ex-managers of 86 failed financial institutions, which amounted to a total of 5.4 trillion Korean won in damages. Such actions are based upon Art. 21-2 Korean Depositor Protection Act.

[40] *See* generally Joseph F. Johnston, Jr., *Corporate Indemnification and Liability Insurance for Directors and Officers*, 33 Bus. Law. 1993 (1978).

[41] Art. 400 KCC. Effective from 15 April 2012, according to Para. 2 of Article 400 of the amended KCC partially exempts directors from liability under the articles of incorporation of a company in addition to the release of directors' liability by the consent of all shareholders. Under the new standards for mitigation or exemption of directors' liability, the company, through its articles of incorporation, may exempt a director from liability for amounts in excess of six times (three times for an outside director) his remuneration (including bonuses and gains from the exercise of stock options, etc.) for the year immediately preceding the date of the acts leading to such liability. However, the amended Article 400 also states that in case (i) the director caused losses intentionally or by gross negligence or (ii) violated

However, such a release with respect to a public company is unrealistic since the unanimous shareholder consent of a public company is almost impossible to obtain. Therefore, as recommended in the Report and Legal Reform Recommendations to the Ministry of Justice prepared by a group of international experts, the liability of at least the outside directors should be limited in cases in which they have acted in good faith. The Report recommended that the KCC should be amended "to provide that the personal liability of an independent director will be limited, in the case of non-willful breaches of duty not involving personal benefit to the director or the director's family, to a multiple (such as 5 times) of the director's total annual compensation from the company (including the value of non-cash compensation)."[42] By way of comparison, the 2001 revision of the Japanese Commercial Code introduced the three-way exoneration mechanism. It provides that the directors' liability can be released by (1) a supermajority (2/3) vote of the shareholders' meeting; (2) a decision of the board of directors when authorized by the articles of incorporation; or (3) a contract signed by the company and director when authorized by the articles of incorporation.[43]

As the validity of indemnification of directors' liability by their companies is being disputed more frequently by legal scholars in Korea, it is

---

(a) the provision on the prohibition of competitive business for directors (KCC Article 397), (b) the provision on the prohibition of misappropriation of business opportunities (KCC Article 397-2), or (c) the provision on the prohibition of transactions between companies and their directors (KCC Article 398), the liability of the director shall not be mitigated or exempted. That is, a director may have his liability mitigated or exempted only in the case of negligence which does not rise to the level of gross negligence and does not involve a violation of the provisions related to the prohibition of competitive business, misappropriation of business opportunities and transactions between companies and their directors. Particularly noteworthy is that the amendments differentiate between the limitations on liability for inside directors and for outside directors based on the reality that the latter is inferior to the former in terms of legal status and access to the company's internal information. The different treatment incentivizes outside directorship as a result. The amended KCC provisions regarding the mitigation or exemption of directors' liability applies mutatis mutandis to auditors, members of the audit committee, and executive officers (KCC Articles 415, 415-2 paragraph 7, and Article 408-9). Shin & Kim, Recent Amendments to the Korean Commercial Code – Mitigation or Exemption of Directors' Liability, Legal Update, 13 July, 2011.

[42] Bernard Black et al., *Corporate Governance in Korea at the Millennium: Enhancing International Competitiveness*, 26 J. Corp. L. 537, 579–80 (2001).

[43] *See* Art. 266, Para 7, 12 and 19 Japanese Commercial Code. *See generally*, Tomotaka Fujita, Transformation of Management's Liability Regime in Japan: A Decade After 1993 Revision (Working Paper presented at 4th Asian Corporate Governance Conference, 20 May 2005).

becoming common practice among public companies to purchase liability insurance for directors and officers (D&O insurance) for their directors. Directors can obtain D&O insurances from a number of Korean insurance companies against certain civil (but not criminal) liabilities. Coverage provided by such insurance usually includes damages resulting from such wrongful acts of directors (as well as legal fees resulting thereof) but generally will not include damages resulting from a director's pursuit of illegal personal profit, willful misconduct or compensation claimed by major shareholders of the company.

B. No *Caremark* Yet

Under *Caremark*, directors are liable if, and only if, they failed to prevent a loss as a result of a systematic failure to attempt to control potential liabilities. Directors can be sued derivatively by the shareholders when the company vicariously pays a huge fine for the illegal acts of employees. According to the decision of the Delaware Chancery Court,[44] however, the board of directors of Caremark International satisfied its responsibility through exercising a good faith judgment that the company's internal control system was adequate to assure that appropriate information would come to its attention in a timely manner even though they could not prevent some employees from paying illegal commissions to doctors.

Although, there are generally no formal requirements on Korean companies relating to the internal control of business risks, certain specialized companies are subject to such formal requirements. For example, the KCMA provides that financial-investment-business companies are required to establish internal control standards to ensure that its officers and employees (1) observe the KCMA and subordinate statutes in the course of the performance of their duties, (2) operate the assets of the company in a sound manner and (3) protect customers. In addition, securities companies are also required to have at least one compliance officer responsible for ensuring that such internal controls are being observed.[45] The compliance officer shall also investigate any violations of internal control standards and report the results of such investigation to the statutory auditor or the audit committee.[46] Banking laws and insurance laws

---

44 In Re: Caremark International, Inc. Derivative Litigation, Civ. A. No. 13670.

45 Art. 28 Para. 1 KCMA.

46 Art. 28 Para. 2 KCMA.

also provide similar internal control obligations on banks and insurance companies.[47]

The KCMA is silent on the legal effect of the well-functioning compliance system. But the Korean Insurance Business Act (KIBA) provides that the insurance companies with good compliance system could enjoy certain benefits in terms of governmental supervision.[48] The Korean Financial Supervisory Commission's (currently Financial Services Commission) internal guideline also provides that the securities companies with good compliance system may enjoy certain benefits in terms of governmental supervision.[49]

Perhaps it is too early to see a Korean version of the Caremark case. It would be highly doubtful whether Korean judges would be willing to render a decision that the Caremark court rendered even if the directors of a qualified company appear as defendants before the court. However, an effective board in Korea would also need a Caremark protection especially when it is subject to enhanced level of fiduciary duties.

V. IS TAKEOVER DEFENSE BUSINESS JUDGMENT?

It is too early to predict whether takeover defensive tactics would be contested in terms of directors' fiduciary duty and the business judgment rule in Korea.[50] However, two recent lower court decisions dealt with the

---

47 The December 2003 amendments to the Act on External Auditors of Joint Stock Companies requires the relevant companies to prepare internal accounting control regulations and run an operational organization for drafting accounting information and disclosing it publicly. The new law also requires the auditor to evaluate the internal accounting control system each fiscal year and report the results to the board of directors.

48 *See* Art. 17 Para. 8 KIBA.

49 *See* Korea Financial Supervisory Service Press Release, 5 February 2003.

50 Korean companies adopt various pre-offer as well as post-offer takeover defensive tactics, including golden parachute, supermajority vote requirements, staggered board, lock-ups, and rights offering to a friendly party. It is understood that the poison pill and dual-class common stock as they are used in the United States are not allowed under the KCC. For takeover defensive tactics in Korea, *see generally* Hwa-Jin Kim, M&A and Corporate Control, chapter 5 (3rd ed. 1999) (Korean). Tender offers appear to be picking up the pace again in Korea. Tender offers grew in number recently, but, more notably, the types of and purposes for tender offers have also become more diversified. It is plausible that this trend will continue and tender offers may soon be used for a greater variety of purposes and in equally as many forms in Korea.

legality of the takeover defensive tactics,[51] and it has been reported that the defendants argued that their tactics were legal and also justified as business judgment. Perhaps, the U.S. takeover law will be imported and adapted to the Korean circumstance in the future.

A. Hyundai Elevator Case

In November 2003, Kumgang Korea Chemical, having acquired, directly or indirectly, approximately 44.39 percent of the issued and outstanding shares of Hyundai Elevator, the flagship company of the Hyundai Group, announced its plan to acquire the control of Hyundai Elevator and other companies of the Hyundai Group. The board of directors of Hyundai Elevator, in an attempt to defend Kumgang's hostile takeover attempt, resolved to issue 10 million new shares, which was 178 percent of the then outstanding shares, at a 30 percent discount, with a condition that the number of the newly-issued shares to which any one person may subscribe cannot be more than 300 shares. Kumgang sought a preliminary injunction of the proposed issuance of new shares by Hyundai Elevator arguing that the proposed issuance was improper as it infringed on the preemptive rights of the existing shareholders and was an attempt only to perpetuate the current management.[52]

The Suwon District Court found that the proposed issuance of new shares was in breach of the KCC and infringed on the preemptive rights of the existing shareholders, and it granted the requested preliminary injunction.[53] The court reasoned that since any attempt to defend a takeover bid should be made within the confines of the laws and regulations and the articles of incorporation of the company concerned, Hyundai Elevator's proposed issuance of new shares, which would be allowed only to the

---

[51] *Cf.* Center for Good Corporate Governance (Korea), Issue Report dated 12 January 2004 (Korean summary of the two court cases mentioned below).

[52] Under the KCC, shareholders have preemptive rights. Each shareholder of a corporation has the right to purchase a proportionate share of any new shares of the corporation issued. Notwithstanding the foregoing, the corporation may issue new shares to a third party without first offering them to the existing shareholders if, and only if, (a) such possibility is specified in the articles of incorporation of the corporation and (b) such issuance is necessary for the business of the corporation, e.g., for induction of new technology or improvement of financial structure. Art. 418 KCC. The issuance of new shares for the purpose of perpetuation of the current management, however, would generally not be considered to be necessary for the business of the corporation and would not be allowed, unless the new shares are first offered to the existing shareholders.

[53] Case No. 2003-Kahap-369, 12 December 2003.

extent necessary to raise funds for the business of the company under the KCC and the articles of incorporation of the company, was not proper for the apparent purpose of perpetuating the status of the existing controlling shareholder(s) or management.

Notwithstanding the foregoing decision of the court with respect to Hyundai Elevator board's action, the court did not completely rule out the possibility of issuing new shares as a means of takeover defense. Specifically, the court stated that the following scenarios may be an exception to the general rule in which the company concerned may issue new shares in an attempt to avert a hostile takeover: (1) if preserving the existing controlling shareholder(s) and/or the existing management of the target company is beneficial to the company itself or the shareholders in general, or there are other specific public reasons and (2) if the target company has taken all reasonable steps in making the decision to issue new shares, such as soliciting the opinions of the disinterested shareholders or independent experts. According to the court, if these conditions were met, the issuance of new shares may not be invalidated because it would have been done for the proper business purposes as stipulated in the company's articles of incorporation and the KCC.[54]

B. SK Corporation Case

The directors of SK Corp., one of the major shareholders of SK Telecom, in response to a demand by the then largest shareholder of SK Corp., Sovereign Asset Management, to replace the existing management and to suspend the subsidization of an affiliated company, decided to sell 13 208 860 treasury shares (accounting for approximately 10.41 percent of the issued and outstanding shares) to certain parties friendly to the existing management.[55] Sovereign sought a preliminary injunction of the directors'

---

[54] However, the incumbent management of Hyundai Elevator has successfully defended its control over the company through various defensive tactics.

[55] The KCC strictly regulated a corporation's acquisition of its own shares. Accordingly, under the KCC a corporation was allowed to acquire its own shares for the purpose of capital reduction, in the course of a merger or in other exceptional cases. However, the KCMA allows public companies to acquire own shares subject to certain regulations under the KCMA, without satisfying the requirements of the KCC. The KCMA allows public companies to acquire own shares only through on-exchange transactions, tender offers or from trust business entities. Also, disposal of treasury shares of a public company must, in principle, comply with the procedure laid out in the KCMA. Under the KCMA, the company would first have to obtain approval from its board of directors for the disposal of its treasury shares and then file a report on the disposal of treasury shares with

decision. It claimed that SK Corp.'s decision to sell its treasury shares to friendly parties caused the dilution of Sovereign's voting rights, and therefore, it was being prevented from fairly exercising its voting rights in the 2004 general meeting of shareholders of SK Corp.

The Seoul District Court, however, refused to grant the preliminary injunction.[56] The court opined that the disposal of any treasury shares should not be prevented even in the midst of a dispute for control of the company, provided however, that the shares have not originally been acquired to perpetuate the existing management and the controlling shareholder(s). The decision to sell the treasury shares in the court's view was justified as a business judgment which the directors may exercise in the face of a hostile takeover threat.[57]

VI. DIRECTORS' CRIMINAL LIABILITIES AND THE BUSINESS JUDGMENT RULE

A. The Crime of Up-mu-sang Bae-Im and the Business Judgment Rule

In Korea, an officer or a director of a company might end up in prison for his or her failure in business judgment in respect to the investments and the operation of the company. At issue is the crime of Up-Mu-Sang

---

the Korea Financial Services Commission. In case the company disposes of its shares through on-exchange transactions, the order for the shares must be placed in a certain way and the asking price will have to be within a certain range. To be sure, selling at significant discount may expose the company's directors to charges of breach of their fiduciary duty and the company to claims for damages. *See* Art. 165-2 KCMA. Self-tender offer is allowed under the KCMA and can be used as an effective defensive tactic. In 2001, in connection with the dispute over the control of the management of Union Steel Manufacturing between the largest shareholder and the second largest shareholder, Union Steel faced delisting of its shares from the Korea Exchange because it would be difficult to satisfy the Korea Exchange's share distribution requirement. As minority shareholders of the company may incur losses from the illiquid stocks of the company due to such development, Union Steel made a tender offer to repurchase its own shares to protect the minority shareholders. This was Korea's first self-tender offer and launched in the hope that the second largest shareholder would also tender. The dispute was finally resolved through a private sale and purchase made between the largest and second largest shareholders in 2003.

[56] Decision of 23 December 2003.

[57] The incumbent management of SK Corp. was successful in the proxy contest and, consequently, has prevailed in the general meeting of shareholders. *See* The Korea Economic Daily, 13 March 2004, at A13.

Bae-Im.[58] The elements of the offense, according to the law, are that the wrongdoer (1) owes a fiduciary duty to an entity, (2) breaches that fiduciary duty with intent, and (3) obtains pecuniary gain or causes a third person to obtain it (4) to cause financial harm to the entity. Courts have interpreted the "intent" requirement so as to mean "reckless disregard" for the probability of one's action causing financial harm to the company.

The concept of Up-Mu-Sang Bae-Im may not be a foreign concept to many jurisdictions. For instance, the German Criminal Code and the Japanese Criminal Code contain comparable provisions.[59] However, whereas German and Japanese laws regard the act as fraud, the crime of Up-Mu-Sang Bae-Im does not involve intent to defraud the company. In fact, the law does not require that one take or convert another's money or property to one's own use. This is why Korean courts can impose much stricter criminal liability on directors and officers of companies who have failed to manage their business organizations. Consequently, the courts have been criticized by legal scholars for applying the Up-Mu-Sang Bae-Im case so widely that the judiciary ended up creating a separate crime based upon an unconstitutional "Auffangstatbestand."[60]

The crime of Up-Mu-Sang Bae-Im, thus, has important practical implications for corporate governance in Korea. In a country where the possibility of facing shareholders' derivative suits and/or a hostile takeover attempt has been not as substantial as in other jurisdictions, the crime of Up-Mu-Sang Bae-Im has been utilized in challenging corporate managers and/or officers' business actions. For example, in one case, the CEO of a large corporation was found guilty of committing the crime of Up-Mu-Sang Bae-Im for acquiring the newly issued shares of a financially distressed company at their face value.[61] In essence, what was challenged was the CEO's business judgment.

However, in July of 2004[62] a sign of change was detected in the Korean court's willingness to tolerate the use of the crime of Up-Mu-Sang Bae-Im

---

[58] A person who, in administering another person's business, by an act in breach of one's duties obtains pecuniary gain or causes a third person to obtain it and thereby causes pecuniary loss to that other person, is punishable for criminal "breach of duty of occupation." ("Up-Mu-Sang Bae-Im" in Korean) Art. 356 Korean Criminal Code. There are special laws which will strengthen the penalty under certain circumstances.

[59] Art. 266 German Criminal Code; Art. 247 Japanese Criminal Code.

[60] *See, e.g.*, Sang-Don Yi, *Business Failure and Criminal Liabilities* (Korean), 560 Korean Law. Ass. J. 61 (2003).

[61] The Supreme Court, Case No. 2004-Do-520, 24 June 2004.

[62] Case No. 2002-Do-4229, 22 July 2004.

as a tool to challenge the business judgment of the officers and/or directors of a company. In particular, the Supreme Court of Korea rendered a judgment that departed from its previous decisions on the crime of Up-Mu-Sang Bae-Im. The factual background of the case is as follows. A representative director of a company was charged with the crime of Up-Mu-Sang Bae-Im for issuing an insurance coverage to an entity that subsequently went bankrupt. In fact, the director's company was in the business of serving as a guarantor, in return for certain premium payments, for entities that needed to borrow money for business purposes. According to the company's business model, if everything went well, the borrower paid off the loan and the company made money from the premium payments received thus far. On the other hand, should the borrower go bankrupt, the company had to pay off the loan on behalf of the insured and as a result possibly suffer a financial loss. The latter was the case at bar. The borrower went bankrupt and the company, as the borrower's guarantor, was forced to pay off the loan in the amount that would cause financial harm to the company. Subsequently, the representative director was accused of committing the crime of Up-Mu-Sang Bae-Im for allegedly breaching his fiduciary duty owed to the company by issuing the insurance coverage to the borrower and causing financial harm to the company as a result.

The Supreme Court, however, acquitted the representative director in the case and stated the rationale for its decision in a language that surprisingly resembles that of a U.S. court applying the business judgment rule. Specifically, according to the Supreme Court, it is in the nature of any business that even when a director/officer of a company – with care, diligence and prudence – makes a corporate decision, the results show that what he or she did was unwise and as a result the company suffers financial losses. Therefore, to employ the crime of Up-Mu-Sang Bae-Im to challenge such business decisions, otherwise made with care, diligence and prudence without any conflict of interests, is to stifle the spirit of entrepreneurship and to violate the legislative intent of the law. This in return will be a loss to society as a whole, stated the Court. In the end the court stated that "[j]ust because a company suffered a financial loss due to what turned out to be a poor business judgment of a director, this Court, without more, shall not find a director of a company guilty of committing the crime of Up-Mu-Sang Bae-Im."

The Court thus reduced the threat to corporate managers in Korea of facing a criminal charge based on their unwise business decisions, which can result in financial harm to the companies. The implications of the decision on the Korean corporate governance structure, however, remain to be seen.

B. The Leveraged Buyout and Directors' Criminal Liabilities

A leveraged buyout (LBO) is a purchase of a corporation in which the acquiring company obtains a significant portion of the funding from investors, such as financial institutions, and provides the assets of the acquired entity ("target company") as security to secure the purchase price. Because it is the assets of the target company that are being provided as security for the LBO, the management and directors of the target company must inevitably be involved. In an LBO, the target company's asset-liability ratio increases and the possibility of disposition of the secured assets becomes higher because the assets are being provided as collateral for the debt. On the other hand, the direct benefits of or the profits from the funding and the security go to the acquiring company or the financial institutions from which the funding is obtained. Because of this disparity between the burden and the benefits, the transaction raises the issue of whether the directors of the target company may be held liable.

The Seoul High Court has recently ruled, in its highly publicized judgment of 6 October 2004,[63] that the act implementing a leveraged buyout transaction cannot be viewed as a crime of Up-Mu-Sang Bae-Im under certain circumstances. This case involved the issue of the liability of the representative director of the target company for breach of his fiduciary duty in an LBO transaction. In deciding on whether pecuniary loss[64] has been incurred on the target company, the court stated that "although the target company provided its assets as security for the LBO and thus created the risk that the secured assets may be disposed of in the future, if existing liabilities of the target company were extinguished through the funding for which the security was established, then such pledging of the assets cannot be said to have caused loss on the company."

Another element of the crime of Up-Mu-Sang Bae-Im is that the director or a third person must obtain pecuniary gain from the director's actions. In this case, the defendant representative director of the target company had not obtained personal gain from the funding which was secured by the target company's assets, and which came into the company's account as the share purchase price. Thus, the court held that the director of the target company was not guilty of a crime of Up-Mu-Sang Bae-Im because the director had never personally obtained any gain and all of the funding

---

63 Case No. 2003-No-3322.

64 In proving pecuniary loss in terms of the crime of Up-Mu-Sang Bae-Im, the loss need not be ascertained specifically, nor does the loss have to be immediately realized. Pecuniary loss is interpreted as including the case where the "risk" of pecuniary loss is increased.

was applied toward repaying existing loans of the target company and for the purpose of financial restructuring of the target company, and therefore the actions did not include the element of "pecuniary gain" for purposes of the criminal breach of duty.

In connection therewith, there was another criminal case decided in a Korean district court where the court held that the director was criminally liable for the crime of Up-Mu-Sang Bae-Im. In the process of restructuring the affiliated companies of Halla Group, the major shareholder and representative director of the acquired company had established a special purpose vehicle to attract foreign investment. After it had obtained funding, the special purpose vehicle assumed the business of the acquired company and successfully restructured the acquired company. However, the representative director and officers of the acquired company were found guilty of the crime of Up-Mu-Sang Bae-Im. The reason was because in the process of establishing the special purpose vehicle, a portion of the equity of the special purpose vehicle was transferred to the major shareholders and the affiliated companies of the prior existing target company free of charge or at a very low price, thus causing unjust pecuniary enrichment. At the same time, it was in fact causing the target company to see the same amount of pecuniary loss.[65]

VII. CONCLUDING REMARKS

There is a visible shift in the paradigm of corporate governance in favor of the board of directors and managers in Korea. At the surface, shareholder rights supremacy is conspicuous. However, Korean corporate law maintains and consolidates its basic pro-board attitude adopted in 1962. The introduction of the business judgment rule in the wake of the shareholder derivative litigation and securities class action will contribute to the trend. Given that the effective board needs the protection of the business judgment rule, among other things, especially when the impacts of the U.S. Sarbanes–Oxley Act of 2002 are slowly being felt in Korea, this can be viewed as a welcoming development. It is ironic that the recent shareholder activism has strengthened the power of the boards of Korean companies.

The business judgment rule is a doctrine of judicial abstention.[66]

---

65 Seoul Criminal District Court, Decision of 4 October 2002.

66 Ronald J. Gilson, *A Structural Approach to Corporations: The Case Against Defensive Tactics and Tender Offers*, 33 Stan. L. Rev. 819, 823 (1981).

Therefore, application of the rule would sanction virtually all conduct of directors in defending control over and restructuring the company. In the United States, it was reported long ago that "[t]he search for cases in which directors of industrial corporations have been held liable in derivative suits for negligence uncomplicated by self-dealing is a search for a very small number of needles in a very large haystack."[67] As Professor Bernard Black suggests "[t]he case for judicial abstention is even stronger in civil law countries, where judges are often selected through an academic career track and have no practical experience."[68] As seen in the recent cases, the Korean courts seem amenable to such observation although, at the same time, remain reluctant to introduce the U.S. concepts of fiduciary duties of corporate directors. Lawyers and scholars in Korea must be aware, however, that they may be importing a black box that is widely used but not readily understood.[69] Perhaps the experience in the United States may be repeated in Korea. Nevertheless, this clearly will open a new chapter for corporate law in Korea. The corporate control and restructuring cases will definitely serve the test field.

The descriptions in this chapter clearly illustrated that the Korean corporate system gradually adapts to the model accepted by global standards. The common law elements "transplanted" into the Korean legal system would contribute to the development of an advanced corporate governance structure of Korean companies, which ultimately would enhance their competitiveness in the global market.

REFERENCES

Bishop, Joseph, *Sitting Ducks and Decoy Ducks: New Trends in the Indemnification of Corporate Directors and Officers*, 77 Yale Law Journal 1078 (1968)

Black, Bernard S. et al., *Corporate Governance in Korea at the Millennium: Enhancing International Competitiveness*, 26 Journal of Corporate Law 537 (2001)

Black, Bernard S., Brian Cheffins & Michael Klausner, *Shareholder Suits and Outside Director Liability: The Case of Korea*, 10 Journal of Korean Law 325 (2011)

---

67 Joseph Bishop, *Sitting Ducks and Decoy Ducks: New Trends in the Indemnification of Corporate Directors and Officers*, 77 Yale L. J. 1078, 1099 (1968).

68 Black, *supra* note 14, at 16.

69 *See, e.g.*, Henry G. Manne, *Our Two Corporation Systems: Law and Economics*, 53 Va. L. Rev. 259, 270 (1967) (noting that the business judgment rule is "one of the least understood concepts in the entire corporate field").

Black, Bernard S., *The Core Fiduciary Duties of Outside Directors*, Asia Business Law Review 3 (July 2001)
Chung, Dae Hwan, *Introduction to South Korea's New Securities-Related Class Action*, 30 Journal of Corporate Law 165 (2004)
Gilson, Ronald J., *A Structural Approach to Corporations: The Case Against Defensive Tactics and Tender Offers*, 33 Stanford Law Review 819 (1981)
Kim, E. Han & Woochan Kim, *Changes in Korean Corporate Governance: A Response to Crisis*, Journal of Applied Corporate Finance 47 (Winter 2008)
Kim, Hwa-Jin, *The Case for Market for Corporate Control in Korea*, 10 Oxford University Comparative Law Forum 2 (2009)
_____, *Directors' Duties and Liabilities in Corporate Control and Restructuring Transactions: Recent Developments in Korea*, 7 Oxford University Comparative Law Forum 2 (2006)
_____, *Toward the "Best Practice" Model in a Globalizing Market: Recent Developments in Korean Corporate Governance*, 2 Journal of Corporate Law Studies 345 (2002)
_____, *Living with the IMF: A New Approach to Corporate Governance and Regulation of Financial Institutions in Korea*, 17 Berkeley Journal of International Law 61 (1999)
Kim, Joongi, *A Forensic Study of Daewoo's Corporate Governance: Does Responsibility for the Meltdown Solely Lie with the Chaebol and Korea?*, 28 Northwestern Journal of International Law & Business 273 (2007)
Kim, Jooyoung & Joongi Kim, *Shareholder Activism in Korea: A Review of How PSPD Has Used Legal Measures to Strengthen Korean Corporate Governance*, 1 Journal of Korean Law 51 (2001)
Manne, Henry G., *Our Two Corporation Systems: Law and Economics*, 53 Virginia Law Review 259 (1967)
Pritchard, A. C., *Monitoring of Corporate Groups by Independent Directors*, 9 Journal of Korean Law 1 (2009)
Seo, Jeong, *Who Will Control Frankenstein? The Korean Chaebol's Corporate Governance*, 14 Cardozo Journal of International & Comparative Law 21 (2006)

2. Shareholder suits against Korean directors

Bernard Black, Brian Cheffins and Michael Klausner

I. INTRODUCTION[1]

Korea engaged in extensive corporate governance reform after the 1997–98 East Asian financial crisis. The reforms included a mandate that outside directors constitute a significant fraction of public company boards (25 percent for all public companies; a majority for large companies). Suing directors also became easier due to the introduction of new fiduciary duty rules, a procedure for securities class actions, a much lower ownership threshold for shareholders to bring a derivative suit, and changes in attorney fee rules.

These reforms were motivated by the belief that outside directors can play an important role in monitoring and constraining potentially wayward or self-interested managers and controlling shareholders, and that outside directors will be more effective if they face a threat of liability. There is evidence that the belief in the value of outside directors was not misplaced. Board independence appears to causally predict higher share prices for Korean firms.[2] The "channels" that could explain this impact on

---

1 This article is a shortened and modestly updated version of Black, Cheffins and Klausner (2011). That article, in turn, was prepared for a conference held in 2004, and was only partially updated for publication. The published version of this article will also be available on SSRN, at http://ssrn.com/abstract=913623. We do not read Korean and cite principally English language sources, but were advised by experts in Korean law that our description of Korean law is a fair summary. Earlier versions of this paper were presented at a conference on Corporate Governance and the Capital Market in Korea and at Stanford Law School. We thank KDI School of Public Policy and Management for financial support, and Joongi Kim, KonSik Kim, Hwa Jin Kim, Woo-Chan Kim, Young Sam Kim, Jung Soo Lee, and Ji-Min Park for answering our questions about Korean law and practice.

2 For supporting evidence, see Black, Jang and Kim (2006); Black and Kim (2012); see also Choi, Park and Yoo (2007).

share price include reduced self-dealing between firms and their controlling shareholders and lower capital expenditures against a background of likely overinvestment prior to the crisis.[3] And, for whatever complex mix of reasons, major Korean firms have continued to prosper, despite the 2007–2009 financial crisis and the Korean economy has continued to grow.

The reforms to lawsuit procedures also appear to have succeeded, at least by one crude measure. Derivative suits against directors, previously almost unheard of, have become reasonably common. There were no derivative suits filed before 1997, but at least 20 had been filed by early 2003, and 55 by the end of 2010, including suits against directors of firms that are part of leading *chaebol* groups, including Samsung, LG, and Hyundai Motors.[4] At the same time, commentators, echoing fears voiced in other countries, have worried that excessive legal risk might cause some good outside director candidates to decline to serve, and "that Korean companies will be deprived of honest and competent directors precisely at a time when they are most needed."[5]

In this article, we seek to put into context the Korean outside director reforms, with particular reference to director liability. Based on extensive research concerning the experience in other countries, we predicted in 2004, when we presented an initial draft of a related article at a conference in Korea, that there would be few cases of "personal liability," in which outside directors of Korean public companies paid damages or legal expenses out of their own pockets and were not reimbursed by the company or by directors' and officers' (D&O) insurance. Our research indicated that once self-dealing was put to one side (self-dealing should be rare for outside directors), in none of the countries we studied did outside directors face a large risk of personal liability from serving as directors. Even, in the United States, where outside directors are sued much more often than elsewhere, they rarely pay damages or legal expenses personally as a result of suits by shareholders or creditors. Instead, if a suit survives the defendants' efforts to have it dismissed at an early stage, it will almost always be settled prior to trial with any damages and legal fees paid entirely by the company, by directors' and officers' (D&O) insurance, or both.

---

[3] For evidence on these channels, see Black, Kim, Jang, and Park (2012). Another possible channel is better behavior during an economic or financial crisis. See Johnson et al. (2000); Bae et al. (2012).

[4] The 2003 figure is from Park and Lee (2003); data through 2010 is from Rho and Kim (2011).

[5] Park and Lee (2003), at 17.

Our cross-country analysis indicates that if the risk of personal liability is effectively zero, market forces that might limit this risk will be weaker (for example, many firms will not think it worthwhile to buy D&O insurance, or will not focus on the policy terms, leading to potential loopholes). Moreover, political pressure may well emerge for directors to face *some* risk if they engage in truly egregious behavior. On the other hand, when events occur that threaten to make personal liability a significant risk for outside directors, political or market forces typically emerge to reduce this risk to a very low level.

This international experience led us to predict in 2004 that there might be occasional instances where outside directors of Korean public companies paid damages or legal expenses personally, but these cases would be uncommon. We also predicted that if personal payments occurred with any frequency, this would be likely to provoke political and market responses to ensure that personal liability remained rare.

In 2012, with the benefit of eight years of hindsight, our predictions have proven to be largely correct, so far. To date, we know of no confirmed instance in which an outside director made a personal payment as a result of an investor lawsuit. Moreover, recent amendments to the Korean Commercial Code, effective in 2012, provide additional protection for outside directors by permitting companies to adopt liability caps in their corporate charters.

Is Korea's current level of director liability risk a good policy outcome? We believe that for outside directors, very low but non-zero risk of personal liability is a reasonable outcome. A substantially higher degree of risk might cause more harm than good by deterring good director candidates from serving and by inducing too much caution in making business decisions. At the same time, we believe that *some* exposure to personal liability is likely to be salutary, particularly with respect to transactions between companies within *chaebol* groups and other related-party transactions. In our judgment, the new liability caps may go too far in protecting outside directors.

This chapter proceeds as follows. Section 2 briefly discusses outside director liability risk in the other countries we have studied. Section 3 discusses the Korean situation in light of the experiences of these other countries. Section 4 discusses the policy implications of our analysis.

We focus on outside directors of public companies. We do not consider unlisted companies, and do not address the personal liability risk faced by inside directors (executives and representatives of a controlling family or group) except to illustrate points we make concerning outside directors. We also exclude cases, which should be rare, where outside directors engage in self-dealing or otherwise act with a conflict of interest. Thus, we focus on outside directors' duties to be vigilant, including controlling self-dealing by controllers, not their separate duty to place the shareholders' interests before their own.

II. PERSONAL LIABILITY OF OUTSIDE DIRECTORS IN OTHER COUNTRIES

We summarize here briefly the conclusions from our studies of outside director liability in a representative sample of developed countries, including both common law countries (Australia, Britain, Canada, and the U.S.) and civil law countries (France, Germany, and Japan).[6]

A. Personal Liability in the U.S.

We consider the U.S. first and in greater detail because outside directors of U.S. public companies face a much higher risk of being sued under company and securities law than directors in Korea or the other countries we studied. Under securities law, directors are potentially liable for a company's failure to comply with public disclosure rules.[7] Under company law, directors can be liable for breach of their fiduciary duties. Procedural rules for these suits, coupled with the ability of plaintiffs' lawyers to bring cases on a "contingency" basis, in which they receive a fee only if the suit is successful, and rules under which each side pays its own legal expenses regardless of the outcome, provide incentives to plaintiffs' lawyers to bring suits against companies, their executives, and their directors under these laws. There are numerous lawsuits every year in which outside directors of U.S. public companies are named as defendants. In many of those suits plaintiffs are successful in the sense that they receive payments – nearly always in settlements prior to trial. Those payments, however, almost never come from the pockets of the directors themselves.[8]

The apparent anomaly of frequent shareholder suits and virtually non-existent outside director liability is the product of four factors: (a) legal rules that screen out suits that fail to meet a threshold degree of gravity,

---

[6] We draw here on Black, Cheffins and Klausner (2006a) and Cheffins and Black (2006). We provide only minimal citations. Fuller citations and additional details and nuances can be found in those sources and in Black, Cheffins, and Klausner (2011).

[7] Securities Act of 1933, § 11; Securities Exchange Act of 1934, § 10(b), and related Securities and Exchange Commission Rule 10b-5.

[8] Black, Cheffins, and Klausner (2006a).

(b) broad powers given to companies to indemnify directors against both legal expenses and damages, (c) directors' and officers' (D&O) liability insurance, which covers directors if indemnification is unavailable, and (d) settlement dynamics that result in payments from the corporation and its insurer rather than from outside directors (or even executives) in the vast majority of cases.

Legal rules governing both securities lawsuits and fiduciary duty suits under company law set a high bar for plaintiffs' lawyers to surmount before a case may proceed past an initial pleading stage. In a securities suit, the lawyers must allege specific facts indicating that the defendants both committed acts that constitute a violation of law and had the requisite mental state in doing so. In cases involving a public offering, the requisite state of mind is one of negligence. In all other cases, either intentional misconduct or a high degree of recklessness is required – mental states that are difficult to support with the needed specificity without the benefit of discovery. In fiduciary duty cases, the bar is even higher. Due to the "business judgment rule" and provisions in the charters of essentially all public companies, directors face personal liability only for self-dealing, which is rare among outside directors, or for "conscious disregard of duty," which due to judicial construction is almost impossible to prove.

If plaintiffs' lawyers allege concrete facts that meet these threshold requirements, a case will be able to survive a motion to dismiss if made, the plaintiffs will be able to obtain discovery, and the case will either be settled or, uncommonly, go to trial. There remains, however, ample protection for directors. Indemnification by the company will cover both litigation expenses and amounts paid to settle a securities case so long as the company is solvent and the director has not engaged in self-dealing or conscious disregard of his duties. The rules for indemnification in fiduciary duty cases brought as direct suits by shareholders are similar to those governing securities cases. In fiduciary duty cases brought as derivative suits, indemnification is available for litigation expenses, but not for amounts paid following trial or in a settlement.

Where indemnification (or lack thereof) leaves directors financially exposed (principally where damages are payable in derivative suits or where the company is insolvent and cannot pay), D&O insurance, carried by almost all U.S. public companies, almost always fills the gap. D&O insurance covers legal expenses and damage payments that directors incur in both fiduciary duty cases and securities cases. The primary exclusions from these policies are for cases in which a director has committed "deliberate fraud" or obtained "illegal profits."

A final source of protection for directors is settlement dynamics. All parties to a case prefer settlement over trial. Trials are expensive and risky.

In a securities suit, the company is a defendant along with the named executives and directors. Moreover, the company itself is typically both solvent and covered by D&O insurance, so the plaintiffs typically cannot expect to recover more dollars by insisting on a payment from the directors. Instead, the defense will typically offer a settlement in which only the company and its insurer make payments. Even if the directors were to agree to pay something, the company would usually indemnify them.

If the company is insolvent, the plaintiffs' lawyer may seek additional funds paid by the executives and the directors beyond what is available from the insurance policy, but these defendants will resist. The outside directors in particular, are normally not directly involved in disclosure decisions, so they can credibly threaten to go to trial, where the plaintiff may be unable to prove that they had the legally required state of mind for a violation. Also, D&O policies are "wasting" policies, in that the defendants' (often large) legal expenses are paid out of the policy, reducing the amount available to the plaintiffs. Thus, to chase the defendants' personal assets, the plaintiffs must believe the expected recovery from them exceeds the diminution in recovery from the D&O policy. Experience shows that the plaintiffs nearly always settle with no funds coming out of the directors' pockets.

The dynamics are similar in fiduciary duty suits. The company can indemnify directors for damages payments in direct suits if it is solvent, but not in derivative suits. But even if the company cannot indemnify the directors, the plaintiffs have strong incentives to settle with the defendants within the D&O policy limits.

Ultimately, based on experience to date, outside directors of U.S. public companies face a meaningful risk of personal liability in shareholder suits only if there is a "perfect storm;" the company is insolvent; there is strong evidence of outside director culpability; D&O insurance is inadequate; and one or more outside directors have serious personal wealth.[9] These perfect storms are rare.

The equilibrium in which suits against outside directors are frequent but personal liability is rare has been stable over several decades. When judicial rulings have increased liability risk, the D&O insurance market and lawmakers have responded to shield outside directors. This response of lawmakers is not accidental. Not only are corporate managers a powerful lobbying force with a strong interest in protecting themselves as both

---

9 The presence of just one rich outside director may not change the plaintiffs' calculus due to the securities law rule that caps liability based on proportionate fault.

executives and outside directors, there are strong policy reasons to protect outside directors from more than a modest amount of liability risk.[10] There is no constituency that favors increased liability risk for outside directors. While institutional shareholders frequently lobby for stronger shareholder rights, they do not advocate greater liability exposure for outside directors.

B. Personal Liability in other Countries

To assess whether the U.S. situation of low actual out-of-pocket risk was similar in other countries, we investigated up to 2005 the situation in Australia, Great Britain and Canada (all common law countries) and France, Germany, and Japan (all civil law countries). We found that in each of these countries, outside directors face only a remote risk of personal liability. The legal rules differ substantially across borders, but the bottom line is the same: unless self-dealing is involved, personal liability is rare. While we have not thoroughly studied other countries, the factors that limit liability in the countries we have studied are likely to be present, and if so, outside director personal liability should be rare.[11]

In each of the countries we studied in detail, directors owe duties to their companies to act with care and skill and to act in their companies' best interests. Also, in each country, investors have a cause of action against directors of a public company that has distributed false or misleading documentation in support of a public offering of shares. In Australia, Britain, France, and Germany, severe financial distress creates additional legal responsibilities for directors who fail to take appropriate steps to preserve assets for creditors. In addition to civil liability, outside directors in each of the six countries can face administrative penalties or fines for infractions that they commit personally or that their company commits.[12]

---

10 Black, Cheffins and Klausner (2006b).

11 In Black et al. (2007), two of us participated in a review that included the European Union, Austria, Italy, Latvia, and Russia, which found similar results.

12 We put aside one additional risk, not currently important in Korea: a regulator may seek damages paid personally by directors, in order to "send a message" to other directors. Private plaintiffs generally want to maximize recovery. A regulator, in contrast, might refuse to settle without a personal payment. This "government risk" is currently of concern in Australia, where the securities regulator has obtained personal payments from outside directors in several cases over the last decade. It exists elsewhere, to a lesser degree. But regulators have limited resources and other battles to fight. Moreover, this "government risk" is likely to be bound by political reaction from managers and directors against the regulator, if the regulator acts too aggressively.

While in all six countries, outside directors face some liability risk, the risk of a personal payment is small. One reason is that suits against directors are much less common than they are in the United States. A combination of procedural hurdles and practical considerations discourage litigation. For instance, in the U.S., plaintiffs' lawyers are typically paid only if they win a case. Their fees and other expenses are part of a settlement negotiated with the defendants, reviewed by the court, and typically paid by the company or the D&O insurer. In practice, plaintiffs' lawyers earn enough in the cases they win to cover the cost of bringing the cases that they later lose. The procedural rules in other countries do not provide a comparable way to compensate plaintiffs' lawyers. Consequently, unless a shareholder or a small group of shareholders is willing to bring a suit and to pay legal fees regardless of whether they win or lose the case (often the fees of both sides under a "loser pays" rule), no suit will be filed even if a valid claim of mismanagement exists.

Procedural rules in each of the six countries create additional impediments to securities law suits against outside directors. In none of the countries we analyzed is the class action as well-developed as it is in the U.S., and in several, multi-party litigation is largely unknown. Also, in each of the countries a "loser pays" litigation rule discourages shareholders and their lawyers from naming outside directors as defendants. Under this rule, if a suit against outside directors is unsuccessful, the plaintiffs will likely be required to pay the directors' legal expenses, even if the suit succeeds against the company or inside directors. Moreover, by suing the outside directors, the plaintiffs take the risk of a larger legal costs award without doing much to increase the potential recovery. With the stakes for suing outside directors unbalanced in this way, focusing on the company and the (likely more culpable) inside directors will often be sensible. Even if a company is insolvent, focusing on the inside directors and deeper-pocketed defendants, such as auditors, investment bankers, or other professional advisers, will often be the preferred strategy.

As in the United States, when events occur that increase the risk of personal liability for outside directors, political and economic forces often respond to restore the status quo ante of very low risk. For instance, litigation involving outside directors prompted Japanese lawmakers in 2002 to give companies the option to introduce a cap on damages payable by directors and led to a 2004 statutory change in the U.K. expanding the company's power to indemnify directors for legal expenses.

One also commonly sees a market response to the threat of personal liability, principally through companies purchasing D&O insurance with policy limits high enough so that settlement within limits is financially attractive to plaintiffs. With this "deep pocket" of insurance in place, shareholders are more likely to sue outside directors, but the directors' risk of personal liability is still likely to decline. With insurance in place, the directors' legal fees will be reliably covered. Moreover, the settlement dynamics discussed above, which encourage settlement without a personal payment, will apply.

We have not investigated instances of outside director liability in any depth since the mid-2000s, but we are unaware of any trend toward greater personal liability in these six countries, or elsewhere. We also find in separate work that in the U.K., suits under company law against company directors are nearly non-existent.[13] It is unclear whether the lack of personal liability is due to obstacles associated with suing directors, to D&O insurance coverage or a combination of both. Regardless, personal liability has been and remains rare in both the U.S. and other major industrialized countries.

III. THE KOREAN SITUATION

A. Legal Reform and Director Liability

Prior to the East Asian financial crisis of 1997–98, many Korean firms had no outside directors. Moreover, until 1997, there were, to our knowledge, no lawsuits filed against either inside or outside directors under either company law or securities law. Thus, directors' liability risk was effectively zero.

To be sure, Korean law is unusual in making directors directly liable to third parties if they "have neglected to perform their duties willfully or by gross negligence."[14] Thus, the duties of Korean directors can be enforced by creditors, contract counterparties and other third parties. If the company is solvent, third parties have little reason to sue the directors, because they can recover more easily from the company. But if the company is insolvent, third parties may sue the directors, seeking amounts they cannot recover from the company. In our comparison countries, in contrast, the fiduciary duties of directors generally are enforceable only by the company and its shareholders. Creditors can only bring a claim for breach of duty in limited circumstances.

Korean insolvency law has no analog to rules in Australia and Britain that create insolvency-specific liability for "wrongful trading" or

---

13 Armour, Black, Cheffins and Nolan (2009).

14 Korean Commercial Code art. 401.

"insolvent trading."[15] But insolvency increases the risk that directors will be sued for breach of their duties by creditors or an insolvency custodian, in circumstances where two normal protections against personal liability – the company paying damages or indemnifying the directors – are not available.[16] Still, in practice, prior to the crisis, there were no suits against directors under this provision.

In response to the East Asian financial crisis, Korea introduced various reforms that gave outside directors a greater governance role and created greater risks that both inside and outside directors will face a lawsuit challenging their conduct. We summarize here the more important reforms. One reform required all listed firms to have at least 25 percent outside directors. Banks and companies (companies with assets greater than 2 trillion won, around $2 billion) were required to have a majority of outside directors and an audit committee with at least 2/3 outside directors, one of whom must act as chair. New fiduciary rules for company directors were introduced.[17] Korea also reduced the shareholding requirements for bringing a derivative suit from 5 percent to 1 percent for private companies, and to 0.01 percent for public companies. Shareholding requirements for access to company records were lowered, from 5 percent to 3 percent for private companies, to 0.1 percent for public companies, and to 0.05 percent for public companies with over 100 million won ($100 million) in capital.[18] Finally, Korea adopted a new class action procedure specifically for securities suits.[19] Previously, class actions of any sort did not exist. As we discuss below, these reforms led to a significant number of lawsuits, and thus potentially exposed directors to personal liability.

For companies that adopt a liability cap, the actual risk to outside directors of being sued for conduct covered by the cap – let alone making

---

15 See Cheffins and Black (2006), at 1417–19, 1440.

16 The Korean Insolvency Law facilitates these suits by providing an expedited procedure for creditors or the bankruptcy custodian to obtain court authorization to bring such a suit. Korean Insolvency Law arts 115 and 352.

17 Korean Commercial Code art. 382-3.

18 See Korean Commercial Code arts 542-6(6) (derivative suits against public companies), 542-6(4) (access to public company records), 542-8 (outside directors), 542-11 (audit committees); Banking Act arts 22, 23-2 (outside director and audit committee rules for banks); Korean Commercial Code arts 403 (derivative suits generally), 466 (access to company records generally).

19 Securities Class Action Act (2004). The class action procedure has been available for larger companies beginning in 2005 and for all public companies beginning in 2007.

a personal payment – will fall to nearly zero.[20] Assuming a potential suit is motivated by financial recovery, if damages are limited to three times the compensation paid to outside directors, it is unlikely to be worthwhile suing outside directors, even if several are potentially liable. Occasional suits might still be brought, perhaps by shareholder activists, to make an example of particular directors and thus deter others.

B. Suits Against Inside Directors

A number of shareholder suits against inside directors of Korean public companies illustrate that these directors do face some personal liability risk as a result of a derivative suit. We are aware of four derivative suits that led to a finding of liability. Two resulted in out-of-pocket payments; one did not. In a fourth case, the court has found liability, but the case is not yet finally resolved.

The first case with out-of-pocket payments by inside directors arose from a 1997 derivative suit (apparently Korea's first derivative suit) brought by the People's Solidarity for a Participatory Democracy (PSPD), a Korean non-governmental organization with a strong shareholder rights orientation.[21] The suit was brought against four former inside directors of Korea First Bank for failure to oversee Korea First's lending practices (the company had no outside directors). The trial court awarded damages of 40 billion won ($40 million). On appeal, after Korea First Bank failed and the plaintiff shareholders were wiped out, Korea First Bank (now controlled by the government) took over the litigation and struck a compromise under which the defendant directors agreed to pay 1 billion won ($1 million). Assuming this amount was split equally by the four directors, it is a serious amount, but likely not a bankrupting one. The settlement could well reflect the amount that the defendants could reasonably afford to pay.

A 1998 derivative lawsuit, brought by PSPD against nine inside directors of Samsung Electronics (the company again had no outside directors) for approving a bailout of a related company, led to the defendant directors personally paying 12 billion won ($12 million) in damages.[22] A

---

20 Korean Commercial Code § 400(2) (effective 2012). The cap is based on remuneration for the year immediately preceding the acts leading to liability.

21 On *PSPD*'s corporate governance efforts and influence, see Kim and Kim (2001); Milhaupt (2004).

22 Samsung's chairman and one director paid an additional 7.5 billion won to compensate Samsung for bribes that they had caused Samsung to pay to government officials. For more details on the Korea First and Samsung cases, see Kim and Kim (2001); Hwa-Jin Kim Yi (2006). The court decisions are Suwon District

third case, involving LG Petrochemical, is discussed in more detail in the next sub-section. It led to a finding of liability for both inside and outside directors but no out-of-pocket payments by the directors. The fourth is a 2011 case involving Hyundai Motor where the controlling shareholder, who was also a director, was ordered to pay 83 billion won ($83 million) and another inside director was held liable for 8 billion won ($8 million).[23] The company's outside directors were not sued. The decision has been appealed, and it is too early to know whether any directors will make personal payments.

We are also aware of seven cases over the last decade in which inside directors of Korean public companies that became insolvent were found liable, either to creditors or to the company. In a case concerning Daewoo Corp. and Daewoo Heavy Industry, two directors who apparently served on the boards of both companies were found liable to creditors after engaging in accounting fraud and a third was found liable for failing to monitor sufficiently and to deter this wrongdoing.[24] A second case, concerning Kohap, also involved liability to creditors for accounting fraud.[25] Four other cases involved liability to the company. The companies involved were Dongbang Peregrine, Cheong-gu Construction, Korea Life Insurance, and Dongah Construction.[26] A final case, concerning Daehan Investment Banking Corp., involved liability to the company for reckless lending, which breached the directors' duty of care.[27]

Details on any amounts actually paid by inside directors in these seven insolvency cases are not available. In some cases, the directors may have been protected by D&O insurance. Nevertheless, these cases confirm that shareholder and creditor suits against inside directors under corporate law are viable in Korea. They also confirm that in Korea, as in our comparison countries, there is heightened risk for directors after insolvency. For example, insolvency is a key element in the "perfect storm" that is

---

Court Decision on 2001.12.27 (awarding 90 billion won in damages), 1998-gahap-22553; Seoul High Court Decision on 2003.11.20, 2002-na-6595 (reducing award to 12 billion won); Supreme Court Decision on 2005.10.28, 2003-da-69638 (affirming appellate decision).

23 Seoul Central District Court Decision on 2011.2.25, 2008-Gahap-47881.

24 Supreme Court Decision on 2008.09.11, 2007-da-31518.

25 Supreme Court Decision on 2008.02.14, 2006-da-82601.

26 Supreme Court Decision on 2004.12.10, 2002-da-60467, 60474 (Dongbang Peregrine); Supreme Court Decision on 2007.09.20, 2007-da-25865 (Cheong-gu Construction); Supreme Court Decision on 2007.9.21, 2005-da-34797 (Korea Life Insurance); Supreme Court Decisions on 2007.10.11, 2007-da-34746 and on 2007.12.13, 2007-da-60080 (Dongah Construction).

27 Supreme Court Decision on 2007.07.26, 2006-da-33609.

usually needed for outside directors to make personal payments in the United States. The statutory reforms that authorize Korean companies to cap liability of executives at six times' annual compensation will likely discourage future suits, but how strongly remains to be seen.

C. Suits Against Outside Directors[28]

In Korea, PSPD and other shareholder rights activists have initiated many of the high-profile suits against managers under corporate law. Thus far, to our knowledge, these activists have not included outside directors as defendants in their lawsuits. We are aware, however, of two cases in which outside directors of Korean public companies were held liable after trial, in both cases together with inside directors. In one, it is not known whether the outside director paid damages personally; in the other the outside director did not pay damages.

The first case involved grave misconduct by an insider of Daesun Brewery, which the sole outside director, a university professor, took no action to prevent. The company was subsequently acquired in a hostile takeover, and the bidder sued Daesun Brewery's directors, including the outside director.[29] The court awarded damages of 140 billion won ($140 million). The case settled during the appeals process, and no information on who paid the damages is available.

The second case was brought against eight former directors of LG Chemical (currently, LG Corporation). Two outside directors (one was the former President of Seoul National University) participated in the board's decision to approve the sale of LG Petrochemical shares to the company's controlling shareholders and executive directors at a below-market price. In 2006, the Seoul Central District Court found the directors liable, and awarded damages of 40 billion won ($40 million) to the company, but limited the outside directors' share of the damages to 10 percent of this amount (4 billion won).[30] The court's decision, which departed from the usual rule of joint and several liability and lacked a direct basis in the Korean Commercial Code, suggests reluctance to impose a large financial penalty on the outside directors. The controlling shareholders who

---

28 The discussion in this section relies on the discussion of Korea, prepared by Hwa-Jin Kim, in Black, Cheffins, Gelter, Kim, Nolan, Siems and Linia Prava (2007, 2008). Professor Kim confirmed to us that he knows of no additional cases in which outside directors were found liable.

29 Busan Ilbo, May 12, 2004, at 014; court decision on 2004.04.14, 2002-gahap-16791, 2003-gahap-1066.

30 Case No. 2003-gahap-1176.

benefited from the sale of shares paid all damages, so neither the outside nor the inside directors paid anything.

Given these cases, outside directors in Korea clearly face some legal risks. But outside directors also enjoy a set of protections that collectively make personal liability a remote possibility, in our judgment, absent self-dealing. We have already discussed two important protections, these being the limits on damages in corporate lawsuits and rules discouraging frivolous securities class actions. Below, after spelling out the key sources of director liability, we identify three others, namely the loser pays rules for legal expenses, corporate indemnification, and D&O insurance.

D. Sources of Director Liability

To understand the extent to which legal reforms in Korea have increased the likelihood of lawsuits being brought against outside directors, and the directors' exposure to personal liability, it is helpful to analyze separately liability under corporate law and securities law.

Corporate law

The Commercial Code creates a duty of care, but does not directly specify a standard of liability by which breach of that duty is measured. It states, in article 382-3, that "Directors shall perform their duties faithfully for the good of the company in accordance with the relevant acts, subordinate statutes and the articles of incorporation."[31] Article 399 then provides that directors who participate in a board decision are jointly and severally liable to the company if they "acted in violation of any Acts and subordinate statutes or of the articles of incorporation or have neglected to perform their duties."[32] One might read these two provisions together as implying a simple negligence standard, especially if one compares article 399 on liability *to the company* to article 401 (quoted above), which contains an explicit gross negligence standard for liability *to third parties*. Nonetheless, some Korean courts, when interpreting this provision, have been receptive to a business-judgment-rule defense in cases that do not

---

31 Korean Commercial Code art. 382-3. The title of this article is "Directors' Duty of Loyalty." Some Korean commentators in Korea regard the title as misleading, and suggest that this provision creates both a duty of loyalty and a duty of care. Others view the duty of care as deriving from Korean Civil Code art. 681. There seems agreement that such a duty exists. The decided cases tend not to clearly distinguish between the duty of care and the duty of loyalty, and have not resolved this dispute among scholars.

32 Korean Commercial Code art. 399.

involve self-dealing.[33] This defense, if generally adopted, would provide an additional layer of protection for outside directors for cases in which the plaintiffs claim that the directors merely made bad decisions.

Even before the recent reforms allowing companies to limit directors' liability, Korean courts were apparently developing their own theory to limit the amounts for which directors are liable. They have been willing to exercise discretion to reduce substantially the amount of liability based on mitigating factors such as the director's prior contribution to the firm's success. The courts have justified this discretion on the basis of a general good faith principle in the Civil Code.[34]

Derivative litigation is now a realistic means of enforcement of directors' duties in Korea. Shareholding requirements for derivative suits are now low enough so that derivative suits are feasible, if a major institutional investor, or a shareholder group such as PSPD, is willing to bring them. Moreover, plaintiffs in derivative suits are exempt from Korea's usual loser-pays attorney fee rules unless the judge finds that the case was brought in bad faith. Also, for successful plaintiffs in derivative suits, the Commercial Code authorizes the plaintiff to be reimbursed by the company for reasonable litigation costs.[35] The filing of 55 derivative actions between 1997 and 2010, with just over half involving public companies, indicates that such litigation is feasible in Korea.[36]

Securities law

Korean securities law creates potential liability for outside directors. The 2004 securities class action law potentially makes these lawsuits feasible. Unlike derivative suits, the representative plaintiffs do not have to own a minimum percentage of the company's shares to bring a securities class action, though they do have to own shares.[37] At the same time, because securities class actions are still rare, with only one suit filed to date, it may take some time for courts to develop procedures to handle them.

---

33 Hwa-Jin Kim (2006).

34 Rho and Kim (2011), citing the *LG Petrochemical* case, Seoul Southern District Court 2003-gahap-1176 (Aug. 17, 2006); the *Dongbang Peregrine* case, Supreme Court 2002-na-60467, 60474 (Dec. 10, 2004); and Seoul Central District Court 2008-gahap-47867 (Feb. 8, 2010). One plausible way to understand the liability caps, permitted by Korean Commercial Code § 400(2), which apply absent gross negligence, is that they limit liability in many of the same cases in which a business judgment rule would protect directors from liability.

35 Korean Commercial Code art. 405.

36 Rho and Kim (2011).

37 Securities Class Action Act arts.11, 12(1)-1.

One reason securities litigation has been less common is that Korean securities law liability has been, until recently, narrower than U.S. liability. Korean directors are liable for faulty disclosure in a public offering, under standards similar to those in the United States. However, for secondary trading, until 2009, there was no basis for liability.[38] In addition, one interpretation of the class action law is that the judge must be persuaded of the merits of the case before it can proceed past a preliminary stage. If this view prevails, outside directors will often have an opportunity to seek early dismissal from a securities lawsuit, if they are named to begin with.[39]

A further factor discouraging securities litigation in Korea is uncertainty under Korean law as to the compensation available to plaintiffs' counsel in a successful suit. The Securities Class Action Law provides for attorneys' fees to be paid out of the recovery to the plaintiff class.[40] However, in the analogous case of fees for derivative suits, some fee awards have been quite low, both in dollar terms and as a percentage of the recovery. Also, the company itself will also be liable for securities violations directors might commit, has a "deeper pocket," and has fewer defenses (in particular, no due diligence defense). This is likely to deter both suits against directors and, if a suit succeeds, efforts are made to collect from the directors, rather than the company.

Korea's loser-pays rule for attorney fees may also come into play here. When plaintiffs know they have to reimburse the defendants if they lose in court, they will tend to focus on the most culpable defendants, who in securities litigation are unlikely to include outside directors. On the other hand, Korean attorney fee awards are based on a formula that significantly understates actual fees, which should mute this deterrent effect.

---

[38] Financial Investment Services and Capital Markets Act § 178 (adopted 2010) creates liability for "unfair trading," similar to U.S. Securities Exchange Act § 10(b) and Rule 10b-5. For securities offerings, directors are liable for misstatements by the company in the offering materials, but have a due diligence defense.

[39] For a class action lawsuit to proceed, the judge must find that it is "an efficient instrument which is appropriate for the realization of rights of the class and the protection of their interests." Securities Class Action Act art. 12(1)(3). One can read this as requiring only that procedural prerequisites, such as the predominance of common issues, are met. But one can also read it more broadly as permitting the judge to reject a class action, either altogether or against certain defendants, if he decides that the merits are weak.

[40] Securities Class Action Law art. 44.

E. Indemnification

Beyond the procedural and substantive rules that bear on the likelihood that plaintiffs will pursue outside directors, two additional shields will often protect directors from the risk that such suits will result in personal liability. These are indemnification by the company and D&O insurance. We discuss indemnification here and D&O insurance below.

Korea's Commercial Code is silent on the power of companies to indemnify directors against damages and case law has not yet addressed this issue. We asked for the opinions of several Korean scholars on the extent to which indemnification is likely to be permitted. There was agreement that in a derivative suit, indemnification will not be available for damages and likely will not be available for legal expenses if a director is found liable for damages. There was also agreement that indemnification for expenses should be available if the director is successful in defending against a suit, regardless of the nature of the suit.

There was disagreement as to whether indemnification for legal expenses or damages would be available in a securities case, or a corporate suit brought directly rather than a derivative suit, in which the director or the company pays damages. Our guess, though, is that in securities cases, indemnification is likely to be permitted as to both legal expenses and damages, especially if securities lawsuits become more common. Korea's civil code is German-derived, so the view of German scholars, that a silent civil code will likely be interpreted to permit indemnification, may be persuasive. Japanese scholars have advised us informally that a pro-indemnification outcome is considered likely there as well.[41] The permissibility of indemnification for direct suits under company law is harder to predict.

Legal uncertainties aside, we predict that, as in other countries, so long as the company is both directly liable and solvent, indemnification will rarely be an issue in practice. The company will hire and pay joint counsel, so directors' legal expenses will not be a concern. The company will also probably pay any damages, usually through a settlement.

F. D&O Insurance

D&O insurance provides directors with a further layer of protection against the risk that exposure to lawsuits will translate into significant

---

[41] For Germany, see Baums (1996). For Japan, see Cheffins and Black (2006), at 1461-62.

Table 2.1 D&O insurance in Korea

Year	Total no. of policies
1996[a]	1
1997[a]	5
1998[a]	105
1999[a]	320
2000[b]	101
2001[b]	264
2002[b]	386
2003[b]	372
2004 (est.)[c]	500

Note: The information in this table is taken from several sources, indicated by letter in the table, with citations in the accompanying footnote. The drop in number of policies from 1999 to 2000 likely reflects different data sources rather than an actual decline.

Sources: a=Financial Supervisory Service (2000) (in Korean, summarized in Kim and Kim (2003)). The one policy reported by this source for 1996 could be an error, since the reported premium was only 2 million won (around $2,000), which is implausibly low. b=Korea Insurance Development Institute (2004) (in Korean, selected information provided to us by Joongi Kim). c=Information provided to us in October 2004 by Young-Sam Kim of Marsh and McLennan.

exposure to personal liability. In Korea, as in other countries, D&O insurance will be available even in situations where indemnification by the company is not permitted, or not available because the company is insolvent. As we discuss above for the U.S., there will also be strong incentives for cases to settle with any payments coming from the D&O policy, the company, or both.

The Korean market for D&O insurance developed in the late 1990s, in response to the first derivative suits, brought by PSPD in 1997 and 1998.[42] Table 2.1 indicates how D&O policies grew in popularity.

We anticipate the number of Korean companies with D&O coverage has grown substantially since the mid-2000s. Moreover, while we know few details about the nature of D&O coverage that Korean companies currently purchase, we suspect that the market either has – or readily can, if the demand exists – develop policies offering thorough protection for outside directors, similar to that available in the U.S. One of us (Black) was an outside director of a public, U.S.-listed Korean company, and had first-hand experience with obtaining the broad coverage that is the norm in the

42 See Kim (2006).

United States. The company had coverage, but with huge loopholes (for example, advancement of legal expenses was at the insurer's discretion).[43] After protracted effort, the company ultimately obtained coverage that was acceptable in amount and was based on a good American policy. The policy was in English, which reduced the chance that loopholes could be introduced in translation.

This experience suggests to us that if lawsuit risk drives companies or their directors to bolster D&O coverage, insurers will likely adapt and provide broad coverage, if only by copying practice elsewhere. The likelihood that the legislature would react by limiting the scope of permissible insurance seems small. We would expect instead, given other countries' experience, that political pressure will be mostly the other way, toward limiting the scope of directors' liability, expanding the scope of permissible insurance, and clarifying the availability of indemnification. With insurance available, the settlement incentives we discuss above for the United States would likely emerge in Korea as well.

IV. IMPLICATIONS

In every country we have studied, outside directors of public companies face a very small but non zero risk of personal liability. Korea has been no exception, and seems unlikely to become one. Securities class actions have yet to occur with any frequency. Derivative suits under corporate law have occurred, but only in moderate numbers, and outside directors have not been the primary targets of most of these suits.

We believe that with outside directors, Korea likely has had the balance at least roughly correct over the period from the East Asian crisis to today. It was sensible for Korea to facilitate lawsuits against directors of public companies because previously such litigation was virtually unknown. We worry that the new limits on monetary liability of outside directors will lead, in practice, to their facing almost no risk of being sued. The challenge with caps on the amount of liability, to which there is no easy solution, is ensuring that plaintiffs and their lawyers retain financial incentives to bring suits in the first place.

At the same time, we believe that it would be counterproductive for Korea to expose outside directors to a significant risk of personal liability. We begin with the potentially positive effects of exposing outside directors to lawsuits, perhaps leading to settlements in which money changes hands,

---

43 A predecessor company first obtained coverage in 1999.

but not to actual personal liability. In such a world, the threat of a lawsuit should prompt directors to be more careful even if personal liability is highly unlikely.[44] Directors may be concerned about loss of reputation if they, or their company, are sued and lose or settle, even if the directors do not pay anything. The threat of lawsuits can also reinforce directors' professional norms, and provide a basis for outside directors to say no to a questionable transaction that management proposes. Moreover, a lawsuit is not fun. The time and aggravation entailed in being sued may be a significant deterrent without more.

On the other hand, a significant risk of personal liability could be counterproductive. For instance, outside directors might become too cautious. A high degree of care can be desirable when policing conflict of interest transactions involving management or a controlling shareholder, but not when overseeing business decisions generally. Absent the unusual circumstance in which an outside director owns a large block of stock, the director's upside from accepting a business gamble is limited, especially compared to the downside of possibly devastating liability if something goes wrong. Reducing the caution that might flow from this asymmetry of risk and reward provides a strong reason to limit outside directors' exposure to personal liability when no conflict of interest is involved.

Fear of personal liability risk could also result in a counterproductive effort by directors to establish and follow bureaucratic procedures and create a paper record for everything they do. Up to some unquantifiable point, the threat of a lawsuit can help to induce a well-structured deliberative process and careful deliberation. Beyond that point, however, fear of liability could be counterproductive, with boardroom meetings becoming protracted affairs, with more time spent on process and less on substance and business strategy.

An additional consequence of imposing significant personal liability risk on outside directors is that people will be less willing to serve in these positions, especially if they are wealthy and therefore attractive targets for a lawsuit. This could have an adverse impact on corporate governance. In many cases, the ideal outside director is someone who has succeeded in business and as a result has considerable wealth. If many of these people were to decide not to serve, the quality of outside directors could suffer. Already Korean outside directors are often academics and former government officials rather than experienced businessmen.

---

[44] We develop reasons why a moderate level of litigation, and corresponding *nominal liability* (without personal liability) could promote vigilance in Black, Cheffins, and Klausner (2006b).

Wealthy businessmen's fear of liability could deter businessmen from serving where their service would be valuable.

Finally, if there was a significant out-of-pocket risk and individuals agreed to serve as outside directors despite that risk, they would logically demand higher director fees that compensate for that risk. If, however, director fees become a substantial portion of a director's overall income, a valuable measure of independence could be lost. It is important for a director to be willing to walk away from a directorship, or at least to be able to credibly threaten to do so, if management is heading in a direction the he or she believes is ill-advised. As the cost of walking away rises, the likelihood of it happening declines. The risk that high director compensation could undermine independence may be a special concern in Korea, due to Korea's reliance on academics and former government officials as major sources of outside directors. These persons are often not wealthy, so director compensation may well form a substantial part of their income. Fear of losing this income could chill their willingness to speak up in board meetings or to resign if need be.

In assessing the extent to which outside director conduct would be improved by exposing them to a risk of being sued, a (small) risk of personal liability, one must also consider other factors that motivate outside directors. One factor is an outside director's economic interest in the firm. An outside director of a company that performs poorly in the marketplace will be harmed to the extent he holds company shares or options. This economic interest can motivate many outside directors to work hard. Korean companies can improve these incentives by paying directors partly or mostly with stock and stock options, rather than in cash, and expecting directors to hold their shares until after they leave the board.

More generally, outside directors have a reputational interest in doing a good job. If a scandal occurs on their watch, then quite apart from any litigation risk, their credibility may suffer, with damaging consequences for their future business prospects, their sense of personal pride, and what their friends and colleagues think of them. Korea has a vigorous press that is quick to report on business scandals. Such an active press can reinforce directors' concern for reputation.[45] Fear of an adverse outcome should motivate outside directors to be attentive and vigilant. To be sure, it is hard for outsiders to assess the extent to which reputational sanctions will provide incentives for good governance. Still, our sense is that Korean

45 On the role of the business press in addressing corporate misbehavior, see Dyck, Volchkova, and Zingales (2008).

directors are at least as attentive to reputation as their counterparts elsewhere.

As outsiders, we are reticent to offer firm conclusions about the right level of exposure of Korean outside directors to the risk of lawsuits or personal liability. Still, we believe that a moderate level of both derivative litigation under company law and securities class actions, in which outside directors are sometimes named, could be salutary. On the other hand, we do not believe that outside directors should face a substantial risk of personal liability, given that such liability can provide counterproductive incentives and that outside directors already have various reasons to be attentive monitors of corporate executives.

REFERENCES

Almeida, Heitor, Sang Yong Park, Marti G. Subramanyam, and Daniel Wolfenzon, *The Structure and Formation of Business Groups: Evidence from Korean Chaebols*, 99 Journal of Financial Economics 447–475 (2010).

Andrews, Neil, *English Civil Procedure: Fundamentals of the New Civil Justice System* (Oxford University Press, 2003).

Armour, John, Bernard Black, Brian Cheffins, and Richard Nolan, *Private Enforcement of Corporate Law: A Comparative Empirical Analysis of the UK and the US*, 6 Journal of Empirical Legal Studies 687–722(2009).

Armour, John, Brian Cheffins, and Bernard Black, *Delaware's Balancing Act*, Indiana Law Review (forthcoming 2012), available at http://ssrn.com/abstract=1677400.

Aronson, Bruce E., *Reconsidering the Importance of Law in Japanese Corporate Governance: Evidence from the Daiwa Bank Shareholder Derivative Case*, 36 Cornell International Law Journal 11–57 (2003).

ASX Corporate Governance Council, *Principles of Good Corporate Governance and Best Practice Recommendations* (Australian Stock Exchange, 2003), available at http://www.asx.com.au/about/pdf/ASXRecommendations.pdf.

Bae, Kee-Hong, Jun-Koo Kang, and Jin-Mo Kim, *Tunneling or Value Added? Evidence from Mergers by Korean Business Groups*, 57 Journal of Finance 2695–2740 (2002).

Bae, Kee-Hong, Jae-Seung Baek, Jun-Koo Kang, and Wei-Lin Liu, *Do Controlling Shareholders' Expropriation Incentives Imply a Link between Corporate Governance and Firm Value? Theory and Evidence*, Journal of Financial Economics, forthcoming (2012).

Baek, Jae-Seung, Jun-Koo Kang, and Inmoo Lee , *Business Groups and Tunneling: Evidence from Private Securities Offerings by Korean Chaebols*, 61 Journal of Finance 2415–2449 (2006).

Baums, Theodor, *Personal Liabilities of Company Directors in German Law*, 9 International Corporate and Commercial Law Review 318–24 (1996).

Baxter, Colin, *Demystifying D&O Insurance*, 15 Oxford Journal of Legal Studies 537–64 (1995).

Bishop, Joseph, *New Cure for an Old Ailment: Insurance Against Directors' and Officers' Liability*, 22 Business Lawyer 92–114 (1966).
Bishop, Joseph, *Sitting Ducks and Decoy Ducks: New Trends in the Indemnification of Corporate Directors and Officers*, 77 Yale Law Journal 1078–1103 (1968).
Black, Bernard, Brian Cheffins, Martin Gelter, Hwa-Jin Kim, Richard Nolan, Matthias Siems, and Linia Prava law firm, *Report to Russian Center for Capital Market Development: Comparative Analysis on Legal Regulation of the Liability of Members of the Executive Organs of Companies* (2007), available at http://ssrn.com/abstract=1001990.
Black, Bernard, Brian Cheffins, Martin Gelter, Hwa-Jin Kim, Richard Nolan, Matthias Siems, and Linia Prava law firm, *Legal Liability of Directors and Company Officials Part 2: Court Procedures, Indemnification and Insurance, and Administrative and Criminal Liability (Report to the Russian Securities Agency)*, Columbia Business Law Review 1–171, (2008) available at http://ssrn.com/abstract=1010307.
Black, Bernard, Brian Cheffins, and Michael Klausner, *Outside Director Liability*, 59 Stanford Law Review 1055–1159 (2006a), available at http://papers.ssrn.com/abstract=382422.
Black, Bernard, Brian Cheffins, and Michael Klausner, *Outside Director Liability: A Policy Analysis*, 162 Journal of Institutional and Theoretical Economics 5–31 (2006b), available at http://ssrn.com/abstract=878135.
Black, Bernard, Brian Cheffins, and Michael Klausner, *Shareholder Suits and Outside Director Liability: The Case of Korea*, 11 Journal of Korean Law 325–362 (2011).
Black, Bernard, Hasung Jang, and Woochan Kim, 'Does Corporate Governance Affect Firms' Market Values? Evidence from Korea', 22 Journal of Law, Economics and Organization 366–413 (2006), nearly final version available at http://ssrn.com/abstract=311275.
Black, Bernard, and Woochan Kim, *The Effect of Board Structure on Firm Value: A Multiple Identification Strategy Approach Using Korean* Data, 103 Journal of Financial Economics (forthcoming 2012), nearly final version available at http://ssrn.com/abstract=968287.
Black, Bernard, Woochan Kim, Hasung Jang, and Kyung-Suh Park, *How Corporate Governance Affects Firm Value: Evidence on Channels from Korea* (working paper 2012), available at http://ssrn.com/abstract=844744.
Black, Bernard, Barry Metzger, Timothy O'Brien, and Young Moo Shin, *Corporate Governance in Korea at the Millennium: Enhancing International Competitiveness (Report to the Korean Ministry of Justice, May 2000)*, 26 Journal of Corporation Law 537–609 (2001), available at http://ssrn.com/abstract=222491.
Cheffins, Brian R., *Company Law: Theory, Structure and Operation* (Oxford University Press, 1997).
Cheffins, Brian, and Bernard Black, *Outside Director Liability Across Countries*, 84 Texas Law Review 1385–1480 (2006), available at http://ssrn.com/abstract=438321.
Choi, Jongmoo Jay, Sae Woon Park, and Sean Sehyun Yoo, *The Value of Outside Directors: Evidence from Corporate Governance Reform from Korea*, 42 Journal of Financial and Quantitative Analysis 941–962 (2007).
Choi, Stephen, and Kon Sik Kim, *Establishing a New Stock Market for Shareholder Value Oriented Firms in Korea*, 3 Chicago Journal of International Law 277–300 (2002).

Coffee, John C., *Understanding the Plaintiff's Attorney: The Implications of Economic Theory for Private Enforcement of Law Through Class and Derivative Actions*, 86 Columbia Law Review 669–727 (1986).

Cole, Douglas G., *Counsel Fees in Stockholders' Derivative and Class Actions – Hornstein Revisited*, 6 University of Richmond Law Review 259–85 (1972).

Corporate Board Member, *What Directors Think Research Study 2003*, available at http://www.boardmember.com/network/WhatDirsThink2003.pdf.

Dyck, I.J. Alexander, Natalya Volchkova, and Luigi Zingales, *The Corporate Governance Role of the Media: Evidence from Russia*, 63 Journal of Finance 1093–1135 (2008).

Fanto, James A., *The Role of Corporate Law in French Corporate Governance*, 31 Cornell International Law Journal 31–91 (1998).

Financial Reporting Council, *The Combined Code on Corporate Governance* (United Kingdom, 2003), available at http://www.frc.org.uk/about/combined.cfm.

Financial Supervisory Service (Korea), *Report on Directors' and Officers' Insurance* (2000) (in Korean).

Fujita, Tomotaka, *Transformation of the Management Liability Regime in Japan in the Wake of the 1993 Revision*, in Hideki Kanda, Kon-Sik Kim and Curtis J. Milhaupt eds, *Transforming Corporate Governance in East Asia* 15 (2008).

Gilson, Ronald J., *Globalizing Corporate Governance, Convergence of Form or Function*, 49 American Journal of Comparative Law 329–58 (2001).

Government Commission, *German Corporate Governance Code* (2003), available in English at http://www.ecgi.org/codes/country_documents/germany/code_200305_en.pdf.

Gray, Wayne D., *Corporations as Winners under CBCA Reform*, 39 Canadian Business Law Journal 4–35 (2003).

Hodges, Christopher, *Multi-Party Actions* (Oxford University Press, 2001).

Hopt, Klaus J., *Directors' Duties to Shareholders, Employees, and Other Creditors: A View from the Continent*, in Ewan McKendrick ed., *Commercial Aspects of Trust and Fiduciary Obligations*115–132 (Oxford University Press, 1992).

Johnson, Simon, Peter Boone, Alasdair Breach, and Eric Friedman, *Corporate Governance in the Asian Financial Crisis*, 58 Journal of Financial Economics 141–186 (2000).

Kim, Joongi, *Recent Amendments to the Korean Commercial Code and Their Effects on International Competition*, 21 University of Pennsylvania Journal of International Economic Law 273–330 (2000).

Kim, Hwa-Jin, *Toward the "Best Practice" Model in a Globalizing Market: Recent Developments in Korean Corporate Governance*, 2 Journal of Corporate Law Studies 345–366 (2002).

Kim, Hwa-Jin, *Directors' Duties and Liabilities in Corporate Control and Restructuring Transactions: Recent Developments in Korea*, 2006 Oxford University Comparative Law Forum, article 2, at http://ouclf.iuscomp.org/articles/kim.shtml.

Kim, Jooyoung, and Joongi Kim, *Shareholder Activism in Korea: A Review of How PSPD Has Used Legal Measures to Strengthen Korean Corporate Governance*, 1 Journal of Korean Law 51–76 (2001).

Kim, Kon-Sik, and Joongi Kim, *Revamping Fiduciary Duties in Korea: Does Law Matter in Corporate Governance?*, in Curtis Milhaupt ed., *Global Markets,*

Domestic Institutions: Corporate Law and Governance in a New Era of Cross-Border Deals 372–399 (Columbia University Press, 2003).

Korea Insurance Development Institute, *Liability Insurance Annual Statistics Report* (2004), at www.kidi.or.kr.

Knepper, William A., and Dan A. Bailey, *Liability of Corporate Officers and Directors* (6th ed. 1998) (Lexis Law Publishing).

Korn/Ferry International, *Annual Board of Directors Study* (2003).

Milhaupt, Curtis J., *A Relational Theory of Japanese Corporate Governance: Contract, Culture, and the Rule of Law*, 37 Harvard Journal of International Law 3–64 (1996).

Milhaupt, Curtis J., *Nonprofit Organizations as Investor Protection: Economic Theory and Evidence from East Asia*, 29 Yale Journal of International Law 169–207 (2004).

Nakahigashi, Masafumi, Corporate Governance in Japan: Financial Information and Auditing System, unpublished working paper (2003).

Park, Johneth Chongseo, and Doo-Ah Lee, 'The Business Judgment Rule: A Missing Piece in the Developing Puzzle of Korean Corporate Governance Reform', 3 Journal of Korean Law (2003).

Rho, Hyeok-Joon, and Kon-Sik Kim, *Invigorating Shareholder Derivative Actions in Korea*, in Daniel Puchniak and Harald Baum eds, *The Derivative Action in Asia* (Cambridge University Press, forthcoming 2011).

Romano, Roberta, *Corporate Governance in the Aftermath of the Insurance Crisis*, 39 Emory Law Journal 1155–1189 (1990).

Toronto Stock Exchange, *TSX Company Manual* (Toronto Stock Exchange, 2004), at http://www.tse.com/en/productsAndServices/listings/tse/resources/resourceManual.html .

Toronto Stock Exchange Committee on Corporate Governance in Canada, *Report: Where Were the Directors? Guidelines for Improved Corporate Governance in Canada* (Toronto Stock Exchange, 1994).

Towers Perrin, *2003 Directors and Officers Liability Survey* (2004).

Van Duzer, J. Anthony, *The Law of Partnerships and Corporations*, 2nd ed. (Toronto: Irwin Law, 2003).

West, Mark D. *Why Shareholders Sue: Evidence from Japan*, 30 Journal of Legal Studies 351–382 (2002).

3. New squeeze-out devices as a part of corporate law reform in Korea*

Hyeok-Joon Rho

I. INTRODUCTION

When the incorporated entity first emerged, the operation of the corporation was based on mutual agreement among its shareholders.[1] Because the charter was viewed as a contract among shareholders,[2] the management of the corporation was subject to consensus among its shareholders.[3] Thus, the nineteenth-century corporate law effectively allowed all shareholders a veto right whenever their corporation wanted to amend its charter or to adopt fundamental changes in its operation.[4] A veto right, however, turned out to be an easy tool for minority shareholders to use to block a

* This chapter is based upon an article by this author published in the Boston University International Law Journal (29 B.U. Int'l L. J. 41, 2011). For more domestic squeeze-out issues in Korea, including the detailed method of appraisal, readers may refer to the author's other paper in Korean: Hyeok-Joon Rho, *Sosoo-Jooju-Chuckchul-Jedoeu-Doipae-Kwanhan-Yeongoo [Imminent Adoption of Squeeze-out Devices in Korea: What Should be Considered for Balancing Majorities and Minorities?]*, 26 Com. L. Rev. 231-71 (2008).

1 In other words, shareholders in a corporation would stipulate to their rights and obligations, the governance of the corporation, and other material terms on management in the corporate charter and then operate the corporation pursuant to that charter.

2 *See* Elliott J. Weiss, *The Law of Take Out Mergers: A Historical Perspective*, 56 N.Y.U. L. Rev. 624, 627 (1981) ("The basis for this rule was the view that the charter was a contract, both among the corporation's shareholders and between the corporation and the state, in which every shareholder had vested rights.").

3 *See id.*

4 Alexander Khutorsky, *Coming in from the Cold: Reforming Shareholders' Appraisal Rights in Freeze-Out Transactions*, 1997 Colum. Bus. L. Rev. 133, 137 (1997); Barry M. Wertheimer, *The Shareholders' Appraisal Remedy and How Courts Determine Fair Value*, 47 Duke L. J. 613, 618-19 (1998).

change that would serve collective interests, thereby frustrating desirable economic progress.[5]

The appraisal right was developed in response to the inevitable tension between shareholders, as parties to the corporate contract, and the economic reality that granting a veto right to every minority shareholder crippled the governance of large corporations.[6] The appraisal right allowed the majority to decide what they thought was appropriate for the corporation and provided a right of exit to minority shareholders by forcing the corporation to repurchase minority shareholders' shares if the minority disagreed with the majority decision. Corporate statutes in many countries, including Korea, have adopted the appraisal remedy in a bid to enable the majority to operate a corporation with flexibility while providing sufficient protection to the minority for the minority shareholders' investment.[7]

The squeeze-out or freeze-out is another retreat in terms of minority shareholders' rights. Generally speaking, a squeeze-out is a mechanism used by a majority shareholder in a corporation to force out those in the minority.[8] A squeeze-out may be executed through various strategies including a cash-out merger,[9] reverse stock split,[10] two-step merger,[11] or compulsory acquisition.[12] In contrast to the appraisal remedy – where minority shareholders decide whether to follow a blueprint suggested by the majority – under a squeeze-out scheme, it is the majority shareholder who decides the transfer of minority shareholders' shares.

The KCC does not provide shareholders with a veto right when deciding major issues in a corporation. Instead, dissenting shareholders are entitled to an appraisal right when a shareholders' meeting approves a business transfer, a comprehensive share exchange, or a statutory merger. The KCC seemed to be based upon a vested-right theory – the idea that

---

5 *See In re* Timmis, 93 N.E. 522, 523-24 (N.Y. 1910); *see also* Weiss, *supra* note 2, at 629 (describing this phenomenon as "tyranny by the minority").

6 Robert C. Clark, Corporate Law 443-44 (1986).

7 *See, e.g.*, Del. Code Ann. tit. 8, § 262 (2010); Cal. Corp. Code § 1300 (West 2010); the Korean Commercial Code (KCC), Act No.10600, April 14, 2011, art. 299-2 (Kor.).

8 *See* F. Hodge O'Neal, *Minority Owners Can Avoid Squeeze-outs*, 41 Harv. Bus. Rev. 150, 150 (1963); John C. Coates IV, *"Fair Value" as Avoidable Rule of Corporate Law: Minority Discounts in Conflict Transactions*, 147 U. Pa. L. Rev. 1251, 1253 (1999).

9 *See* Clark, supra note 6, § 12.1, at 501-02.

10 *See id.* at 502.

11 *See id.* § 12.2, at 516.

12 *See id.* § 12.1, at 503.

every shareholder has the right to continue his investment in a corporation. As such, the KCC strictly limited squeeze-out transactions.

But the new KCC of 2011,[13] which is effective as of April 15, 2012, contains several provisions on squeeze-out rights. Thus the discussion surrounding squeeze-out rights in Korea has become increasingly important. This paper aims to explore squeeze-out strategies in Korean corporate practice. This paper will also analyze squeeze-out mechanisms in other countries by way of comparison. This article will focus mainly on the "statutory" squeeze-out device, rather than the *de facto* or indirect oppressive methods that the majority may use to drive out the minority.[14]

The balance of this article will proceed as follows. Section II will examine current squeeze-out devices in other countries and will separate those devices into three general categories. Section III will analyze demands for new squeeze-out devices in Korea and review traditional and newly-adopted squeeze-out devices. Finally, Section IV summarizes and concludes this article.

II. COMPARATIVE ANALYSIS: VARIOUS TYPES OF SQUEEZE-OUT LEGISLATION

Given that squeeze-out devices have many positive aspects, what legislative options are available and what are the merits of each legislative alternative? As discussed later, Korea did not provide flexible methods for a squeeze-out until the adoption of the new KCC of 2011. A comparative research into statutory squeeze-out devices adopted in other countries would further elucidate the pros and cons of each legislative option and assist in developing more well-organized squeeze-out regulations in Korea.

Some legislative devices included substantial as well as procedural requirements for squeeze-outs. For example, under early U.S. case law, in order to squeeze-out minority shareholders, a company had to prove that a specific business purpose would be achieved by the transaction.[15] In addition, Securities and Exchange Commission Rule 13e-3 of 1979 required controlling shareholders to disclose the purpose of the squeeze-out and the

---

[13] The Korean Commercial Code, Act No.10600, April 14, 2011.

[14] Joseph A. McCahery et al., *The Economics of the Proposed European Takeover Directive*, *in* Reforming Company and Takeover Law in Europe 591-92, 636 (Guido Ferrarini et al. eds, 2004).

[15] *See, e.g.*, Singer v. Magnavox Co., 380 A.2d 969, 978-80 (Del. 1977). *See also* Weiss, *supra* note 2, at 625 n.4.

reason that controlling shareholders had to choose a squeeze-out among various other methods of achieving the same purpose.[16]

However, the substantial requirements historically imposed in the U.S. were so vague that they did not necessarily function as a safeguard against abusive squeeze-outs: almost every squeeze-out might be viewed as having a business purpose, because, at a minimum, the elimination of minority shareholders would normally reduce some governance costs.[17] Therefore, it may be wiser instead to focus on fair compensation for minority shareholders and procedural requirements (including the threshold for approving squeeze-out transactions) rather than substantial requirements similar to those that have historically existed in the U.S.[18] In tender offer type as opposed to a squeeze-out through a statutory merger a two-step transaction is required: using what process and with how many shares can a majority shareholder force out minority shareholders. From this perspective, squeeze-out legislation can be categorized as one of three types: (1) tender offer type;[19] (2) cash-out merger type;[20] or (3) supermajority type.[21]

A. Tender Offer Type: Compulsory Acquisition in the U.K.

In tender offer type squeeze-out legislation, as opposed to a squeeze-out through a statutory merger, a two-step transaction is required.[22] First, in the tender offer stage, the offeror makes a public offer to attract shareholders in a target company. Second, having successfully acquired the minimum level of shares required by the squeeze-out regulation, the offeror is allowed to acquire shares held by the remaining minority shareholders in the compulsory acquisition stage.[23] After a successful tender offer and the subsequent acquisition of remaining shares, the offeror will

---

16 Rule 13e-3, 17 C.F.R. § 240.13e-3. *See also* Guhan Subramanian, *Fixing Freezeouts*, 115 YALE L.J. 2, 10 (2005).

17 *See* CLARK, *supra* note 6, § 12.2, at 514.

18 *See, e.g.*, Weinberger v. UOP, Inc., 457 A.2d 701, 715 (Del. 1983). *See also* STEPHEN KENYON-SLADE, MERGERS AND TAKEOVERS IN THE U.S. AND U.K.: LAW AND PRACTICE 63-86 (2004); Marc I. Steinberg & Evalyn N. Lindahl, *The New Law of Squeeze-out Mergers*, 62 WASH. U. L. Q. 351, 351-414 (1984); Robert B. Thompson, *Squeeze-out Mergers and the "New" Appraisal Remedy*, 62 WASH. U. L. Q. 415, 423-34 (1984).

19 *See* CLARK, SUPRA note 6, § 12.2, at 531-33.

20 *See id.* § 12.1, at 501-02.

21 *See id.* § 18.3.2, at 775-76.

22 KENYON-SLADE, *supra* note 18, at 514-17.

23 ELIZABETH BOROS, MINORITY SHAREHOLDERS' REMEDIES 262-65 (1995).

have obtained 100 percent ownership of the target company.[24] Where the offeror is an inside controlling shareholder, the aim of the squeeze-out is to take the company private and to eliminate the cost of maintaining minority shareholders in the company.[25] Where the offeror is an outside acquirer, the aim of the squeeze-out might be to enjoy the increased value of the target company exclusively.[26]

A typical tender offer type squeeze-out can be found in the U.K. According to the U.K. Companies Act of 2006,[27] where a takeover offer is made for all shares in a company (or for all shares of any class or classes), and the offeror has acquired nine-tenths of the shares (or nine-tenths of the shares of any class to which the offer relates), the offeror is able to acquire the shares of the dissenting minority shareholders on the same terms as the offer, subject to the right of the dissenting shareholders to apply to the court.[28] Both public and private companies fall within the scope of this legislation, regardless of whether the City Code on Takeovers and Mergers is applied to the squeeze-out transaction.[29] The offeror must provide non-assenting shareholders with a notice informing them of the rights of compulsory acquisition.[30] The notice should be sent to the target company, along with a statement from the offeror declaring that the statutory requirements for giving such notice have been met.[31] Where the terms of an offer give shareholders a choice of consideration, the remaining shareholders in the target company may, within six weeks from the date of the notice, indicate their choice.[32] At the end of the six weeks from the date of the notice, the offeror must pay or transfer the compensation for the shares that are being acquired by the target company.[33]

It is true that the statutory remedy against oppressive or unfairly prejudicial conduct against minority shareholders has been emphasized in common law countries.[34] However, the courts are generally unsympathetic

---

24 *See id.*

25 *See id.* at 306-07.

26 *See id.* at 306.

27 The Directive of the European Parliament and of the Council on Takeover Bids, Council Directive 2004/25, art. 15, 2004 O.J. (L 142) (EC), which took effect on April 21, 2004, was reflected in the Companies Act of 2006.

28 Companies Act, 2006, c. 3, § 979(1-4), § 986(1) (Eng.).

29 TAKEOVERS: LAW AND PRACTICE 573 (Gary Eaborn ed., 2005).

30 Companies Act, 2006, c. 3, § 980(1) (Eng.).

31 *Id.* § 980(4).

32 *Id.* § 981(3).

33 *Id.* § 981(6).

34 *See, e.g.*, Elizabeth Boros, *Altering the Articles of Association to Acquire Minority Shareholdings*, *in* THE REALM of COMPANY LAW 107, 107-08 (Barry A.K.

when minority shareholders challenge compulsory acquisition, because the courts are swayed by the fact that 90 percent of shareholders have approved the transaction.[35] In the absence of special circumstances, therefore, the minority shareholders bear the burden of proof of establishing why their shares should not be acquired.

On the other hand, the Companies Act of 2006 also provides a so-called "sell-out right" for minority shareholders. Under section 983, when an offeror has acquired 90 percent of all the company shares, holders of shares to which the offer relates who did not accept the offer may require the offeror to purchase their remaining minority interest shares on the same terms and for the same consideration as under the offer.[36] The sell-out right is seen as the opposite side of the same coin: a benefit for the minority that mirrors the benefit of compulsory acquisition for the majority.[37]

The U.K. is not the only country that applies this type of squeeze-out. Since the adoption of the European Directive on Takeover Bids in 2004,[38] which is broadly consistent with the U.K. company law concerning squeeze-out devices,[39] many European countries have introduced tender offer type squeeze-outs.[40] Tender offer type squeeze-outs in the U.K. have two distinctive features. First, a tender offer is a prerequisite for the squeeze-out. Second, the shares already held by the offeror or its associate[41] are not counted toward the threshold percentage required for the

---

Rider ed., 1998) ("There is growing judicial sympathy for the complaints of minority shareholders, reflected in part in the increasing role and importance of the statutory remedy against oppressive or unfairly prejudicial conduct.").

35 BRENDA HANNIGAN, COMPANY LAW 912 (2003).

36 Companies Act, 2006, c. 3, § 983(1-2) (Eng.).

37 *See* Joseph Lee, *Four Models of Minority Shareholder Protection in Takeovers*, 16 EUR. BUS. L. REV. 803, 826-27 (2005). *But see* Paul L. Davies, *The Notion of Equality in European Takeover Regulations*, *in* TAKEOVERS IN ENGLISH AND GERMAN LAW 9, 22 (Jennifer Payne ed., 2002) (explaining that some commentators do not agree to accept the equivalence of the sell-out and squeeze-out rights at the 90 percent plus level).

38 Council Directive 2004/25, The Directive of the European Parliament and of the Council on Takeover Bids, art. 15, 2004 O.J. (L 142) (EC).

39 *See* DEPARTMENT OF TRADE AND INDUSTRY (DTI), COMPANY LAW IMPLEMENTATION OF THE EUROPEAN DIRECTIVE ON TAKEOVER BIDS: A CONSULTATIVE DOCUMENT 34 (2005).

40 *See generally* Christoph van der Elst & Lientje van den Steen, *Balancing the Interests of Minority and Majority Shareholders: A Comparative Analysis of Squeeze-out and Sell-out Rights*, EUR. COMPANY & FIN. L. REV. 391 (2009).

41 Companies Act, 2006, c. 3, § 988(1) (Eng.) (explaining that an associate of an offeror means: a nominee of the offeror; a holding company, subsidiary or fellow

second step of the squeeze-out.[42] For example, even where an offeror or its associate has more than 90 percent of the shares (under U.K. law), the offeror or its associate may not squeeze minority shareholders out unless 90 percent of the minority shareholders have tendered their shares.

B. Cash-out Merger Type: Long-form Mergers in the U.S.

In some countries, a statutory merger allows a majority shareholder to force out minority shareholders. Specifically, in a stock-for-cash merger, according to the merger contract between the acquiring company and the target company, minority shareholders in the target company are supposed to receive cash in return for their shares in the target company. Thus, majority shareholders in the acquiring company and those in the target company will decide whether to squeeze-out minority shareholders in the target company. Long-form mergers in the U.S. provide a good example.[43] Pursuant to section 251 of the Delaware General Corporation Law (DGCL), a merger contract, approved by an ordinary shareholders' resolution, may provide that minority shareholders in a target company shall be given cash or securities other than an acquiring company's shares.[44]

In the U.S. it is common to force out minority shareholders through a statutory merger.[45] Why is a merger so closely associated with a squeeze-out? As will be shown by the supermajority type squeeze-out, a squeeze-out mechanism is not necessarily related to a combination of two companies. However, a statutory merger, in which the acquirer generally expects an enormous increase in the value of the target company, would provide a fertile environment for a squeeze-out mechanism, as the acquirer would normally want to eliminate free riders who want to remain as minority shareholders and enjoy the fruits of the merger. In addition, in terms of compensation for minority shareholders, the acquirer, being

---

subsidiary of the offeror or a nominee of such a holding company, subsidiary or fellow subsidiary; a body corporate in which the offeror is substantially interested; a person who is, or is a nominee of, a party to a share acquisition agreement with the offeror, or; (where the offeror is an individual) his spouse or civil partner and any minor child or step-child of his).

42 *Id.* § 974(1), § 977(2).

43 KENYON-SLADE, *supra* note 18, at 12-13.

44 DEL. CODE ANN. tit. 8, § 251 (2010).

45 Subramanian, *supra* note 16, at 9 ("These laws provided the statutory merger mechanism for freezing out minority shareholders, which remains the most common procedure today.").

confident about the positive effects of the merger, might be willing to provide generous compensation for an efficient and smooth transaction.

C. Supermajority Type: German Stock Corporation Act and Short-form Mergers in the U.S.

This type of squeeze-out enables a majority shareholder who has obtained a supermajority threshold ownership in the target company to squeeze-out the minority bloc. Once a dominant shareholder crosses the threshold stipulated by the law, he or she may demand remaining shareholders to sell their shares. Section 327(a) of the German Stock Corporation Act (*Aktiengesetz*) stipulates a squeeze-out right for a dominant shareholder. A shareholder who owns 95 percent or more of a company's legal capital may squeeze-out minority shareholders provided that appropriate compensation is given to them.[46]

Another example of a supermajority type of squeeze-out can be found in U.S. short-form merger. According to section 253 of the DGCL, an offeror who succeeds in obtaining 90 percent of a target company may proceed with a short-form merger.[47] As opposed to a "merger freeze-out" that relies on a statutory long-form merger, a "tender offer freeze-out" is based upon a tender offer and subsequent short-form merger.[48] The tender offer freeze-out in the U.S. is similar to a compulsory acquisition in the U.K., in that both require a two-step transaction comprised of a tender offer and a compulsory acquisition of minority shares. However, U.S. tender offer freeze-outs have an important "supermajority feature." Such a feature requires 90 percent ownership of "all outstanding" shares of the target company.[49] Meanwhile, compulsory acquisition in the U.K. requires 90 percent approval of "shares to which the offer relates."[50] Thus, even where a dominant shareholder has more than 95 percent ownership, he or she cannot squeeze-out minority shareholders should he or she fail to obtain 90 percent of the remaining shares through a tender offer first.

---

46 Nils Krause, *The New German Takeover Law: An Overview of the New Regime*, 4 INT'L & COMP. CORP. L.J. 345, 366 (2002); *see also* Frank Wooldridge, *The New German Takeover Act*, 14 EUR. BUS. L. REV. 86 (2003).

47 DEL. CODE ANN. tit. 8, § 253 (2010).

48 *See* Subramanian, *supra* note 16, at 7 (explaining how some scholars categorize squeeze-out in the U.S. into two groups: tender offer freeze-out which combines tender offer and short form merger, or merger freeze-out which uses statutory cash-out merger (long-form merger)).

49 DEL. CODE ANN. tit. 8, § 253(a) (2010).

50 Companies Act, 2006, c. 3, § 979(2)(4) (Eng.).

III. SQUEEZE-OUTS IN KOREA: THE CURRENT SITUATION AND THE WAY TO REFORM

A. Introduction

The general economic justification for squeeze-outs would apply to Korean businesses. Specifically, some Korean enterprises might want to eliminate minority shareholders in order to cut the costs associated with minority shareholders and to enhance the synergy gains from combining businesses. In addition, in the case of 100 percent ownership, which can be reached through a squeeze-out, companies are able to enjoy benefits under the Korean corporate regulatory regime. For example, under the Monopoly Regulation and Fair Trade Act[51] and its guidelines, a loan by a financial holding company to its wholly-owned financial affiliate at a lower interest rate shall not constitute an unfair transaction between affiliated companies.[52] However, most provisions in Korean corporate or anti-trust law do not differentiate between a company that is wholly-owned and a company that has minority shareholders. Thus, demands for squeeze-out, if any, are normally based upon an economic or business rationale, rather than any marginal legal benefits that are attained through 100 percent ownership.

The question that then naturally arises is whether there is any evidence of a significant demand from Korean companies for squeeze-outs that would justify the introduction of new squeeze-out devices? While it is understood that squeeze-outs can be justified in an economic sense, the government may choose not to introduce new devices as long as the demand for such legislation is not urgent. Thus, we need to evaluate whether there is a demand for squeeze-outs in the Korean business community and assess what devices, if any, would best satisfy this demand.

B. Business Surroundings and New Trends in Korea

1. Shareholder activism and adoption of consolidated tax return system

It seems that minority shareholders have become very active these days in Korea. The Korean courts have recently begun to take a more accommodating position with regards to minority shareholders' activism in

---

[51] Dokjeom gyuje mit gongjeong geooraeae gwanhan beobyul [Monopoly Regulation and Fair Trade Act], Act No. 10303, May 17, 2010 (Kor.).

[52] IV-3-Ma of Guideline for Regulating Unfair Assistance of a Person with Special Interest, *available at* http://www.ftc.go.kr/laws/laws/laws.jsp?lawDivCd=01 (last visited Aug. 31, 2011).

several derivative actions than they have done in the past. For example, in the application of the demand requirement,[53] which requires minority shareholders to demand that the corporation sue the directors before they file a derivative action, the recent case law shows flexibility. Under the traditional approach, a derivative action that was filed without having satisfied the demand requirement would have been dismissed.[54] In a recent case, however, the Seoul District Court ruled that the absence of the demand process was cured, because the plaintiff shareholders had called for the corporation to seek the responsibility of the director right after the commencement of the derivative action, but the corporation didn't pursue the director's responsibility.[55] The liberal interpretation on the demand requirement may also be found in other lower court cases.[56]

Accordingly, shareholder derivative actions have become more frequent these days.[57] For example, in October 2005 the Korean Supreme Court decided that the current and former directors of Samsung Electronics were required to pay 12 billion Korean won (approximately $10 million USD) to Samsung Electronics,[58] a decision that was interpreted as emphasizing the responsibility of directors or shadow directors under the KCC. Additionally, the newly-introduced 2005 Securities Class Action Act[59] may ultimately become a weapon which minority shareholders may use to

---

[53] The Korean Commercial Code (KCC), Act No.10600, April 14, 2011, art. 403 (Kor.).

[54] *See* Changwon District Court [Dist. Ct.], 2001Ga-Hap4231, Sept. 6, 2002 (Kor.); Seoul Central District Court [Dist. Ct.], 2004Ga-Dan232721, Dec. 17, 2004 (Kor.); Daejeon District Court [Dist. Ct.], 2006Ga-Hap4186, Jul. 3, 2006 (Kor.).

[55] Seoul Central District Court [Dist. Ct.], 2005Ga-Hap97694, Nov. 30, 2006 (Kor.).

[56] *E.g.,* Seoul High Court [High Ct.], 2003Na5360, Jun. 27, 2003 (Kor.).

[57] From 1962 to 2001 there were only 18 derivative suits filed in the Korean courts, but from 2002 to 2006, around 30 derivative suits were filed. Jooyoung Kim, *Woori-Nara-Jooju-Daepyo-Sosongae-Jaeso-Hyunwhang-Mit-Pankyul-Kyeonghyangae-Kwanhan-Gochal* [*Survey on Derivative Actions and Analysis on Court Decisions*], 34 CG Review 09/10 (2007).

[58] Supreme Court [S. Ct.], 2003Da69638, Oct. 28, 2005 (Kor.). *See also* Hwa-Jin Kim, *Directors' Duties and Liabilities in Corporate Control and Restructuring Transactions: Recent Developments in Korea*, Oxford U. Comp. L. F. 2 (2006).

[59] Jeunggwon gwanlyeon jipdan sosong beob [Korean Securities Class Action Act], Act No. 7074, Jan. 20, 2004 (Kor.). *See also* Stephen Choi, *Evidence on Securities Class Actions*, 57 Vand. L. Rev. 1465, 1521-22 (2004) (suggesting that deterrent effects on controlling shareholders may be one of the direct benefits of the new Securities Class Action Act); Dae-Hwan Chung, *Introduction to South Korea's New Securities-Related Class Action*, 30 J. Corp. L. 165, 170 (2004) (listing protection of minority shareholders' rights as one of the benefits of the new Securities Class Action Act).

threaten directors and majority shareholders. For directors and majority shareholders who are directly or indirectly engaged in corporate management, stronger protections for minority shareholders may mean increased costs and decreased management efficiency. Thus, the growth in minority shareholder activism and supervision may spark an increased demand by management for companies devoid of minority shareholders altogether.

In addition, the consolidated tax return system took effect in the 2010 fiscal year.[60] According to the new provisions, a holding company and its wholly owned subsidiary may have the consolidated tax return system applied to them with the approval of the Commissioner of the National Tax Service.[61] Under the consolidated tax return system, more holding companies may try to satisfy the 100 percent shareholding requirement, and accordingly, such companies may seek a way to squeeze out minority shareholders from their subsidiaries.

In sum, the growth of shareholder activism is likely to increase the costs associated with minority shareholders. In addition, the new tax return system is likely to reduce the tax burden on wholly-owned subsidiaries once 100 percent ownership of those subsidiaries is first obtained. The combination of these two novel features in Korea's business environment is likely to increase the demand by controlling shareholders or management for devices to squeeze out minority shareholders.

2. Some anecdotal evidence of the increasing demand for squeeze-outs

There is no published survey on the demand for new squeeze-out devices among Korean companies. An analysis of tender offers used for delisting public companies would be helpful towards understanding the business atmosphere surrounding squeeze-outs. This is because voluntary delisting for the purpose of going private usually reflects the intent of the offeror to eliminate minority shareholders – a goal that is pursued by utilizing squeeze-out devices.[62] Although not required by law, most listed companies first announce a tender offer and provide minority shareholders with an opportunity to sell their shares in order to accomplish a smooth delisting. Thus, the current tender offer practices to achieve delisting would

---

[60] Beobin sae beob [Korean Corporate Tax Act], Act No. 10337, May 31, 2010, arts 76-8 to 76-12 (Kor.).

[61] Beobin sae beob [Korean Corporate Tax Act], Act No. 10337, May 31, 2010, art. 76-8 (1) (Kor.).

[62] *See* Chang-Hyun Song et al., *Analysis of Freeze-outs in Korea: Quest for Legal Framework Synchronizing Transactional Efficiency and Protection of Minority Shareholders*, 8 J. Korean L. 277, 283-93 (2009).

Table 3.1 Purposes of tender offer (from Jan. 2002 to Oct. 2010)[a]

Year	2002	2003	2004	2005	2006	2007	2008	2009	2010	Total
Delisting	–	1	12	5	–	2	3	2	1	26
Securing of Managerial Right	1	8	–	3	1	4	2	1	–	20
Meeting Holding Co. Requirement[b]	–	–	–	–	–	8	2	1	6	17
M&A	–	1	3	–	2	2	3	2	1	14
Others	–	–	1[c]	–	–	2	1	–	1	5
Total	1	10	16	8	3	18	11	6	9	82

Notes:

a. Press Release, Financial Supervisory Service of Korea, 2004 Report (Jan. 14, 2005), *available at* http://www.fss.or.kr/kr/nws/nbd/bodobbs_v.jsp?seqno=9392&no=2&gubun=01&menu=nws020100; Press Release, Financial Supervisory Service of Korea, 2006 Report (Feb. 2, 2007), *available at* http://www.fss.or.kr/kr/nws/nbd/bodobbs_v.jsp?seqno=11833&no=11&gubun=01&menu=nws020100; Press Release, Financial Supervisory Service of Korea, 2009 Report (Apr. 14, 2010), *available at* http://www.fss.or.kr/kr/nws/nbd/bodobbs_v.jsp?menu=nws020100&seqno=14299&gubun=01; for information on year 2010, the author looked through the Data Analysis Retrieval and Transfer System (DART), Financial Supervisory Service of Korea, DART, http://dart.fss.or.kr.

b. Dokjeom gyuje mit gongjeong geooraeae gwanhan beobyul [Monopoly Regulation and Fair Trade Act], Act No. 10303, May 17, 2010, art. 8-2 (Kor.) (requiring a certain type of holding companies in a corporate group to acquire and maintain minimum shareholdings in their subsidiaries).

c. The Financial Supervisory Service classified a tender offer by STX Corp. dated Jan. 7, 2004 as having been made for delisting purposes, but the delisting was not aimed at eliminating minority shareholders. Rather, the offer was made for the benefit of preferred-stock owners by way of share repurchase. Thus, Table 3.1 reclassifies the purpose of the offer as "others."

show the demand for squeeze-outs. In fact, the "going private phenomenon" is closely related to the recent trend towards shareholder activism.[63]

An analysis of tender offers in the Korean stock market, as is shown by Table 3.1, illustrates that going private through a tender offer is not a foreign idea any more. A tender offer for delisting purposes was rarely made before 2002.[64] About 31.7 percent (or 26 out of 82 cases) of tender

63 *Id.* at 279.

64 The Financial Supervisory Service of Korea only provides the statistics on the going-private tender offer made after 2002 (*see* www.fss.or.kr.). The author reviewed the tender offer reports between January 1990 and December 2001 through the Data Analysis, Retrieval and Transfer System (DART), but could not find any tender offer proposed for delisting. *See* Financial Supervisory Service of Korea, DART, http://dart.fss.or.kr (last visited Aug. 31, 2011).

offers between January 2002 and October 2010, however, were aimed at delisting.

Eliminating minority shareholders might not be the only reason for tender offers that are undertaken for delisting. For example, a company may be forced to delist when it fails to meet the qualifications for listing companies.[65] In order to find out the precise reason for delisting, one needs to review the tender offer reports submitted by the offeror.

Here, this author analyzed all 26 tender offer reports aimed at delisting from 2002 to 2010. Based on this analysis, this author found that in 19 cases, controlling shareholders tried to get rid of minority shareholders and obtain 100 percent ownership (see Table 3.2). Only seven cases were not directed to secure complete management control.[66] One may need to note two points about these statistics. First, some companies tried very hard to have full ownership. For example, Pulmuone Holdings Co., Ltd. provided its first tender offer on Sep. 22, 2008 in order to raise its shareholding ratio in Pulmuone Co., Ltd. from 57.71 percent to 100 percent. Unsatisfied with the result of the first offer, it made a second offer on Dec. 2, 2008. Similar to Pulmuone Holdings Co., Ltd., Asahi Glass Co., Ltd. placed two tender offers towards minority shareholders in Hankook Electric Glass Co. Ltd. Those repetitive tender offers show the pursuit of full ownership by controlling shareholders. Second, no controlling shareholder, among the 19 cases aforementioned, was able to achieve its goal. The tender offer, which basically depends on voluntary tenders by minority shareholders, has its limit in terms of fulfilling sole ownership.

While these statistics are limited to listed companies and tender offers, they indicate a preference of majority shareholders to drive out the minority.

---

[65] For example, a listed company will get delisted from KOSPI Market where annual financial statements of the company have been disapproved by the auditor, where checks or promissory notes issued by the company have been dishonored, or where the annual turnover fails to reach a certain minimum level. *See* Yuga jeunkwon sijang sangjang kyujeong [KOSPI Market Listing Regulation], art. 80 (Kor.), *available at* http://eng.krx.co.kr/m7/m7_1/m7_1_1/JHPENG07001_01.jsp.

[66] (1) D. Y. Holding Ltd. and (2) Shin Dongbang CP Co., Ltd. were forced to be delisted because of a termination of business and financial difficulties, respectively; in (3) Chohung Bank and (4) Good Morning Shinhan Securities Co., Ltd., the Shinhan Financial Holding Co. did not seek 100 percent ownership, because a comprehensive share exchange was scheduled right after the tender offers; in (5) Pacific Glass Inc., (6) iRevo Co., Ltd., and (7) CDNetwork Co., Ltd., the offerors just set a lower target than 100 percent ownership.

Table 3.2 Tender offers for delisting between Jan. 2002 and Oct. 2010[a*]

No.	Date of Registration	Target Company	Offeror	Offeror's Shareholding Ratio(%)**		
				Before TO	Intended by TO	After TO
1	Oct. 15, 2003	Chemiglas Co., Ltd.	Essilor Korea Co., Ltd.	71.74	100	81.68
2	Mar. 10, 2004	D.Y. Holding Ltd.	D. Y. Holdings Ltd.	83.63	90.74	90.74
3	Mar. 30, 2004	Hanmi Bank	Citibank Overseas Investment Corp.	36.55	100	97.5
4	Apr. 13, 2004	Korea Computer Holdings Inc.	Korea Computer Holdings Inc.	75.4	100	95.7
5	Apr. 20, 2004	Chohung Bank	Shinhan Financial Holding Co.	81.15	84.92	84.92
6	Jun. 17, 2004	Keukdong Electric Wire Co.	Nexans Corp.	45.29	100	50.54
7	Jun. 17, 2004	Nexans Korea Ltd.	Nexans Corp.	50	100	82.03
8	Jul. 20, 2004	Busan Mutual Savings Bank	Park, Yeon-Ho (Individual)	99.09	100	99.55
9	Sep. 9, 2004	Auction Co., Ltd	eBay KTA (UK) Ltd.	97.04	100	99.73
10	Sep. 20, 2004	Good Morning Shinhan Securities Co. Ltd.	Shinhan Financial Holding Co.	56.53	57.44	56.80
11	Oct. 12, 2004	Seah Metal Co., Ltd.	Seah Holding Corp.	79.99	100	92.83
12	Nov. 29 2004	Sewon Chemical Co., Ltd.	Misung Trading Corp.	48.87	100	96.00
13	Dec. 20, 2004	Dongseo Industrial Co., Ltd.	Dongseo Industrial Co., Ltd.	59.58	100	80.11
14	Feb. 2, 2005	Isu Ceramics Co., Ltd.	Isu Corp.	69.55	100	93.08
15	Feb. 17, 2005	Shin Dongbang CP Co., Ltd.	CJ Corp.	94.9	100	98.34

Table 3.2 (continued)

No.	Date of Registration	Target Company	Offeror	Offeror's Shareholding Ratio(%)**		
				Before TO	Intended by TO	After TO
16	Apr. 15, 2005	KDB Capital Inc.	The Korean Development Bank	97.49	100	99.53
17	Apr. 19, 2005	Pacific Glass Inc.	AmorePacific Corp.	76.78	78.68	78.54
18	Aug. 5, 2005	PKL Co., Ltd.	Photronics, Inc.	89.98	100	96.51
19	Jun. 12, 2007	LG Card Co.	Shinhan Financial Holding Co.	85.7	100	93.36
20	Nov. 1, 2007	Hankuk Electric Glass Co. Ltd.	Asahi Glass Co., Ltd	62.76	100	71.47
21	Sep. 22, 2008	Pulmuone Co., Ltd.	Pulmuone Holdings Co., Ltd.	57.71	100	89.12
22	Oct. 15, 2008	iRevo Co., Ltd.	iRevo Assa Abloy Korea Co., Ltd	45.33	90.14	81.52
23	Dec. 2, 2008	Pulmuone Co., Ltd.	Pulmuone Holdings Co., Ltd.	91.97	100	94.67
24	Jun. 19, 2009	CDNetworks Co., Ltd.	Oak Asia Infrastructure, LLC	59.69	86.86	77.62
25	Oct. 30, 2009	Sung Woo Mold Co., Ltd.	Lee, Myung-Geun (Individual)	72.81	100	96.52
26	Oct. 7, 2010	Hankuk Electric Glass Co. Ltd.	Asahi Glass Co., Ltd.	78.57	100	95.87

Notes:

a. All data is from the tender offer reports submitted to the Financial Supervisory Service of Korea. *See* Financial Supervisory Service of Korea, Data Analysis, Retrieval and Transfer System (DART), http://dart.fss.or.kr (last visited Aug. 31, 2011).

* The shadowed boxes (19 cases) indicate voluntary tender offers directed to eliminate all minority shareholders.

** In calculating the ratio, the shares held by those specially related to the offeror (e.g., family members of the offeror) were added to the offeror's shares.

C. Methods of Squeeze-out before the KCC of 2011

Under the KCC, a majority shareholder may try to squeeze out minority shareholders through such oppressive methods as limiting dividends, changing the corporate structure, and siphoning off earnings. However, such oppression has its limits since each share must be treated equally in terms of voting rights and dividend rights under articles 368, 538, and 464 of the KCC. Statutory squeeze-out methods represent an alternative to these traditional, indirect, and oppressive devices. These statutory methods are reviewed below.

1. Cash-out merger

The feasibility of cash-out mergers, the basic method of squeeze-outs in the U.S., has long been debated in Korea. Under a cash-out merger, minority shareholders are forced to sell their shares, provided that the merger is approved by shareholders and fair compensation is made. Under the KCC, shareholders of a target company in a statutory merger are generally expected to receive shares in the acquiring company.[67]

The KCC before its reform of 2011 did not directly address the possibility of cash-out mergers. However, section 4 of article 523 stipulates that the merger agreement should include a cash payment provision if the acquirer has promised to pay cash to the target company's shareholders. Based upon this provision, some Korean scholars argued that the acquiring company may rely upon cash consideration instead of shares in the acquiring company.[68] That being said, most Korean practitioners and scholars construed the application of section 4 of article 523 much more narrowly to allow only the cash consideration described in the section to be used to supplement default consideration, or in addition to the shares provided in the acquiring company.[69] According to this logic, cash consideration should be supplementary and would be allowed if and only if it facilitates an accurate exchange ratio between a target company's share price and an acquiring company's share price. The short-form merger, another major method of squeeze-outs in the U.S., could not be used as a device for squeeze-outs in Korea. Although a company could easily

---

67 *See, e.g.*, Song et al., *supra* note 62, at 296.

68 *See, e.g.*, Jin-Gi Hong, *Joosikhoesaui-Habbyungae-Isseoseoui-Kyobookuem* [*Cash Consideration in a Statutory Merger*], OVERALL LEGAL ISSUES: IN MEMORY OF DR. HONG 385 (1977) (arguing that the acquiring company may offer to each target company's shareholder one nominal share and cash consideration).

69 *See, e.g.*, Chul-Song Lee, HOESABUP-GANGUI [LECTURE OF COMPANY LAW] 838 (12th ed. 2005).

merge its 90 percent subsidiary without shareholder approval,[70] it could not squeeze out the minority shareholders of a subsidiary using cash consideration.[71]

2. Comprehensive share transfer and share exchange

An acquiring company that desires to obtain all of the shares in a target company may do so through a comprehensive share exchange under article 360-2 of the KCC.[72] With the approval of the shareholders of both the acquiring and target companies, all of the shares in the target company can be transferred to the acquiring company, making the acquiring company a holding company with 100 percent share ownership in the target company.[73] Shareholders of the target company would receive shares of the acquiring company, either in the form of newly-issued shares or as the shares already issued and held by the acquiring company. In the case of a comprehensive share transfer under article 360-15 of the KCC,[74] a new company is established. With shareholder approval by a transferring company (the transferor), all of the transferor's shares would be transferred to the new company (the transferee), which would become a holding company that holds 100 percent of the transferor's shares. The shareholders of the transferor would be given shares newly-issued by the transferee. In most cases, share transfer is carried out by several companies together and not by a single transferor. Through collective share transfer, which requires the approval of the shareholders of all of the companies concerned, a newly-established holding company is able to own all of the shares in several companies at the same time.

Both share exchanges and share transfers are "comprehensive;" they do not require individual notification or delivery of possession. Even if a shareholder of the target company or transferor votes against a share exchange or share transfer, his or her shares still must be transferred.

Under the KCC, a comprehensive share exchange is similar to the share-for-share offering scheme in the U.K. The new Korean scheme follows the same steps as the U.K. scheme: (1) the cancellation of all target company

---

70 The Korean Commercial Code (KCC), Act No.10600, April 14, 2011, art. 527-2 (Kor.).

71 Art. 527-2 of the KCC does not provide any exception for the consideration in short-form mergers; the logic about the long-form merger would apply. Lee, SUPRA note 37, at 838.

72 The Korean Commercial Code (KCC), Act No.10600, April 14, 2011, art. 360-2 (Kor.).

73 *Id.*

74 *Id.* art. 360-15.

shares (other than those owned by the offeror), and (2) the issuance of new offeror shares to the former shareholders of the target company as compensation for the cancellation of their shares.[75] As a result, the target company will become a wholly-owned subsidiary of the offeror, and the former shareholders of the target company will own a proportionate equity interest in the offeror – which is incidentally the same result as in a comprehensive share exchange.

The comprehensive share exchange and share transfer were introduced in Korea in 2001, and are viewed as steps towards liberalizing squeeze-outs because they allow for the transfer of target company's shares held by dissenting shareholders to the acquiring company.[76]

3. Other methods

Although a majority shareholder may change the articles of incorporation or reduce the paid-in capital of a company by special resolution, it is impossible to squeeze out dissenting minority shareholders through amending the articles of incorporation or employing selective capital reduction. Based on the traditional vested-right theory, the KCC still emphasizes the equal treatment of all shareholders.[77]

Another device used for the purpose of squeeze-outs is the so-called fractional share. While it is not so common in the U.S., fractional shares resulting from a reverse-split are said to be available as a squeeze-out technique.[78] What about in Korea? For example, a company may try to effect a reverse-split under which ten shares will be merged into seven. If shareholder A has 21 shares and shareholder B has nine, what would happen? In such cases, the KCC does not offer specific provisions for dealing with fractional shares. If shareholder B cannot receive any shares, such as where holders of fewer than ten shares are only eligible to receive cash consideration, shareholder A could become the sole shareholder of the company, allowing for a substantial squeeze-out. However, most Korean scholars agree that the reverse-split provision and fractional shares should not be used to facilitate squeeze-outs.[79] Reverse-splits should be exercised so that the shareholding ratio is not substantially changed. In the above example

---

75 *See* KENYON-SLADE, *supra* note 18, at 576 (outlining details of share-for-share offer by way of a scheme of arrangement).

76 Hwa-Jin Kim, *The Case for Market for Corporate Control in Korea*, 8 J. KOREAN L. 227, 264-67 (2009).

77 *See* the Korean Commercial Code (KCC), Act No.10600, April 14, 2011, arts 368, 538, 464 (Kor.).

78 CLARK, supra note 6, § 12.1, at 502.

79 *See* Lee, *supra* note 37, at 723.

then, shareholder B would receive six shares and remaining cash consideration ($9 \times 7/10 = 6.3$; therefore, he or she has the right to six new shares and 0.3 fractional shares in cash), even though he or she has fewer than ten shares.

In all, it was very difficult to squeeze out minority shareholders using the devices currently in place in the KCC.

D. The Squeeze-out Devices in the New KCC and the Way to Reform

1. The squeeze-out devices in the KCC of 2011

In 2011, the National Assembly of Korea approved the Reform Bill of the KCC.[80] This reform is so comprehensive that it covers almost every major topic in corporate governance and corporate finance. New squeeze-out devices are also adopted in the bill.

According to the new KCC, two types of squeeze-outs become available.

First, a cash-out merger, similar to the U.S. long-form merger, is included. According to the provision, an acquiring company and target company may agree in a statutory merger contract that shareholders in the target company would be given cash or property other than shares in the acquiring company.[81] The available property includes the shares in the acquiring company's parent company.[82] Although not explicitly stipulated by the KCC, the cash-out merger shall be designed in terms of equal treatment of all shareholders. For example, a cash-out merger is not feasible where some shareholders of the target company are forced to receive cash considerations while others are supposed to receive shares in the acquiring company. The unequal treatment among shareholders may threaten the validity of a statutory merger contract. What about providing all the shareholders in the target company with unreasonable but equal cash consideration? A lower court denied the effectiveness of a merger contract that stipulated too low compensation for all the shareholders in the target company.[83] Generally speaking, however, the courts prefer protecting minority shareholders through appraisal remedy to declaring a merger contract null and void.

Second, the new KCC adopted a supermajority-type squeeze-out device. A dominant shareholder who holds 95 percent or more of a company's

---

80 The Korean Commercial Code Reform Bill, Bill No. 1801566, Oct. 21, 2008 (Kor.).

81 The Korean Commercial Code, Act No. 10600, April 14, 2011, art. 523 (4).

82 *Id.* art. 523-2.

83 *See* Incheon District Court [Dist. Ct.], 85Ga-Hap1526, Aug. 29, 1986 (Kor.).

outstanding shares may require minority shareholders to sell their remaining shares in order to accomplish a business objective.[84] In calculating the 95 percent threshold, the dominant shareholder includes shares held by another company that are controlled by the dominant shareholder.[85] While the new KCC requires that the squeeze-out must be approved by the shareholders' meeting and that the dominant shareholder must explain at the meeting the purpose and other details of the squeeze-out,[86] the approval itself shall be easily obtained once the controller has obtained more than 95 percent of the shares. Is the dominant shareholder bound to the price he has suggested in the shareholders' meeting? The dominant shareholder shall not lower the price unless he can prove persuasive reason for such change. To allow unlimited modification to the terms of purchase that were reported to the shareholders' meeting would make the shareholders' meeting requirement meaningless. The dominant shareholder, after the approval by shareholders' meeting, should place an offer to minority shareholders and the minority shareholders should sell their shares to the dominant shareholder no later than two months after an offer is placed.[87] If the dominant shareholder and minority shareholders cannot reach an agreement on the amount of fair compensation, the court will determine a fair price in the same manner as in an appraisal procedure.[88]

As a counterpart to a dominant shareholder's squeeze-out right, minority shareholders are provided with sell-out rights: minority shareholders may require being "cashed out" where there is a dominant shareholder holding more than 95 percent of the shares in a company.[89] This new right seems to be a Korean version of the sell-out right under the 2006 U.K. Companies Act.[90]

2. Analysis of the new KCC and the right way to reform

The new KCC of 2011 would bring about drastic changes to current squeeze-out practices. In Korea, it has been almost impossible to get rid of minority shareholders as long as they want to hold out.[91] Traditional

---

84 The Korean Commercial Code, Act No. 10600, April 14, 2011 art. 360-24 § 1.

85 *Id.* art. 360-24 § 2. The shares held by the companies in which the dominant shareholder has 50 percent or more shares shall be regarded as being held by the dominant shareholder.

86 *Id.* art. 360-24 §§ 3-4.

87 *Id.* art. 360-24 § 6.

88 *Id.* art. 360-24 §§ 7-9.

89 *Id.* art. 360-25.

90 Companies Act, 2006, c. 3, § 983 (Eng.).

91 *See, e.g.*, Song et al., *supra* note 62, at 297.

reluctance of the KCC to allow squeeze-outs raises several questions about new devices adopted in the new KCC. Does Korea need squeeze-out devices? If so, are the two devices in the bill suitable for the Korean business environment? The two questions will be answered based upon the analyses in the preceding section.

(1) Whether or not to introduce new squeeze-out devices Until 2011, comprehensive share exchange and share transfer were in actuality the only means under the KCC for implementing a squeeze-out. However, these devices are far from satisfying the demand from businesses. It is true that through a comprehensive share exchange, an acquiring company may force minority shareholders in a target company to transfer their shares to the acquiring company. But minority shareholders in a target company, while leaving the target company, may still try to influence the target company as shareholders of its 100 percent parent company.[92]

In this author's opinion, it is necessary to introduce new squeeze-out devices in Korea. Provided that minority shareholders are paid fair compensation, there is no reason to prohibit squeeze-outs. When someone invests in a company, he or she has already accepted the possibility that the nature and value of that investment might change as a result of a majority shareholders' resolution. Under the KCC, such change may result from a merger, spin-off, capital reduction and/or liquidation. Also, the allotment of new shares to a third party, already allowed under the KCC in some cases, may legitimately dilute shareholders' rights (e.g., a shareholder's shareholding of 10 percent might be reduced to 5 percent due to an issuance of new shares to a third party). On that basis, why not allow a 10 percent shareholder to be reduced to a 0 percent shareholder, as long as it is accompanied by fair compensation?

In a takeover or a transfer of control, the squeeze-out mechanism can help to attract socially desirable takeover bids, since the bidder would expect to become better off after free-riders have been taken out of the picture. In addition, a holding company may pursue the interests of a whole corporate group without any regard for each subsidiary's minority shareholders, if the holding company fully owns its subsidiaries.

Under Korean constitutional law, an individual is entitled to the peaceful enjoyment of his or her property.[93] However, this does not necessarily

---

92 There was a so-called double derivative suit in 2002 in which shareholders of the parent company brought a derivative action on behalf of its subsidiary against the subsidiary's director. *See* Seoul High Court [High Ct.], 2002Na13746, Aug. 22, 2003 (Kor.); Supreme Court [S. Ct.], 2003Da49221, Sept. 23, 2004 (Kor.).

93 Daehanminkuk Hunbeob [The Constitution of Korea] art. 23 (Kor.).

mean that property rights should be placed above other rights accorded by constitutional law. Minority shareholders' property rights can be limited, under reasonable and objective standards, for reasons of public interest or mutual economic benefit.

Although protecting minority shareholders is a major concern for those who oppose squeeze-outs, such protection could be achieved by the imposition of strict procedural regulations and the payment of fair compensation. Prohibiting squeeze-outs entirely is an excessive measure that does not give fair weight to the importance of majority shareholders' economic activities.

Recent Korean takeover statistics and the trend of going private show an increasing demand in the business community for squeeze-out transactions.[94] The KCC must endeavor to catch up with rapid changes in the Korean business community. It is not a coincidence that a number of other countries have recently introduced more flexible squeeze-out devices in their own legal systems.[95]

(2) What is the best legislation for squeeze-outs in Korea? Creating legislative provisions for new squeeze-out devices would be beneficial for Korean businesses. However, which squeeze-out devices are best suited for the unique Korean business environment requires further analysis. In evaluating the effectiveness of each potential squeeze-out device, we may apply two criteria: (1) the costs of the execution of a squeeze-out; and (2) the protection of minority shareholders.

First, from the cost-execution perspective, the supermajority type mechanism seems to be the simplest of the three squeeze-out devices, provided that the supermajority shares have already been obtained by a controlling shareholder. This is because it does not require a tender offer or a statutory merger. According to the supermajority squeeze-out device in the Reform Bill of 2008, a dominant shareholder with 95 percent or more shares would be able to invoke a squeeze-out without difficulty. It is hard to tell, though, whether a cash-out merger and a tender offer squeeze-out would cost less in practice.

Second, the protection of minority shareholders through fair compensation has critical importance. While new squeeze-out devices are required for various reasons, the interests of minority shareholders should not be

---

94 *See supra* Section III.B.

95 For European countries, see van der Elst & van den Steen, *supra* note 40. Japan also recently adopted cash-out mergers. *See* Kaisha-ho [Company Act], Act No. 86, July 26, 2005, arts 749 (1), 751(1) (Japan).

ignored in designing a new system. In fact, fair compensation to minority shareholders should be provided. However, estimating a precise and fair price for shares is not an easy task. Once the compensation for minority shareholders has been decided by the company, it would be very costly and time-consuming for them to deny the price and to rearrange it. Thus, we need to design the process for squeeze-outs cautiously, so that the majority shareholder may not expropriate the minority shareholders.

Out of the three types of squeeze-out devices, the new KCC of 2011 adopted two: (1) a cash-out merger type; and (2) a supermajority type. The tender offer type squeeze-out was not addressed. We need to compare the three alternatives in the context of the two situations: the "control-transferred" scenario where squeeze-out is designed and executed by outside acquirers who want to obtain 100 percent ownership of the target company in the course of a statutory merger or share acquisition; and the "control-maintained" scenario where squeeze-out is geared by incumbent controlling shareholders who want to eliminate minority shareholders. In the control-transferred situation, the risk of minority shareholders being expropriated is not high. The risk is not high, because there is no controlling shareholder who is in direct conflict with minority shareholders. If a third party has purchased a controlling block before the squeeze-out offer, the purchase price could be a benchmark for fair compensation. Thus, it seems that there would not be a serious threat to the minority. In a control-maintained situation, a tender offer squeeze-out device bears little risk of being abused. Specifically, a majority or even supermajority shareholder cannot entirely ignore the intent of minority shareholders in a tender offer squeeze-out. In a cash-out merger type or a supermajority type squeeze-out, however, a controlling shareholder with sufficient shares can exercise his or her squeeze-out right without regard to minority shareholders.

In this author's opinion, the Korean government should adopt the tender offer type squeeze-out in future legislative amendments. It is true that the supermajority type squeeze-out, as it exists in the new KCC of 2011 (art. 360-24), would provide a cost effective and simple way to undertake a squeeze-out. In addition, one may argue cash-out mergers would be a better squeeze-out device than tender offer squeeze-outs, because the offeror tends to normally offer a higher price than pre-bid or market prices. However, supermajority type or cash-out merger type devices might be misused to undermine minority interests, especially where the controlling shareholders' interests are in conflict with the minority. If the business practice and corporate governance in Korea effectively monitor the majority shareholders and protect minority shareholders from unfair treatment, the conflict between majority and minority may not be an important issue. However, statistics on international corporate governance research demonstrate that minority shareholders in Korea are subject to majority expropriation, and Korean corporate governance has yet to be fully developed.[96]

Two squeeze-out devices in the new KCC already have their own mechanism for protecting minority shareholders: a cash-out merger should be structured in a way that treats all the shareholders equally in the target company. In order for dominant shareholders to squeeze out minority shareholders, they should obtain an approval by shareholders' meeting and prove the business objective to be accomplished through squeeze-out transaction. Those mechanisms, however, often turn out far from being satisfactory. For example, obtaining the approval by shareholders' meeting and demonstrating business objective for squeeze-out seem to be an easy task for a dominant shareholder.

Now that the Korean legislator adopted cash-out merger type and supermajority type squeeze-out devices, special caution should be given in establishing squeeze-out practices. Especially the role of the courts in the appraisal remedy becomes more important and thus additional legislative measures might be necessary concerning the appraisal process: for example, the court may apply a standard favorable to squeezed-out shareholders or impose the burden of proof on the company or the majority when deciding fair compensation to the minority.

IV. CONCLUSION

This article began with a discussion of whether squeeze-out devices should be allowed pursuant to the fundamental corporate law principle of majority rule. In spite of concerns for minority shareholders, it seems reasonable to seek legislation to minimize negative aspects of squeeze-outs rather than to simply deny the mechanism altogether. In order to reduce the risk of the majority shareholders exploiting minority shareholders through squeeze-outs, squeeze-out legislation should be carefully designed to guarantee fair compensation for minority shareholders.

---

[96] For example, according to the GovernanceMetrics International, an international agency for corporate governance rating, Korea ranked 33rd out of 39 countries in a 2009 survey, GOVERNANCE METRICS INTERNATIONAL, COUNTRY RANKINGS AS OF SEPTEMBER 22, 2009 (2009), *available at* http://www.gmiratings.com/Performance.aspx. According to Asia Corporate Governance Association, Korea ranked 6th out of 11 countries in a 2007 survey, ASIA CORPORATE GOVERNANCE ASSOCIATION, CG WATCH 2007: CORPORATE GOVERNANCE IN ASIA (2007), *available at* https://www.clsa.com (last visited Aug. 31, 2011).

For comparative research, this article reviewed squeeze-out devices available in the U.S., U.K., and Germany and classified them into three categories: (1) tender offer squeeze-outs as in the compulsory acquisitions in the U.K; (2) cash-out merger squeeze-outs as in the long-form merger in the U.S.; and (3) supermajority type squeeze-outs as stipulated in the German Stock Corporation Act.

On the other hand, a squeeze-out may be characterized by either controlling shareholder or incumbent management (control-maintained type) or outside investor (control-transferred type). Specifically, tender offer squeeze-outs, whether combined with the control-maintained or control-transferred type, are likely to provide fair compensation. For cash-out merger type and supermajority type squeeze-outs in a control-transfer situation, there is no critical risk of expropriating minority shareholders. However, those two types of squeeze-outs in a control-maintained situation might fail to provide sufficient protections in the process of forcing the minority out.

The article then focused on Korea's business environment and current legislative amendments to explore the use of squeeze-outs in a developing economy with very limited squeeze-out devices. General justifications for squeeze-outs discussed above would apply to the Korean economy as well. In addition, there are a number of pieces of evidence – including the change in the trend in tender offers between 2002 and 2010 – that show that Korean businesses are demanding new squeeze-out devices.

The Korean legislator adopted cash-out merger squeeze-outs and supermajority type squeeze-outs in the new KCC of 2011. This author supports this decision by the Korean legislator to move in the direction of creating more flexible squeeze-out mechanisms. However, the legislator should take into consideration some of the unique features of Korean business practice and the fact that Korea's corporate governance system is based on an economy that is still developing. Specifically, many Korean companies have dominant or controlling shareholders, and the level of general protection for minority shareholders is known to be still limited in Korea.

In this author's opinion, the Korean government should have adopted tender offer type squeeze-out devices. In operating new squeeze-out devices as are stipulated in the KCC of 2011, the Korean government needs to be cognizant of the risk of minority shareholders being expropriated. For example, the court may apply a standard favorable to minority shareholders or impose the burden of proof on the company or its majority when deciding what constitutes fair compensation to be awarded to the minority. A harmonization of the demand for squeeze-outs and the protection for minority shareholders should always be emphasized in future discussions over new squeeze-out legislation.

4. Monitoring of corporate groups by independent directors

A.C. Pritchard[*]

I. INTRODUCTION

Independent directors have become a popular "cure-all" in the United States for whatever the latest malady ailing the modern corporation happens to be. Whenever a corporation has found its way into the headlines as the subject of the scandal *du jour*, it is overwhelmingly the case that it is the managers who are caught with their fingers in the till, having manipulated the numbers, rolling the dice with the shareholders' money, or otherwise abusing the trust of shareholders and other corporate constituencies. They are, after all, the ones in charge of the day-to-day operations of the company. All too frequently the managers, who have charged some outrageous perk to the corporation's bill, or who have relabeled an expense as a capital expenditure, are at the very top levels of the corporate hierarchy, perhaps even serving on the board. Immunity from greed, fear, and other weaknesses of character are apparently not required to advance to the top of the corporate hierarchy.

It is the venality at the very top that most offends. Given the lofty levels of compensation that CEOs in the United States typically receive, it is hard for the average person (or more importantly, the average politician) to understand the desire for further aggrandizement and reluctance to accept responsibility for poor performance. One suspects that sense of outrage at the abuse of trust is mirrored, and perhaps magnified, inside the boardrooms of the corporations caught up in the wrongdoing. The directors who have placed their confidence, and to some extent their reputations,

[*] The author would like to thank the Korea Development Institute for financial support and participants at the Korea Development Institute Conference on the Corporate Governance of Group Companies, in particular Joon Park, for helpful comments on an earlier draft of this article. Wonjin Choi provided very helpful research assistance. Any remaining mistakes are mine alone. An earlier version of this article appeared in 9 Journal of Korean Law 1-25 (2009).

in the hands of the CEO (who generally will also serve as chairman of the board) are likely to feel a sense of betrayal as well as outrage. The outside directors are probably not the last to know, but they may take the most personal offense at the abuse.

How natural, then, is the instinct of policymakers confronted by corporate wrongdoing to want to harness that sense of betrayal and outrage inside the boardroom to make better citizens out of corporations and their officers? If only we could shift power from the inside directors to the outside directors, all would be well. The insiders, most offensively the CEO/Chair, may have been complicit in the wrongdoing. But as for the outside directors, generally the worst that can be said is that they did not know of the accounting shenanigans or outsized bet. Perhaps by shifting power to the latter, relatively innocent group, we could thwart the wrongdoing before it even gets started, or at least root it out before it begins to snowball into a major scandal. Conflict of interest is the problem, goes the story, so shifting authority to individuals whose judgment is unclouded by conflict will greatly reduce the embarrassing problems that keep appearing in the headlines. Agency costs will be kept in check by recruiting faithful agents as independent directors to monitor the insiders; politicians and bureaucrats will avoid the awkward questions that inevitably arise out of corporate scandal: "Why didn't you catch this sooner? Why wasn't there a law to prevent this? What are you going to do to help these investors who have lost all this money?"

The American faith in independent directors appears to have attracted adherents globally – the long-term trend has been toward greater director independence around the world. I will focus here, however, on two countries: Korea and the United States. Both countries have turned to corporate governance reform in the wake of crises. For Korea the impetus was an economy-wide financial crisis that led to the intervention of the IMF in 1998. Weaknesses of corporate governance were widely perceived as exacerbating the financial shock to the Korean economy.[1]

In this regard, the recent Korean experience echoed the American experience with the market crash of October 1929, which was popularly blamed for the subsequent widespread economic hardship that accompanied the Great Depression. That episode led to the first federal securities laws in the United States, the Securities Act of 1933 and the Securities Exchange Act of 1934. Those laws created the essential framework of

---

[1] Hwa-Jin Kim, *Living with the IMF: A New Approach to Corporate Governance and Regulation of Financial Institutions in Korea*, 17 Berkeley J. Int'l L. 61, 69 (1999).

the securities regime that still governs in the United States. In adopting those laws, however, the 1930s Congress generally avoided wholesale incursions into the internal governance of corporations, leaving that area generally for the states (with the limited exception of disclosure relating to proxies). For the United States, the impetus to corporate governance reform was the collapse of the high-tech bubble, which saw the tech-laden Nasdaq index plunge from nearly 5000 to 2000 in one year.[2] That collapse was accompanied by a salient scandal which fueled the drive to reform. A series of high-profile accounting imbroglios (e.g., Enron, Worldcom, Healthsouth, etc.), reflected any number of violations of existing disclosure and anti-fraud requirements. As a result, the United States has witnessed a number of criminal indictments and convictions for those disclosure violations. Prosecution, however, was not deemed a sufficient response (except perhaps by those indicted), so the accounting scandals have also produced a number of governance reforms which apply to the guilty and innocent alike. None of these reforms seem to have helped with the next crisis, which stemmed from inadequate risk management, perhaps fueled by poorly structured incentive compensation that rewarded executives of financial institutions for placing enormous wagers on the direction of the housing market.

Korea is further along from its motivating financial crisis. It has made great strides during the intervening period in bringing its corporate governance requirements up to international standards. Korea, infected like other countries by the crisis in the United States, must now face the question of whether it has renewed its appetite for governance reform. Are further reforms needed? If the answer is yes, does Korea have the political will to finish the job of reforming its governance standards? Has Korea done enough to prevent the fraud next time?

The United States by contrast, already boasted governance standards – arising from a combination of state corporate law, exchange listing standards, and best practices – that were among the most stringent in the world when it faced its spate of the accounting scandals. Nonetheless, those governance controls proved inadequate to prevent the sort of attention-getting frauds that typically lead to corporate and securities fraud reform. The regulatory backlash in the United States has led to the enactment of best practices as a matter of federal law in the hope that doing so will help prevent fraud in the future. Were those toughened standards needed, or

---

2 The Nasdaq closed at 5,048.62 on March 10, 2000 and 1,923.38 on March 12, 2001. *Available at* http://finance.yahoo.com.

were they overkill? Will the United States' rigorous new standards prevent the fraud next time?

Obviously the reform drives of these two countries have significantly raised governance standards in both countries. More interesting, perhaps, is the fact that the gap between the two has narrowed. Korean governance standards – at least on paper – have many similarities to the standards now in place in the United States. This facial similarity between the governance regimes in the two countries overlooks one critical fact – the corporate environment varies dramatically between Korea and the United States. Although the Korean economy continues to be dominated by the *chaebol* groups of affiliated companies, the American economy is dominated by publicly-held companies with widely dispersed shareholders. One question raised by Korea's move to upgrade to international best practices is whether the practices appropriate for a country like the United States, which has very few controlling shareholders, can be translated into Korea's complex web of corporate groups. What implication does this wide divergence in the two countries' corporate environments have for determining the appropriate standards for corporate governance? Most importantly for the purpose of looking at the role of outside directors, does independence have the same meaning and purpose in the context of a corporate group? Does the notion of independence need to be adjusted to fit into a group context? Should directors' independence be measured with respect to the group as a whole, or only with respect to the individual affiliated company within the group?

In Section 1 and 2 of this chapter, I discuss the current state of corporate governance in Korea and the United States and the recent changes to the two regimes. In Section 3, I compare the very different governance problems faced in those two countries and analyze whether the independent director is the answer to the problems faced in either country. I conclude that the independent director is unlikely to eliminate fraud and self-dealing from the American capital markets, as it proponents may have hoped. I also conclude, however, that the use of independent directors, if properly bolstered by other governance measures, could help mitigate the problems fostered by the *chaebol* system in Korea.

II. CORPORATE GOVERNANCE IN KOREA

A. The Dominance of the *Chaebol*

The defining characteristic of corporate governance in Korea is the predominance of *chaebols*, a group of affiliated firms, which although they are legally independent, are nonetheless tied together by cross shareholdings.[3] The group is commonly dominated by a controlling shareholder or family. Although common shares carry one vote per share in Korea (dual class shares are prohibited for now[4]), the strategic use of cross ownership results in the controlling shareholder exercising voting power over the affiliated companies substantially greater than the controller's economic rights. From 1997 to 2005, controlling shareholders of *chaebol* firms held an average of 69 percent of the voting rights, but only 22 percent of the cash flow rights for those shareholders.[5]

In part to maintain this control, *chaebol* firms rely heavily on debt.[6] Indeed, this is the principal benefit afforded by affiliation with the *chaebol* group: affiliated firms have greater access to financing than non-*chaebol* firms, which is the result of cross-debt guarantees among *chaebol* member firms.[7] Moreover, the importance of the *chaebol* to the Korean economy means that they were historically "too big to fail," enjoying the implicit guarantee of a bailout from the government.[8] That guarantee now appears to have been withdrawn, as evidenced by the demise of the Daewoo group. Perhaps the recently enacted prohibition of loans and guarantees to specially-related persons will put pressure on the *chaebol* to reduce their debt levels.[9] The available evidence suggests that substantial improvement has been made already, with the debt load of the *chaebol* substantially reduced from where it stood at the time of the IMF crisis.[10]

---

[3] Cross shareholding is not permitted between two firms, but this restriction is readily circumvented through the use of three or more firms. Sea Jin Chang, *Ownership Structure, Expropriation, and Performance of Group-Affiliated Companies in Korea*, 48 ACAD. MGMT. J. 238, 238 (2003).

[4] SANGBEOP [KOREAN COMMERCIAL CODE] art. 369-1. The Ministry of Justice has drafted legislation that would allow dual-class stock.

[5] E. Han Kim & Woochan Kim, *Changes in Korean Corporate Governance: A Response to Crisis*, 8 J. KOREAN L. 23, 30 (2008).

[6] Jae-Seung Baek et al., *Corporate Governance and Firm Value: Evidence from the Korean Financial Crisis*, 71 J. FIN. ECON. 265, 267 (2004) (the average debt to total assets ratio in the top 30 *chaebol* firms was 77.18% in 1993–98).

[7] Hyun-Han Shin & Young S. Park, *Financing Constraints and Internal Capital Markets: Evidence from Korean 'Chaebols'*, 5 J. CORP. FIN. 169, 172–73, 190 (1999).

[8] Curtis J. Milhaupt, *Privatization and Corporate Governance in a Unified Korea*, 26 J. CORP. L. 199, 207 (2000).

[9] Cross-debt guarantees of chaebol group companies are tightly regulated by law. Dokjeomgyuje mit Gongjeonggeorae e gwanhan beomnyul [KOREAN MONOPOLY REGULATION AND FAIR TRADE ACT], art. 10-2. I am indebted to Joon Park for this point.

[10] According to the analysis of the Financial Supervisory Service, the largest five *chaebol* groups reduced their average total liabilities-to-equity ratio from 352

B. Evidence on the Effect on Minority Shareholders

Unfortunately, the benefits afforded by greater access to debt carry substantial costs for equity holders. The "separation of ownership and control" enjoyed by the controlling shareholders of the *chaebol* has important implications for minority shareholders in Korean firms. Although this separation of cash flow rights from control rights may reduce the cost of debt (perhaps because it aligns the interests of default-averse creditors with the interests of under-diversified controlling shareholders), it may also leave minority shareholders vulnerable to expropriation by controlling shareholders. The directors charged with protecting those minority shareholders are scant protection: "chaebol affiliates' boards of directors are generally filled with insiders and friends of chaebol families."[11] Thus, the discretion of the controlling shareholder is largely unchecked by the formal authority supposedly held by the board.

There is considerable evidence that controlling shareholders use this discretion to appropriate wealth from the minority. For example, minority shareholders in *chaebol* firms typically lose out when the firm makes an acquisition, but the controlling shareholder benefits.[12] Controlling shareholders also appear to manipulate their ownership interests in group firms to concentrate their economic rights in the most profitable members of the group.[13] Conversely, controlling shareholders may reduce their equity exposure in group members' firms that have provided debt guarantees to more risky firms within the group.[14] So the greater access to debt that *chaebol* firms enjoy may again come at the expense of minority shareholders.

This divergence between control and economic rights may also manifest itself in diminished profitability. Controlling shareholders in *chaebol* groups may be more concerned with avoiding losses to their under-diversified wealth than they are with maximizing the profits of the firms

---

percent (December 31, 1998) to 125 percent (December 31, 2002); other *chaebol* groups reduced their average ratio from 427 percent (December 31, 1998) to 172 percent (December 31, 2002).

[11] Chang, *supra* note 3, at 241.

[12] Kee-Hong Bae et al., *Tunneling or Value Added? Evidence from Mergers by Korean Business Groups*, 57 J. FIN. 2695, 2737 (2002).

[13] Woochan Kim et al., *What Determines the Ownership Structure of Business Conglomerates?: On the Cash Flow Rights of Korea's Chaebol*, ECGI – Finance Working Paper No. 51/2004; KDI School Of Public Policy & Management Paper No. 04-20 (2004), at 30, *available at* http://ssrn.com/abstract=594741.0; Chang, *supra* note 3, at 250.

[14] Chang, *supra* note 3, at. 242.

affiliated with the group. Minority shareholders, by contrast, are more likely to be fully diversified (and therefore effectively risk-neutral) and less likely to have equity holding in each of the members of the group. There is evidence that the ownership structure of the *chaebol* may hurt profitability. For example, Joh shows that *chaebol* firms experienced lower operating profits during the pre-crisis period.[15] Monitoring by the controlling shareholder appears to promote the interests of the group as a whole, not the firm for which the individual works. So top executive turnover in *chaebol* firms appears to be unrelated to firm-level performance, whereas it is significantly related for non-*chaebol* firms.[16] In addition, executive compensation correlates with stock-market returns and return on assets for non-*chaebol* firms, but there is no significant relation between these performance measures and executive compensation for *chaebol* firms, despite the fact that *chaebol* firms pay their executives more.[17]

Not surprisingly, the stock market appears to recognize this risk of abuse by the controlling shareholders of *chaebol* firms: Baek, Kang & Park find that firms in which the controlling shareholders' voting rights exceed his or her economic rights, had significantly lower returns during Korea's financial crisis.[18] By contrast, firms with the largest non-managerial blockholder concentration experienced significantly greater stock returns during the crisis.[19] These findings suggest that concentrated ownership is not the problem; it is the separation of control from cash flow entitlements. In addition, transparency helps mitigate the problem; firms with cross-listed ADRs (thereby subject to more stringent disclosure regimes) and firms with substantial foreign institutional investment also enjoyed significantly less negative returns.[20] Monitoring of management

---

15 Sung Wook Joh, *Corporate Governance and Firm Profitability: Evidence from Korea before the Economic Crisis*, 68 J. FIN. ECON. 287, 318–19 (2003); Terry L. Campbell & Phyllis Y. Keys, *Corporate Governance in South Korea: The Chaebol Experience*, 8 J. CORP. FIN. 373, 389 (2002).

16 Campbell & Keys, *supra* note 15, at 390.

17 Takao Kato, Woochan Kim & Ju Ho Lee, *Executive Compensation, Firm Performance and Chaebols in Korea: Evidence from New Panel Data*, 15 PACIFIC-BASIN FIN. J. 36 (2007).

18 Baek et al., *supra* note 6, at 310. Interestingly, the lower stock market returns of the *chaebol* firms were not matched by lower accounting profitability during the crisis – *chaebol* firms had greater profits (although the difference is not statistically significant) than their non-*chaebol* counterparts. *Id.* at 307.

19 *Id.* at 302.

20 *Id.* This fact is noteworthy in light of the fact that the flight of foreign capital played an important role in exacerbating the effects of the financial crisis. Milhaupt, *supra* note 8, at 295, 297.

by large investors – without the risk of expropriation by the controlling shareholder – benefits *all* of the investors.

C. Reforming the *Chaebols*

Reforming the corporate governance of the *chaebols* to discourage misappropriation from minority shareholders has been a principal focus of the government since the financial crisis of 1997–98. The IMF and World Bank identified weak corporate governance as an important cause of the crisis.[21] Prior to these reforms,

> Principal shareholders commanded all facets of corporate affairs, including board decisions, the selection of directors or auditors, and shareholder meetings. Principal shareholders single-handedly appointed directors and auditors. Candidates were selected from company employees, with one of the most important criteria being personal loyalty to the principal shareholders.[22]

Now, directors owe an explicit fiduciary duty to the corporation.[23] In addition, thresholds have been lowered for the bringing of derivative suits and removing directors.[24] The former change has resulted in a significant increase in the number of derivative actions.[25]

Large firms (i.e., those with assets greater than 2 trillion won) are singled out for especially stringent corporate governance requirements. Large firms must draw at least half of their directors from outside the firm, have an audit committee with at least two-thirds outside directors, and have a nominating committee for outside directors.[26] Substantial numbers of smaller firms have adopted these reforms voluntarily.[27] All of these reforms are major departures from practices prevailing prior to the financial crisis.

Chaebol firms have also received special attention. Principal shareholders who act as *de facto* directors or otherwise influence company management now owe a fiduciary duty to the corporation, whether or not they

---

21 Joongi Kim, *Recent Amendments to the Korean Commercial Code and Their Effects on International Competition*, 21 U. Pa. J. Int'l Econ. L. 273, 275 (2000).

22 *Id.* at 279–80.

23 Korean Commercial Code, art. 382-3.

24 Korean Commercial Code, art. 385 & 403.

25 Kim, *supra* note 21, at 295.

26 Korean Commercial Code, art. 542-8 & 542-1.

27 Bernard Black & Woochan Kim, *The Effect of Board Structure on Firm Value: A Multiple Iidentification Strategies Approach Using Korean Data*, J. Fin. Econ. (Forthcoming 2011).

serve formally as directors.[28] Moreover, conflict of interest transactions involving the firms in the groups with more than 5 trillion won of total assets must be approved by the board of directors.[29] There is evidence that a similar provision adopted by the SK Group in its articles of incorporation has been effective in preventing at least some overreaching by the controlling shareholder.[30] It is worth noting that the provision in question may have been adopted as a result of pressure from foreign investors.[31]

These requirements appear to have had some effect, as *chaebol* firms do not have significantly worse governance than other Korean firms.[32] There is evidence that improvements in corporate governance have a real payoff – Black, Jang, and Kim find that better corporate governance correlates with significantly greater market valuation.[33] For example, having a majority of outside directors correlates with a roughly 40 percent greater share price.[34]

To summarize, the main challenge facing the Korean system of corporate governance is the predominance of the *chaebol* system. Korea has made great strides over the last few years to try and bolster the protections afforded to minority shareholders, but more must be done. I will turn to that topic in Section 3.

III. CORPORATE GOVERNANCE IN THE UNITED STATES

A. Dispersed Public Ownership

The pattern of corporate ownership in the United States differs substantially from the one found in Korea. Controlling shareholders, while not unheard of, are the exception rather than the rule. The typical ownership pattern in the United States is one of dispersed public ownership, with no single shareholder holding more than a small percentage of the company's

---

28 KOREAN COMMERCIAL CODE, art. 401-2.

29 KOREAN MONOPOLY REGULATION AND FAIR TRADE ACT, art. 11-2.

30 Kim, *supra* note 21, at 325.

31 Kim, *supra* note 21, at 324-25.

32 Bernard S. Black, Hasung Jang & Woochan Kim, *Predicting Firms' Corporate Governance Choices: Evidence from Korea*, 12 J. CORP. FIN. 660, 677 (2006).

33 Bernard S. Black, Hasung Jang & Woochan Kim, *Does Corporate Governance Predict Firms Market Values? Evidence from Korea*, 22 J. L. ECON. & ORG. 366 (2006).

34 *Id.*

shares. The need for diversification and certain regulatory restrictions ensure that even institutional investors will not ordinarily hold more than a small bloc of shares in any one company. Moreover, cross-ownership is relatively rare. American companies own shares in other companies, but they are typically a joint venture between companies. More typically, a parent corporation will own 100 percent of the shares of a subsidiary, essentially obviating conflict of interest concerns, or different businesses within a corporation will simply be operated as separate operating divisions, without the formality of separate incorporation. (The downside of the latter arrangement, of course, is that all of the company's assets will be placed at risk if one of the operating divisions sustains liabilities that it cannot satisfy on its own.)

In this system of dispersed public ownership, the principal concern for abuse of power by those in control is not the risk posed by controlling shareholders, but rather, the potential for overreaching by managers. Given the dispersion of ownership, the voting mechanism will only be a weak check on managerial abuse and incompetence. Managers (particularly CEOs) in practice have a great deal of say over who will be named to the company's board, so the ability of the shareholders to affect the company's direction through their power to elect directors will be diffuse at best. Recognizing these weaknesses in direct accountability to widely dispersed shareholders, the corporate governance regime in the United States aims to protect the interests of largely powerless shareholders from overreaching by managers. Controlling shareholders are a concern, but a secondary one. The principal role of independent directors in the corporate regime of the United States is to restrain the CEO and other managers.

B. Evidence on the Effect of Independent Directors

What does the available evidence from the United States show about the success of independent directors in restraining managers? Most notably, on the subject presumably of greatest interest to shareholders, there is no evidence to show that more independent boards correlate with better firm performance.[35] So shareholders cannot rely on independent directors to bolster the bottom line. This should hardly be surprising – if outside directors were a magic elixir, somehow boosting corporate performance, we would hardly need governance mandates to encourage greater board

---

[35] Sanjai Bhagat & Bernard Black, *The Non-Correlation Between Board Independence and Long-Term Firm Performance*, 27 J. Corp. L. 231, 259 (2001).

independence. Companies would bring more independent directors on board purely out of self-interest.

Independent directors do appear to have an effect, however, at certain critical junctures for the corporation. Those junctures arise when the board is asked to make certain high stakes decisions. Being an outside director has historically been a part-time job, but at times it can capture the director's full-time attention. More independent boards are more likely to replace the CEO after a period of poor performance.[36] This finding suggests that independent directors take this paramount monitoring task seriously. Turning to other salient situations likely to capture the focus of independent directors, more independent boards generally extract higher takeover premia in takeovers.[37] Companies adopting a "poison pill" shareholder rights plan experience a positive stock price reaction if their board is majority independent, but a negative reaction otherwise.[38] What explains these findings relating to takeovers? Perhaps more independent boards limit the ability of target company managers to extract side payments from potential acquirers, which the pill may facilitate. On the other side of the fence, acquiring companies announcing takeovers experience *less* of a drop in their stock price if they have a majority of independent directors.[39] Independent directors may check excessive managerial optimism and a penchant for empire building.

These findings that independent directors guide salient decisions are promising. The evidence on whether more independent directors contribute to more accurate financial reporting, however, is mixed. On the one hand, board independence does not appear to have any significant effect on a company's exposure to securities fraud class actions, one of the principal unfortunate consequences stemming from inaccurate financial reporting in the United States.[40] On the other, there is evidence that weak governance, including a lack of board independence, is associated

---

[36] Michael S. Weisbach, *Outside Directors and CEO Turnover*, 20 J. FIN. ECON. 431, 458 (1988).

[37] James F. Cotter et al., *Do Independent Directors Enhance Target Shareholder Wealth During Tender Offers?*, 43 J. FIN. ECON. 195, 216 (1997).

[38] James A. Brickley et al., *Outside Directors and the Adoption of Poison Pills*, 35 J. FIN. ECON. 371, 388 (1994).

[39] John W. Byrd & Kent A. Hickman, *Do Outside Directors Monitor Managers? Evidence from Tender Offer Bids*, 32 J. FIN. ECON. 195, 219 (1992).

[40] Marilyn F. Johnson et al., *Do the Merits Matter More? The Impact of the Private Securities Litigation Reform Act*, 23 J.L. ECON. & ORG. 627, 642 n.14 (2007).

with enforcement actions by the Securities and Exchange Commission.[41] This finding is confirmed in a study looking at a broader range of fraudulent behavior.[42] These studies, however, rely on data that may have little bearing on current practice because governance practices in the United States have considerably less variation today than they did ten to twenty years ago. Virtually all of the boards of American public companies are now "above average," at least when compared with the governance practices of a generation ago.

C. Reforming the Role of Independent Directors

The corporate governance reforms in the United States have not been directed toward areas in which independent directors have been shown to have a positive influence on shareholder returns. Instead, the reforms are pinned to the hope that independent directors can encourage more accurate financial reporting. That focus reflects the scandals that give rise to the impetus for reform. The reforms came in response to a series of accounting scandals at large public companies, most notably Enron, Worldcom, Adelphia and Tyco. Unlike the Korean crisis of 1997–98, the stock market decline that accompanied these headlines of scandal did not have any appreciable effect on the overall economy. Notwithstanding the limited economic impact of these scandals, the widespread wrongdoing at those prominent firms raised concerns that it might reflect a broader pattern of misleading financial statements and self-dealing. Among the concerns raised were:

(1) the perception that managers focused too narrowly on showing earnings growth from quarter to quarter, which may have created a temptation to shade the numbers in order to show that growth;
(2) the closely-related concern that incentive-based compensation, which was supposed to align managers' interests with those of shareholders, again may have tempted managers to play fast-and-loose with accounting-based measures of performance; and

---

[41] Patricia M. Dechow et al., *Causes and Consequences of Earnings Manipulation: An Analysis of Firms Subject to Enforcement Actions by the SEC*, 13 CONTEMP. ACCT. RES. 1, 21-22 (1996); Mark S. Beasley, *An Empirical Analysis of the Relation Between the Board of Director Composition and Financial Statement Fraud*, 71 THE ACCT. REV. 443, 463 (1996).

[42] Hatice Uzun et al., *Board Composition and Corporate Fraud*, 60 FIN. ANALYSTS J. 33, 41 (2004).

(3) a limited form of self-dealing involving not related-party transactions of the sort seen in the *chaebol*, but instead enormous pay packages to managers, seemingly unchecked by too quiescent independent directors.

Politicians quickly stepped in to exploit the opportunity created by this very public airing of corporate dirty laundry. The Sarbanes–Oxley Act of 2002 was the political response to the accounting crisis in the United States.[43] Not surprisingly, given that the impetus for legislation arose out of accounting problems, the governance reforms adopted in response to the accounting scandals revolve around the relation of public companies to their external auditors. Those external auditors were perceived to be lacking in the independence. A variety of restrictions were adopted to foster auditor independence; the reform involving the board was to make the external auditors solely accountable to independent directors.

Although anxious to be seen "doing something" about corporate misbehavior, Congress took pains to avoid responsibility for the details of the reforms to be adopted. Instead of requiring that audit committees be made up solely of independent directors, Congress instead directed national securities exchanges to adopt listing standards requiring wholly-independent audit committees.[44] The distinction between laws and listing standards is largely cosmetic, given that changes in listing standards are subject to approval by the Securities and Exchange Commission. In effect, the delegation of this task to the exchanges was a *de facto* takeover of an important aspect of corporate governance from state corporate law (its traditional domain in the American system). The takeover was done, however, with a self-regulatory veneer, useful because the exchanges have imposed governance standards, of varying degrees of intrusiveness, for decades.[45] Those listing standards now require not only that all members of the audit committee be independent (as directed by Congress), but also require that those members be "financially literate" or possess "financial sophistication."[46] Sarbanes–Oxley also requires that the independent audit committee have exclusive authority over the retention and compensation of auditors.[47] Auditors also must report to the audit committee

---

43 Pub. L. No. 107-204, 116 Stat. 745 (2002).

44 Sarbanes–Oxley Act, Pub. L. No. 107-204, § 301, 116 Stat. 745 (2002).

45 Standards Relating to Listed Company Audit Committees, Exchange Act Release No. 34-47654 (April 25, 2003).

46 NYSE Listed Company Manual § 303A.07; Nasdaq Rule 4350(d)(2).

47 Sarbanes–Oxley Act, § 301, *supra* note 43.

material accounting decisions.[48] Finally, the law establishes "whistle-blowing" procedures for employees to report concerns about accounting to the audit committee.[49]

The requirement of the independent audit committee supplements the requirement that the board of directors have a majority of independent directors. Both the New York Stock Exchange and Nasdaq listing standards now mandate that independent directors predominate.[50] In and of itself, this requirement is uncontroversial, but the definition of independence is circumscribed by a number of relationships with the company which are specified as inconsistent with independence.[51]

A more direct challenge to the power of the CEO is reflected in changes in the selection of directors. Nomination of directors is placed in the hands of independent directors: the NYSE requires a nominating committee consisting solely of independent directors, while the Nasdaq allows a choice between such a committee and nomination by a majority of the independent directors serving on the board as a whole.[52] The exchanges split similarly on the question of CEO compensation: the NYSE requires a compensation committee consisting solely of independent directors, while the Nasdaq again gives a choice between such a committee and allowing a majority of independent directors to determine compensation.[53] The division between the NYSE and Nasdaq reflects the difficulty that some smaller companies, largely concentrated on the Nasdaq, may have in finding enough qualified independent directors to serve all the mandated committees. The requirements relating to CEO compensation probably codify, in large part, existing practice: CEO compensation would be subject to an entire fairness review by the courts if not ratified by the independent directors.

Congress, apparently not satisfied with the performance of compensation committees, has further bolstered the requirements. The Dodd–Frank Wall Street Reform and Consumer Protection Act, passed in 2010, requires the SEC to direct, by rule, the national securities exchanges and

---

48 Sarbanes–Oxley Act, § 204, *supra* note 43.
49 Sarbanes–Oxley Act, § 301, *supra* note 43.
50 NYSE Listed Company Manual § 303A.01; Nasdaq Rule 4350(c)(1).
51 NYSE Listed Company Manual § 303A.02(a); Nasdaq Rule 4200(a)(15).
52 NYSE Listed Company Manual § 303A.04(a); Nasdaq Rule 4350(c)(4)(a).
53 NYSE Listed Company Manual § 303A.05(a); Nasdaq Rule 4350(c)(3)(a). This change appears to have had some effect; Vidhi Chhaochharia and Yaniv Grinstein find that the introduction of these listing standards correlates with reduced CEO compensation. *CEO Compensation and Board Structure*, 64 J. Fin. 231, 232 (2009).

national securities associations to prohibit the listing of any equity securities of public companies unless the compensation committees of the public companies' boards are made up exclusively of independent directors.[54] The independence requirement for the board compensation committee parallels the independence requirement for the board audit committee implemented as part of the Sarbanes–Oxley Act. Moreover, the Dodd–Frank Act imposes a variety of responsibilities on compensation committees. For example, compensation committees must be directly responsible for the hiring and supervision of compensation consultants.[55] In another incursion into corporate governance, the Dodd–Frank Act also requires that companies disclose whether the same person holds both the CEO and chairman of the board positions, and explain why the position is combined or not.[56]

All of these committee requirements have put substantial new responsibilities on independent directors; compliance with all of these new requirements has forced independent directors to work more. Not surprisingly, companies have been forced to pay correspondingly more for independent directors' services.[57] The trend is unlikely to abate; the recent subprime crisis has brought calls for a greater role by independent directors in risk management.[58] Given these greater responsibilities, boards may have to expand to accommodate the greater work load. Expansion of the board, however, may be bad news for investors, as larger boards correlate with weaker firm performance.[59]

---

[54] Dodd–Frank Wall Street Reform and Consumer Protection Act, Pub. L. No. 111-203, § 952, 124 Stat. 1376 (2010).

[55] *Id.*

[56] Dodd–Frank Act § 972, *supra* note 54.

[57] Towers Perrin, *Compensation for Corporate Directors Rose Modestly in 2008*, *available at* http://www.towersperrin.com/tp/showdctmdoc.jsp?country=global&url=Master_Brand_2/USA/News/Monitor/2009/200910/mon_article_200910c.htm (reporting decline in director compensation in 2008 after yearly increases of 10 percent).

[58] Press Release, National Association of Corporate Directors Launches Campaign to Strengthen Corporate Governance (Mar. 24, 2009), *available at* www.nacdonline.org/DirectorChallenge.

[59] David Yermack, *Higher Market Valuation of Companies with a Small Board of Directors*, 40 J. Fin. Econ. 185, 209 (1996).

IV. THE ROLE OF INDEPENDENT DIRECTORS IN KOREA AND THE UNITED STATES

A. Korean and United States' Independent Directors Compared

Table 4.1 opposite summarizes the recent reforms relating to independent directors for large, public firms in Korea and the United States discussed above.

Placing the two countries' reforms side-by-side in the chart highlights the fact that Korea's corporate governance provisions, by and large, have more in common with the requirements in the United States than differences. One might conclude from this overall similarity, and given their relative states of capital market development, that both countries have adopted roughly appropriate models of corporate governance. I would argue, however, that the opposite conclusion is warranted: given their relative states of capital market development, Korea requires *more* stringent corporate governance mandates than does the United States. Korea cannot be content to follow the American lead in corporate governance if it hopes to attain the depth and liquidity of the American capital.

B. The Path Forward for Independent Directors in Korea

Korea's public companies continue to be dominated by the *chaebol*; that dominance is unlikely to end any time soon. As a result, the *chaebol* are the face of Korean companies for many potential investors. As the research discussed in Section 1 demonstrates, minority shareholders in those firms face very substantial risks of expropriation by the controlling shareholder. They face an even more substantial risk that the *chaebol* group will be managed to minimize the losses to the controlling shareholder. Potential investors have good grounds to be wary of placing their money in the hands of the controlling shareholders.

The combination of *chaebol* dominance and controlling-shareholder abuses means that the *chaebol* present a difficult "chicken-and-egg" problem for Korean reformers. On the one hand, the available evidence suggests that the shareholders of the *chaebol* companies would benefit the most from improvements in corporate governance. Korea cannot encourage a culture of investor confidence in Korean companies (with the attendant benefits that this would create for economic growth) without taming the power of the controlling shareholders of the *chaebol* and protecting minority shareholders from their overreaching. *Chaebol* shareholders, as a group, would be better off if governance were improved, but the benefits would accrue primarily to minority shareholders at the expense

Table 4.1 Board independence in Korea and the United States

	Korea	United States
Board	> 50 % independent[a]	> 50 % independent[b]
Audit Committee	Required 67 % outside directors and non-outside director member must satisfy statutory independence test[c] Must have at least one finance or accounting expert[d]	Required 100 % independent directors[e] Must possess "financial sophistication" or "financial literacy"[f] Auditors must report to audit committee[g]
Nominating committee	Required for outside directors ≥ 50% independent[h]	Required 100% independent directors on committee or majority of independent directors[i]
Compensation committee	Not required	Required 100% independent directors or majority of independent directors[j]
Related-party transactions	Board approval required[k] Loans and guarantees prohibited (except for certain limited circumstances)	Independent directors' approval required (otherwise subject to legal challenge)[l] Loans to officers prohibited[m]
Cumulative voting	Required absent opt out in charter; many firms have opted out[n]	Permissible, but not required and not common[o]

Notes:

a. KOREAN COMMERCIAL CODE, art. 542-8.
b. NYSE Listed Company Manual § 303A.01; Nasdaq Rule 4350(c)(1).
c. KOREAN COMMERCIAL CODE, art. 542-11 & 415-2.
d. KOREAN COMMERCIAL CODE, art. 542-11.
e. NYSE Listed Company Manual § 303A.07(b); Nasdaq Rule 4350(d)(2).
f. *Id.*
g. NYSE Listed Company Manual § 303A.07(a).
h. KOREAN COMMERCIAL CODE, art. 542-8.
i. NYSE Listed Company Manual § 303A.04(a); Nasdaq Rule 4350(c)(4)(a).
j. NYSE Listed Company Manual § 303A.05(a); Nasdaq Rule 4350(c)(3)(a). See also Dodd–Frank Act § 952, *supra* note 54.
k. KOREAN COMMERCIAL CODE, art. 542-9.
l. NYSE Listed Company Manual § 307.00; DEL. CODE ANN. tit. 8, § 144 (2009); N.Y. BUS. CORP. LAW § 713 (2009); CAL. CORP. CODE § 310 (2009).
m. Sarbanes–Oxley Act § 402, *supra* note 43.
n. KOREAN COMMERCIAL CODE, art. 542-7.
o. See MODEL BUS. CORP. ACT § 7.28 cmt. Statutory comparison (2008).

of controlling shareholders. Thus, controlling shareholders, anxious to preserve their substantial discretion, are likely to pose a substantial obstacle to further reform. As a result of their wealth and central role of their businesses in the Korean economy, the controlling shareholders exercise tremendous influence in policy discussions. Slicing this Gordian knot to promote a system that facilitates the confidence of minority investors is the central challenge facing Korean regulators today.

Can the knot be cut? Unfortunately, the answer to this critical question is: "Not overnight." The path in the United States to predominance by independent boards was a long one.[60] Moreover, the task will take considerable political will. The hope is that independent directors may be the "camel's nose under the tent" that eventually brings true transparency and accountability in Korea's corporate boardrooms. The power of independent directors will need to be bolstered, however, to achieve this end. But any increase in the power of independent directors is likely to draw opposition from the controlling shareholders of the *chaebol*. To overcome that opposition, Korean reformers must strategically take advantage of the periodic opportunities for reform – created by financial crisis and scandal – to press for further power in the hands of boards dominated by independent directors. Every incident in which a controlling shareholder is publicly disgraced is an opportunity for further reform.

The governance reforms already adopted in Korea are critical first steps. Much reliance is placed, however, on independent directors to ensure that these reforms translate into actual protection for minority shareholders. To achieve this goal, independent directors need to be independent in more than just name. At a minimum, independent directors need to be independent of other members of the *chaebol* group, in addition to independent of the company on whose board they serve. The current rule is that independent directors cannot be employees of affiliated companies of the *chaebol* group.[61] They are not barred, however, from service as directors for *chaebol* affiliates.[62] Service as a director might not be thought to be sufficient to compromise independence. The fees paid to directors are, after all, relatively modest when compared to the typical directors' wealth and income. So one might perhaps conclude that service as a director of an affiliated company should not be deemed to compromise independence. On the other hand, directors owe a duty to each of the companies

---

60 A comprehensive, and illuminating, history can be found in Jeffrey N. Gordon, *The Rise of Independent Directors in the United States, 1950-2005: Of Shareholder Value and Stock Market Prices*, 59 STAN. L. REV. 165 (2007).

61 KOREAN COMMERCIAL CODE, art. 382.

62 *Id.*

on whose boards they serve, and in the *chaebol*, these duties are likely to come into conflict.

The problem, however, may go deeper than a conflict of interest or legal duty, either perceived or real. What is needed is a counter to controlling shareholders' manipulation of transactions among the *chaebol* affiliated companies. From this perspective, an independent director loyal to the group, rather than the individual company, is not likely to help. The independent director must be independent from the group in order to be fully independent from the controlling shareholder. To be sure, this will impose costs on group cohesiveness, but that is the point. If the controlling shareholder wants a free hand to transfer assets among affiliated companies, the companies should be merged, or the minority shareholders should be bought out and the structure changed to a parent/subsidiary one with 100 percent ownership. Requiring independent directors for all members of the group imposes a tax on an interlocking corporate structure that has been shown to harm minority shareholders. Controlling shareholders can avoid this tax by moving to a holding company structure, which would carry with it substantially improved transparency.[63]

Finding enough independent directors for all group companies will not be easy. A more daunting challenge for reformers, however, is cultural rather than legal. It will take time for Korea to develop a culture of independence necessary for outside directors to have the desired effect on management. The institution of independent directors is starting from a very low level:

> Korea has no tradition of active discussion within the Board of Directors, and experience with independent directors has been limited. Most have been lawyers, accountants, academics and retired government officials. Concerns have been expressed about the effective independence of many independent directors and about their lack of business experience. Newly-appointed directors often complain about lack of access to the information they consider necessary for informed decision-making.[64]

This cultural weakness suggests that reformers must take stronger formal steps to ensure that independent directors are tough-minded defenders of the interests of *all* shareholders. It is worth considering whether the roles of CEO and Chairman should be separated to provide a

---

63 Hwa-Jin Kim, *The Case for Market for Corporate Control in Korea*, 8 J. Korean L. 227, 248 (2009) (discussing reorganization of SK Corporation in response to a hostile takeover attempt).

64 Bernard S. Black et al., *Corporate Governance in Korea at the Millennium: Enhancing International Competitiveness*, 26 J. Corp. L. 537, 557 (2001).

stronger voice for the independent directors in the boardroom. As noted above, the Dodd–Frank Act now takes a step in this direction through a disclosure requirement.

Another mechanism to bolster independent directors as monitors is to strengthen the role of institutional investors. The role of independent directors could be greatly enhanced if shareholders were to take advantage of the provision allowing shareholders holding at least 1 percent of the company's shares to nominate candidates for director.[65] Unfortunately, one weakness currently limiting the effectiveness of institutional investors in Korean corporate governance is that many Korean institutions are affiliated with the *chaebol* and as a result provide little in the way of independent monitoring.[66] One avenue for overcoming this problem is to encourage foreign institutions to take larger positions in Korean companies. (This is already an important trend; foreign ownership of Korean listed companies has gone from 13 percent in 1996 to 37 percent in 2006.)[67] Such institutions are accustomed to standards of corporate transparency substantially greater than those currently practiced in most Korean companies. To be effective in demanding transparency, however, these institutions will want some assurance of representation in the boardroom. For this reason, restrictions on share ownership for outside directors should be repealed.[68] Ownership of shares – if less than a controlling stake – is a powerful incentive to work hard on behalf of minority shareholders. In addition, the provision of the Korean Commercial Code [Sangbeop] allowing companies to remove cumulative voting through their charter provision should be repealed.[69] Many companies have taken advantage of this position to eliminate the threat posed to the controlling shareholder's power by institutional investors, thus rendering the cumulative voting provision ineffective.[70] There are now limits on controlling shareholders voting their shares to remove cumulative voting.[71] These limits also apply to undoing the charter provisions that already restrict cumulative voting.[72] But who will initiate such a change? For outside investors to have an effective voice

---

65 Korean Commercial Code, art. 542-6.

66 Black et al., *supra* note 64, at 552.

67 Kim & Kim, *supra* note 5, at 25.

68 Korean Commercial Code, art. 542-8; Sangbeop Sihaengryung [Korean Commercial Code Presidential Decree], art. 13.

69 Korean Commercial Code, art. 382-2.

70 Bernard S. Black, *The Role of Self-Regulation in Supporting Korea's Securities Markets*, 3 J. Korean L. 17, 27 n.9 (2003).

71 Korean Commercial Code, art. 542-7.

72 *Id.*

in the direction of the company, cumulative voting should be mandatory for the foreseeable future.

Cumulative voting would give institutions real clout in determining *who* the independent directors will be. Setting the agenda for voting is also important. Although (as I discuss below) it is difficult to justify the inclusion of any inside directors on the audit committee, the inclusion of inside directors on the nominating committee raises a more problematic question. Including inside directors on this committee may help ensure that the outside directors chosen are a good "fit." But if insiders choose the outsiders, how closely will the board scrutinize the conduct of the insiders? Here the conflict between the board's role as a team decision-maker and its role as a monitor is particularly acute. I think, however, that in the context of Korea's controlling shareholder-dominated corporate governance, the incremental independence that might result is worth the loss in board solidarity. As transparency and accountability increase, this question might need to be rethought.

The role of the audit committee also should be broadened and its independence bolstered. The requirement that boards approve related-party transactions over a certain size threshold is a step in the right direction.[73] The dynamics of the boardroom, however, and the desire to get along with one's fellow board members, make this provision less effective than is needed. Given the pervasiveness of related-party transactions among *chaebol* members and the evidence that such transactions are manipulated to benefit controlling shareholders, stronger medicine is needed. Related-party transactions should require approval of the company's audit committee, not the board. Moreover, the audit committee should be made up exclusively of independent directors. (Some firms have already taken an essentially equivalent step by creating related party-transaction review committees consisting exclusively of outside directors.[74] This approach may be preferable if there are concerns with demanding too great a time commitment from outside directors.) The audit committee, if properly empowered and staffed by the right people, is potentially the single most effective mechanism for protecting the rights of minority shareholders against overreaching by controlling shareholders and managers. The internal auditor, as an employee of the firm, should report to the audit committee, but should not be part of that committee, particularly if the audit committee's responsibilities are expanded. Putting insiders in the audit committee's meeting room, even if they meet statutory tests for

---

73 Korean Commercial Code, art. 542-9.
74 Kim, *supra* note 21, at 275.

independence, can only dampen the vigorous independence that is needed there. Giving the independent directors the separate space afforded by a relatively autonomous audit committee may well encourage a certain solidarity among them, and corresponding willingness to stand together to make tough decisions in the face of demands from strong-willed controlling shareholders. This monitoring role could be further enhanced by requiring that the company pay the reasonable expenses of advisors – accountants, lawyers, etc. – for the audit committee.[75]

C. Independent Directors in the United States: The Path Forward?

If Korea would be well served by giving independent directors more power, does it necessarily follow that the United States is equally well served? The new independence requirements for boards that have been adopted in the United States put the tension between the two roles of corporate boards in stark contrast. One vision of the role of the board – call it the "cooperative" model – sees independent directors as part of a team that helps devise business strategy, offers the CEO and other managers useful advice based on extensive business experience, and provides useful business contacts that help promote the firm's profitability. The cooperative model sees outside directors as useful because they broaden the range of expertise and experience available to firm decision-making. The other vision of the role of the board – call it the "adversarial" model – sees directors, particularly those independent of management, as monitors of management, charged with uncovering self-dealing, fraud, other forms of malfeasance, and now, excessive risk taking. The adversarial model sees outside directors as useful because they bring vigilant suspicion to bear on management's activities. One suspects that the vigilant "monitor" is not much of a "team" player. Moreover, one can have doubts about who is benefiting from the monitoring. Is it the shareholders of the firm, disabled by collective action problems from monitoring on their own? Or is it the regulators, attempting to leverage their enforcement resources by conscripting agents inside the firm to ensure that the corporation lives up to its social responsibilities? If shareholder voting does not suffice to ensure that directors will monitor on behalf of shareholders in the way that government regulators believe that they should, the theory goes, perhaps other (more intrusive) mechanisms can help ensure that directors do their job.

The tension between the independent director's twin roles – advisor and monitor – is inevitable. In the fervor of reform frenzy, it is easy to lose

---

75 Black et al., *supra* note 64, at 563.

sight of the important role that independent directors can play in making the business more profitable. No one expects the board of directors to actively manage the company, but the directors may have an important (non-monitoring) role to play in developing an overall strategy and vision for the corporation. Despite the emphasis that regulators put on the role of directors in ensuring the corporation's managers comply with the law, independent directors typically are chosen on the basis of their business expertise, not their monitoring capabilities. So CEOs of other companies are several times more likely than lawyers to serve on the boards of public companies.[76] One assumes that it is not because the CEOs are more vigilant monitors. The experience of top-level management is apparently more valuable in devising business strategy than the instruction provided in law school. Deputizing independent directors as corporate cops inside the boardroom may have very real costs in the ability of the board to help guide the business. The United States needs to worry about how it may be undermining board effectiveness by fostering too much of an adversarial relationship between independent directors and management; Korea has far to go before this will be a concern.

These costs might be worth paying in the United States if enhanced independence was likely to substantially reduce the incidence of fraud and self-dealing, as it may do in Korea. But the United States is starting from a much lower incidence of fraud and self-dealing than Korea (and most other countries in which controlling shareholders dominate public companies). Dispersed share ownership – and the corporate disclosure that promotes such ownership – is the norm in the United States. There is a culture of accountability by corporate managers to the market, as well as the board, that serves as the background for policy efforts to discourage fraud and self-dealing. Fraud and greed will always be with us; closing off one avenue simply pushes the fraudsters and the greedy to find another weakness in the system. The quest for regulatory perfection is illusory, but the costs of that quest – which ultimately will be paid by the shareholders who are supposed to benefit from regulation – will be all too real.

V. CONCLUSION

My focus in this paper has been on the convergence between Korea and the United States on the role of independent directors in corporate

---

[76] Stephen P. Ferris et al., *Too Busy To Mind the Business? Monitoring by Directors with Multiple Board Appointments*, 58 J. Fin. 1087, 1094 (2003).

governance. Korea has come a long way toward the United States model in the last few years as it responded to a devastating financial crisis, even as the United States raised the bar still higher in response to a corporate crisis of its own. For this effort, Korean reformers are to be congratulated.

Unfortunately, there is still work to be done in Korea. The self-dealing and lack of transparency of the *chaebol* are the principal impediments to a culture of investor confidence in Korea. Independent directors – preferably selected by institutional investors – can play an important role in making the changes that are needed. To do so, however, their independence must be further strengthened.

The United States, by contrast, now risks overdosing on independence. Independence facilitates monitoring, but it discourages the trust and candor that are essential to building an effective team. Independence, therefore, should be deployed with caution, and not as the cure-all for the latest scandal to catch the attention of politicians. Time will tell whether the United States has used the appropriate caution in adopting its latest governance reforms.

5. Piercing of the corporate veil in Korea: case commentary[1]

Joseph Cho and Eun Young Shin

I. INTRODUCTION

Today's corporations set up subsidiaries for a variety of reasons including optimal corporate governance and diversification of business. In the context of a parent-subsidiary relationship, there may be situations where, from a legal standpoint, each constituent company exists as a separate entity, whereas, from an economic viewpoint, the subsidiary in effect operates under uniform control of the parent. In situations involving such a corporate group, treating the parent company and its subsidiary as distinct legal entities may result in an outcome that, depending on the facts involved, defies the principle of justice and equity. The utility of piercing the corporate veil[2] has been debated in Korea in an ongoing bid to redress such possible inequity. Arguably, while the concept of veil piercing[3] is not confined to the realm of parent company-subsidiaries, cases involving a single economic unit would, in general, be more prone to veil piercing than others. In fact, the doctrine of veil piercing is likely to foment more issues and controversies in the parent-subsidiary context than any other.

In the case at hand,[4] the plaintiff put forward the allegation that the defendant's denial of liability behind the façade of a subsidiary controlled by it amounted to an abuse of corporate personality in contravention of

---

1 This is an updated version of a piece that was originally published in *Journal of Korean Law*, Vol. 9, No. 1 in December, 2009.

2 *See* Black's Law Dictionary 1168 (7th ed. 1999) (defining "piercing the corporate veil: the judicial act of imposing liability on otherwise immune corporate officers, directors, and shareholders for the corporation's wrongful acts. Also termed disregarding the corporate entity").

3 In Korea, the term "*Bub-in-kyuk-bu-in*" (disregarding the corporate entity) is used to describe this judicial action.

4 Judgment of 25 Aug., 2006 (2004 Da 26119) (Supreme Court of Korea) [hereinafter *2004 Da 26119*].

the principle of good faith,[5] but the Supreme Court of Korea held that the facts of the case did not warrant the corporate veil to be lifted. In so holding, the Court spelled out the criteria for disregarding the corporate entity under Korean company law.

In what follows, we will first examine the existing case laws in Korea on veil piercing followed by an appraisal of *2004 Da 26119* from the perspective of bringing veil piercing into play in the parent company-subsidiary context.

II. CASE LAWS IN KOREA ON CORPORATE VEIL PIERCING[6]

A. Judgment of 13 Sept., 1977, 74 Da 954 (Supreme Court of Korea)

1. Facts of 74 Da 954

The facts of *74 Da 954* are as follows. Origin Co., Ltd. ("Origin") was a limited liability company incorporated by defendant *Bong-Gil Kim*, his wife, brother-in-law, other close relatives, and law clerk on 10 July, 1967. The business name of Origin later changed to *Taewon* Co., Ltd. ("*Taewon*") as of 12 November, 1968. From its inception as Origin, *Taewon* was incorporated as a shelf company through arbitrary use by the defendant of the names of his wife, next of kin, and law clerk. The defendant appointed himself as the Representative Director of *Taewon* with virtually all of the working capital personally financed by him. As a consequence, the defendant could readily position himself as the controlling shareholder, and the allotment of shares to the name-only equity holders including his wife and others was made at the whim of the defendant in the form of gift or contributory stocks. Also, the capital of KRW 5 million at the time of incorporation (later increased to KRW 10 million) was relatively small for the volume of overseas exports *Taewon* was engaging in (amounting to $10000). Further, the basic assets of *Taewon* consisted

---

[5] In *2004 Da 26119*, the plaintiff also alleged the presence of a guaranty and of an intent to create an agency at the end of the defendant, ratification of acts of an agent with no authority, issuance of work direction in violation of Article 401.2 of the Commercial Code [*Sang Bup*] (S. Korea), and establishment of joint torts as the grounds of appeal, and the Supreme Court ruled thereon. Such rulings, however, are beyond the scope of this Commentary.

[6] It is noted that there is no express statutory basis in Korea for corporate veil piercing. Pertinent case laws seem to have based veil piercing on the principle of good faith as codified in the Civil Code [*Min Bup*] (S. Korea); *see infra* note 8.

of only a few parcels of industrial land at *Hwa-yong Dong, Sung-dong* District in Seoul. On account of its unsound financial conditions, *Taewon* evidently relied on outside credit facilities for management purposes including those from the plaintiff.

In addition, the business office of *Taewon* was located inside the defendant's law office, and the company was effectively run as the defendant's privately owned business with the requisite legal formalities either kept to a bare minimum or ignored outright. Further, the assets of *Taewon* and the defendant's personal assets were improperly mixed. As such, when there was a pressing need to settle the accounts of *Taewon*, the defendant's personal assets were used towards that end, and as the liabilities of *Taewon* mounted resulting in increased risk of attachment against certain assets of the company, the defendant effected the provisional registration of such assets under his name and subsequently disposed of the same, thereby siphoning off corporate assets and leaving creditors with little or no recourse.

As the company drifted further into the doldrums, the defendant ran *Taewon* like a sole proprietorship by turning a blind eye to corporate formalities including those on shareholders' meetings, board of directors' resolutions, and invocation of the right to auditing. In effect, *Taewon* was but a sham sugarcoated with the appearance of a limited liability corporation.

In the meanwhile, *Taewon* issued several promissory notes to the plaintiff from 3 June, 1969 to 26 August, 1969 for a total of KRW 8240000. When these promissory notes were not honored as they became due, the plaintiff instituted an *in personam* proceeding against the defendant to enforce its creditor rights.

2. Judicial holdings of 74 Da 954 and comments

At the appellate level, the Seoul High Court affirmed abuse by the defendant of the corporate personality of *Taewon* from the facts that: (1) the defendant used *Taewon* as a façade; (2) the company was in effect operated as the defendant's personal enterprise; (3) *Taewon* was undercapitalized; (4) the defendant ignored corporate formalities and protocols; and (5) the defendant siphoned off corporate assets for the purpose of preempting creditor claims and enforcement actions against *Taewon*.[7]

The court held that the foregoing acts of abuse would not only render the very purpose of corporate entity, a legal fiction concocted to acclimate societal and economic impacts of the corporation, meaningless, but

7 Judgment of 8 May, 1974, 72 Na 2582 (Seoul High Ct.).

also dispel substantive justice and the principle of good faith.[8] As such, the high court ruled in favor of the plaintiff regarding its creditor claims involving the liabilities of *Taewon*.

Subsequently, the Supreme Court overturned the high court with a brief ratio that the company was not a mere façade and did not further articulate on the contours of veil piercing that had been adopted in the affirmative at the appellate level.[9]

In respect of the Supreme Court ruling, legal commentators critiqued the Court as having erred in refusing to lift the corporate veil for the reason that *Taewon* was a legitimate one man company, for such refusal stemmed from an apparent mischaracterization of veil piercing.[10]

B. Judgment of 22 November, 1988, 87 Daka 1671 (Supreme Court of Korea)

1. Facts of 87 Daka 1671

The facts of *87 Daka 1671* are as follows. Defendants *Hyundai Mipo* Dockyard ("HMD") and Samsung Aerial Services provisionally attached a commercial vessel (the "Subject Vessel") to preserve the enforcement of their individual monetary claims against Chipstead Co., Ltd ("Chipstead"). Plaintiff Grand Harmony Inc., the owner of the Subject Vessel, commenced a third party action challenging the validity of the provisional attachment. Chipstead was not privy to the suit.

The plaintiff was a Liberian company with its main offices at 80 Monrovia Broad Street.[11] On 1 April, 1981, the plaintiff and Touchest Shipping Ltd., a Liberian company with the same main office as plaintiff ("Touchest"), entered into a maintenance contract in respect of the Subject Vessel. The signatories to this contract were Daniel Puchieh Lee on behalf of the plaintiff and Denis Puping Lee on behalf of Touchest, respectively. On the same day, Touchest signed off a sub-agency contract with Chipstead whose main office was at Kennedy Road, Hong Kong, for maintenance of the Subject Vessel. The signatories to the sub-agency

---

[8] *Id.* The principle of good faith is codified in Article 2.1 of the Civil Code [*Min Bup*] (S. Korea), which provides: "The exercise of rights and the performance of duties shall be in accordance with the principle of trust and good faith."

[9] *74 Da 954.*

[10] Jae-Hyeong Chang, *Pan-rye-eh-na-ta-nan-bub-in-kyuk-bu-in* [*The Doctrine of Corporate Veil Piercing in Case Law*], 15-1 SEOUL BAR ASSOCIATION CASE LAW STUDY 147, 154 (2001).

[11] *87 Daka 1671*, at 64.

contract were Denis Puping Lee on behalf of Touchest and Daniel Puchieh Lee on behalf of Chipstead, respectively.

The de facto address of Touchest was identical to that of Chipstead, and they shared phone and facsimile numbers.[12] The chairman of Touchest was Dennis Puping Lee, who served as the president of the plaintiff company, and Touchest's president was Daniel Puchieh Lee, who was also the executive director of the plaintiff. The directors of Chipstead consisted of Daniel Puchieh Lee and Denis Puping Lee, who were siblings. Upon a direction to get the Subject Vessel fixed at HMD, the vessel was arranged to enter the port of Ulsan on 1 April, 1985; at the time of the entry, Chipstead Hong Kong was recorded as the owner of the vessel. Later, when *Suk-Lock Lee*, who served as Head of the Tokyo Branch of Chipstead, signed off a service contract with HMD on 10 June, 1985 in consideration of repair services to be dispensed by HMD, *Lee* put Chipstead on the contract as the vessel owner. As such, HMD undertook repairs with the knowledge that the Subject Vessel legitimately belonged to Chipstead.

The Court also noted that it is customary in the international shipping industry for a ship owner to set up a shelf company in such places as Panama or Liberia, as opposed to the country of the owner's nationality or of the corporate origin, register the ship under the name of such shelf company, hoist the flag of the country of registry, and so sail. Following or concurrently with the registration process, the actual owner enters into a maintenance contract with the shelf company and purports to merely act as a managerial entity. This practice enables ship owners to indulge in jurisdiction shopping and benefit from variances in finance, labor and regulatory regime between the owner's country of origin and the country of registry, for ease and maximal efficacy in management.[13] In light of this trade practice, it is customary for dockyards and related businesses to sign off contractual arrangements with the managing corporation who is the actual owner of the ship, as opposed to the registered owner, and get remunerated as such.[14]

2. Judicial rulings of 87 Daka 1671

Affirming the appellate court decision, the Supreme Court noted that even though Touchest and Chipstead were disparate entities outwardly, Chipstead had in fact incorporated the plaintiff and Touchest, both of which shared the same corporate office and management, for managerial

---

12 *Id.* at 65.
13 *Id.* at 65-66.
14 *Id.* at 66.

convenience. In view of this finding, the Court denied the plaintiff its plea alleging the distinct legal entity of Touchest and Chipstead, as such claim was aimed at avoidance of obligations and hence counter to the principle of good faith.

The majority of Korean jurists touted *87 Daka 1671* as squarely affirming the principle of veil piercing.[15] The decision, however, was subject to criticism as it merely adumbrated the principle without articulating its four corners.[16] That is, some scholars suggested that the Court in *87 Daka 1671* had failed to ascertain a sufficient factual basis for finding any abuse of corporate entity, other than the sharing of the same office and management as between Touchest and Chipstead.[17] Other jurists suggest that *87 Daka 1671* was not a case about veil piercing per se, but an attempt at analogizing veil piercing with perceived violation of the principle of good faith and trust.[18] Accordingly, there is a lingering doubt as to whether *87 Daka 1671* embodies a true landmark affirming veil piercing for the first time at the Court level. *87 Daka 1671* is nevertheless meaningful in that it served as a judicial vehicle for igniting scholarly debates in Korea on the contours of veil piercing.

C. Judgment of 19 Jan., 2001, 97 Da 21604 (Supreme Court of Korea)

1. Facts of 97 Da 21604

The facts of this decision are as follows. Defendant *Samjin* Co., Ltd. ("*Samjin*") whose Representative Director was *Jung-Su Lee* who was also a co-defendant in the case, was in the business of selling units of a

---

15 Although the facts of *87 Daka 1671* do not fit the mould of the typical veil piercing case, in which liability is usually sought against the company's shareholders or officers, the Court appears to have affirmed veil piercing in this case following the enterprise liability doctrine developed in the U.S. Under this doctrine, U.S. courts sometimes disregard "multiple incorporations of the same business under common ownership," especially where a business is divided into several affiliate or sister entities owned by the same investor(s). *See* Alan R. Palmiter *Corporations* 556 (5th ed. 2006). For the representative case under the doctrine, *see Walkovsky v. Carlton*, 223 N.E. 2d 6 (N.Y. 1966). Since, as surveyed above, *87 Daka 1671* involved multiple incorporations (i.e. Touchest and Chipstead) under common ownership, it might have proved an apt occasion for the Court to adopt the enterprise liability doctrine in the affirmative.

16 *See, e.g.*, Chan-Hyung Jung, *Bub-in-kyuk-bu-in-ron* [*Doctrine of Corporate Veil Piercing*], 226 CASE LAW MONTHLY 29, 35-36 (Jul. 1989).

17 *See*, Dong-yun Chung, *Bup-in-kyuk-bu-in-eron-eh-kwan-han dae-bup-won-pan-rye-eh-chu-ei* [*Trend of Supreme Court Cases on Veil Piercing*] Lawyer v. 20 (Jan. 1990).

18 Jung, *supra* note 16, at 35-6.

commercial high-rise (a seventeen-story building with a five-story basement) to be constructed by *Kunyoung* Co., Ltd. ("*Kunyoung*"). On 19 June, 1991, the plaintiff entered into a sale and purchase contract with *Samjin* for the purchase of a unit (Unit No. 502) of the high-rise.[19] Thereafter, the plaintiff made a down payment and two interim payments up until 30 March, 1992. *Samjin*'s original plan was to finance the high-rise project with the sale proceeds. Yet as *Samjin*'s sale of the high-rise went sour, payments to *Kunyoung* were delayed, and *Kunyoung* eventually halted construction as of August, 1992.[20]

In the meanwhile, defendant *Jung-Su Lee* was carrying on the business of selling commercial premises and offices in his own name or under the names of entities over which he exerted de facto control.[21] As part of this business, *Lee* purchased the shares of *Samjin* on 3 May, 1991 from the company's then Representative Director *Il-Hyoung Choi* and became thereby *Samjin*'s new Representative Director.

The number of *Samjin*'s issued shares was five thousand which, for recordkeeping purposes, was divided among four equity holders including *Lee* (*Lee* owned two thousand of these shares with the rest equally divided up among the remaining shareholders who were all related to *Lee*). In fact, however, the vast majority of *Samjin*'s issued shares were in the hands of *Lee*.[22] In addition, *Lee* practically made all managerial decisions of *Samjin* without observing corporate formalities. By the time the plaintiff filed its suit against the defendants, the offices of *Samjin* had been permanently shut down.

From the sale proceeds of the high-rise amounting to KRW 7.8 billion, the defendant used approximately KRW 3 billion to purchase the land for the high-rise in his name and arranged for the levying of provisional registration thereon in the name of a third party, before having the same annulled in anticipation of subsequent creditor claims. As for the remaining proceeds, *Lee* put them to untraceable use. As evidenced by the foregoing, the corporate assets of *Samjin* and the personal assets of *Lee* were improperly intermingled. In addition, despite the large-scale of the high-rise project, *Samjin* was heavily undercapitalized with its capital amounting to a meager KRW 50 million. At the end of the day, *Samjin* was virtually insolvent.

---

19 *97 Da 21604*, at 485.

20 *Id.* at 486.

21 *Id.* at 487.

22 *Id.* at 488.

2. Rulings of 97 Da 21604 and comments

The Supreme Court held that the plaintiff would be entitled to demand the sale proceeds back from either *Samjin* or *Lee* who wielded de facto control on *Samjin* from behind the corporate veil. Specifically in relation to the issue of veil piercing, the Supreme Court enunciated in the following vein.

When a business entity maintains the public appearance of a corporation, but such appearance is merely a sham and the entity, in essence, is reduced down to a private enterprise of the principal behind the corporate veil or to an instrument for staving off legal effects at the helm of the principal, it would be egregious to impute liability arising from what is ostensibly an act of the corporation to the corporation alone, and not to the principal, based on the former's separate legal persona.[23] Such imputation of liability, if accepted by courts, would form an abuse of corporate personality undermining the principle of good faith and hence run afoul of justice and equity. From this analysis, it would be sensible to hold both the company and the principal jointly liable for the corporate act in question.

In the case at hand, in view of the relevant facts including the backdrop against which the defendant had acquired the ownership of *Samjin*, the form and extent of *Lee*'s control over *Samjin*, the degree of asset intermingling between *Lee* and the company, the state of *Samjin*'s business operation and usage of the sale proceeds, the size of *Samjin*'s commercial real estate business, and overall status of corporate asset and solvency – it was incontrovertible to the Court that, while *Samjin* took on the form of a limited liability company, it in effect was *Lee*'s sole proprietorship.[24] Therefore, even though *Samjin* became the party who sold the high-rise in this case, it was no more than an external appearance and, in substance, the business of selling the high-rise was conducted by *Lee* as his private business.

In this account, trial records indisputably indicated that *Lee* was relying on the distinct legal entity of *Samjin* in denying liability in his personal capacity. Such denial, in the Court's view, would be at loggerheads with the prevailing precepts of justice and equity.

In this case, the Supreme Court typified veil piercing into the following two broad categories: (1) abuse of corporate personality (i.e. where the corporation is used by the principal as an arbitrary instrument for escaping legal liability); and (2) incorporation as a mere formality (i.e. even with the formalities of a corporation, such external appearance is but a

---

23 *Id.* at 487.
24 *Id.* at 488.

veneer, and the corporation, in effect, amounts to a private business of the principal lurking behind the corporate veil).

The Court further noted that the criteria for discerning incorporation as a mere formality rest on a showing of de facto governance by shareholders of the company, commingling of assets, lack of separate accounting apparatus, intermingling of business status and corporate transactions, undercapitalization, and failure to observe corporate protocols mandated by law.[25] *97 Da 21604* was lauded as the first decision in Korea ushering the remedy of veil piercing into an actual adjudication setting.[26]

D. Judgment of 12 Nov., 2004, 2002 Da 66892 (Supreme Court of Korea)

1. Facts of 2002 Da 66892

The facts of *2002 Da 66892* are as follows. The plaintiffs leased portions of a building owned by *Angunsa* Co., Ltd. ("*Angunsa*") in *Sinsa-Dong*, *Eunpyung* District, Seoul and completed the registration of *jeonse-kwon*[27]

---

[25] Of recent, however, the Supreme Court denied lifting of the corporate veil in a case involving a similar set of facts. In the Judgment of 11 Sep., 2008, 2007 Da 90982 (Supreme Court of Korea), the defendant held de facto control over Company I. Later on, the defendant wound up Company I on the brink of its bankruptcy, while setting up Company 2 that took over both the goodwill and personnel of Company I. The defendant also took control of Company 2. The defendant subsequently dissolved Company 2 and incorporated in its place Company 6 in the name of a third party. Against this backdrop, the Daegu High Court ruled that the defendant's denial of payment obligations vis-à-vis the plaintiff on account of the separate personhood of Company 2 would embody an abuse of corporate personality in violation of the principle of good faith, as well as justice and equity. The Supreme Court, however, overturned the High Court by noting that: (1) there had been no substantial mix of assets between Company 2 and the defendant to the point of stripping Company 2 of its separate legal entity. Even when considering all the factual elements probed by the High Court, the Court could not ascertain that Company 2 had somehow amounted to a private business of the defendant in that the defendant was simply borrowing the corporate form of Company 2 in carrying on legitimate private business; and (2) under the principle of limited liability, there is nothing illicit about winding up a corporation that is no longer a going concern, and subsequently setting up and managing a new corporation via fresh injection of capital in so far as such sequential measures are not aimed at harming creditors. In light of the extent to which the assets of Company 2 and the defendant were commingled, which was far from substantial, the Court was unable to identify any abuse by the defendant of the corporate personality of Company 2 and, as a result, remanded the case back to the High Court.

[26] Han-sung Cha, *Bub-in-kyuk-bu-in-ron [Doctrine of Disregard of the Corporate Entity] Study of Civil Case Laws* Vol. XXIV 568, 597 (Bak-young-sa 2002).

[27] In Korea, there is a unique way of renting a house called *Jeonse*, in which

on their respective leases. *Angunsa* went bankrupt shortly thereafter, and the above building was auctioned off to a third party at the request of Korea Exchange Bank, a secured creditor with a higher ranking than the plaintiffs, and, in the process, the plaintiffs' individual *jeonse-kwon* were invalidated. As a result, the plaintiffs could not secure their rental deposits back from *Angunsa*. In the midst of this imbroglio, the plaintiffs commenced an action at the Western District Office of the Seoul District Court against *Angunsa* for return of their rental deposits, and *Angunsa* was ordered to pay them back to the plaintiffs.

In the meanwhile, following the bankruptcy of *Angunsa*, the defendant company came into existence. *Angunsa* and the defendant were identical or akin to each other in trade name, commercial emblems, objects of operation, address of the main office, and composition of overseas affiliates.[28] Also, the two companies were similar when it came to the makeup of executives and shareholders in that they mainly consisted of close relatives or employees of *Yong-Sik An* who assumed the dual roles of the controlling shareholder, Representative Director at *Angunsa*. In terms of the actual management, the defendant held itself out to be synonymous with *Angunsa* since *An* assumed the Representative Directorship at the defendant company. As such, *Angunsa* and the defendant were treated equally by outsiders, and the defendant won certain projects on such basis.

2. Judicial rulings of 2002 Da 66892

On the issue of veil piercing, the Supreme Court reasoned as follows in favor of the plaintiffs. If an existing company has set up a new entity that is identical in substance and form to itself for the purpose of eluding existing legal obligations, such act of incorporation embodies an abuse of the corporate law system in furtherance of illicit objectives.[29] In such

---

a tenant makes a lump-sum deposit on a rental space, instead of paying monthly rents, and gets back the entire deposit when the tenancy comes to an end. *Jeonse-kwon*(權) refers to a tenant's right to such leasehold machination.

28 *2002 Da 66892,* at 2015.

29 *Id.* at 2014. In this regard, however, the Court has made it clear in a recent decision that veil piercing is also possible where a corporation abuses the corporate entity of another already existing entity for illicit purpose. Accordingly, veil piercing is not confined to cases involving incorporation from scratch of a new entity for evading financial or legal obligations. Thus in the Judgment of 13 May, 2011, 2010 Da 94472 (Supreme Court of Korea), the plaintiff who owned a parcel of land entered into an agreement with *Filco* Co., Ltd. and *Sinsol* Construction Co., Ltd., under which the plaintiff agreed to convey her land to *Filco*, a sales agent, in consideration of an apartment suite to be constructed by *Sinsol*, a construction company ("Agreement"). Subsequently, while the construction was

a context, therefore, allowing a claim asserting the separate legal entity of two putatively distinct companies vis-à-vis the creditors of the existing company cannot be accepted, since such claim aims at vitiating the principle of good faith and trust. Thus, a creditor of the existing company will be entitled to demand the fulfillment of financial obligations against either of the two companies.

In the present case, the defendant company was identical or similar to *Angunsa* in various aspects including trade name and objects of operation. The vast majority of directors and shareholders of the defendant were either *An*'s close relatives or his former employees at *Angunsa* where *An* had held the Representative Directorship in his capacity as the controlling shareholder. The defendant was deemed equal to *Angunsa* in carrying out marketing and sales activities. In the eyes of outsiders, therefore, the defendant was viewed as the alter ego of *Angunsa*, and captured projects as such. In addition, *An* continued to carry on his roles and responsibilities as the Chairman of the defendant.[30] Moreover, faced with a judicial order forcing the defendant to assume the obligations of *Angunsa*, *An*'s son and others set up a company named Mutech Korea and won projects related to the defendant. Further, on 20 October, 1999,

---

under way, *Filco* and *Sinsol* assigned both the plaintiff's land and their rights in the construction project to *Sangwoo Gunyoung* Co., Ltd. and GFM Construction Co., Ltd., who in turn assigned the same to *Sinpyoung* Construction Co., Ltd. *Sinpyoung* refused to convey the suite in question to the plaintiff. The appellate court refused to lift the corporate veil in favor of the plaintiff in that the incorporations of *Filco, Sinsol, Sangwoo,* GMF, *and Sinpyoung*, had all predated the Agreement. As such, the court was unwilling to let the plaintiff enforce contractual performance by *Sinpyoung* of the Agreement. Based on the above facts, however, the Court found that: (1) where a corporation has utilized another existing corporation that is identical in form and substance to itself for the evasion of liabilities and subsequently vanishes, the creditors of the vanished corporation can seek a remedy from the remaining entity; (2) whether the corporate entity of the remaining corporation has been abused for fraudulent purpose is to be determined from a totality of pertinent facts including the state of overall managerial and financial soundness at the time of the now non-existing firm's dissolution, transfer of assets, if any, between the two entities, and payment of arms length dues relative to such asset transfer, if any; and (3) in light of the fact that *Filco, Sinsol, Sangwoo,* GMF, and *Sinpyoung* were all under common ownership and of other factors revealing abuse of the corporate entity for fraudulent purpose, the plaintiff would be entitled to enforce specific performance of the Agreement against *Sinpyoung*. *2010 Da 94472* is meaningful in that the Court has clearly acknowledged the possibility of lifting the veil, coupled with the criteria for reifying such possibility, where the legal entity of a pre-existing corporation is put to use for the evasion of liabilities.

30 *Id.* at 2015.

Angunsa transferred its interior construction business to the defendant. In light of these evidentiary elements, the Court found it sufficient to hold that *Angunsa* had incorporated the defendant, which was substantially identical to *Angunsa* in corporate form and substance, for the purpose of jettisoning its own financial obligations. As such, the Court could not allow the defendant to hide behind *Angunsa*'s corporate personhood. Holding otherwise, the Court opined, would not comport with the principle of good faith.[31]

In *2002 Da 66892*, the Supreme Court imputed liability to the defendant company, which was set up in a way effectively identical to *Angunsa* in corporate form and substance for the purpose of avoiding away the pecuniary liabilities of *Angunsa*. It is submitted that this case is factually distinguishable from other cases in that there was no direct shareholding between the defendant and *Angunsa*, both of which were controlled by a single shareholder.

Typically, the principle of veil piercing comes in handy where a creditor seeks to hold shareholders of a company personally accountable for the company's obligations. Yet, with time, abuse of the corporate entity has taken on a diversity of forms, one of which is sequential incorporations of the same business under common ownership. As a matter of principle, there is nothing illicit about winding up a corporation that is no longer a going concern, and subsequently setting up and operating a new corporation through fresh injection of capital in so far as such successive measures leave creditors' rights intact. In a context involving sequential incorporations, a question nevertheless arises on whether the successor company may assert the separate legal entity of both its own and of its predecessor against the creditors of the predecessor. It hence becomes increasingly important for courts to set out under what circumstances and specific criteria the successor's assertion is viable.

Beginning with *2002 Da 66892,* the Court has probed in cases involving sequential incorporations by a common owner whether the principal possessed an intent to evade legal obligations in deciding to pierce the veil or not. Specifically in *2002 Da 66892*, the Court listed an identity of corporate form and substance between the predecessor and the successor

---

[31] It appears that the Supreme Court affirmed the principle of corporate veil piercing in this case based on the unity of ownership and financial stakes, and presence of illicit purposes as exemplified by evasion of pecuniary obligations. In addition, albeit not explicitly stated, the Court here appears to have applied the enterprise liability doctrine in that, not unlike *87 Daka 1671*, the facts of *2002 Da 66892* also involved multiple incorporations (namely, *Angunsa* and the defendant company) under common ownership. *See supra* note 29.

as a key ingredient for probing the principal intent.[32] The Court in *2006 Da 24438*[33] further refined *2002 Da 66892* by requiring an appraisal of the totality of pertinent circumstances including the overall state of managerial affairs at the time of the predecessor's dissolution and the payment of arm's length dues regarding transfer of assets, if any, from the predecessor to the successor.

In this respect, certain jurists may balk at extending veil piercing to sequential incorporations since such extension may signal dilution of limited liability. Despite such concern, judicial expansion of the outer boundaries of veil piercing is welcome and seems warranted in that rapid changes in commercial practice will ineluctably diversify ways in which abuse of corporate entity are maneuvered through. As such, courts will need to reckon with this commercial reality by turning to the remedy of veil piercing, where appropriate, on a case-specific basis guided by the principles of justice and equity.

III. ANALYSIS OF 2004 DA 26119

A. Basic Facts

Korea Telecom Philippines Inc. ("KTPI"), a wholly owned subsidiary of defendant in the Philippines, entered into two separate contracts for Project Management, Supply and Installation of Outside Plant Facilities (collectively "OSP Agreement") with Philippine Telegraph and Telephone Corporation ("PT&T") on 11 October, 1995 and 12 November, 1996, respectively, for communication network extension projects near Manila (collectively the "Project").[34] In connection with the Project, KTPI acted as the project manager and subcontracted portions related to the supply of materials, provision of services, and installation of communication lines to certain Korean companies including the plaintiff. The plaintiff signed off two agreements with KTPI, the first on 13 October, 1995 and the other on 12 November, 1996 pertaining to communication line installation and supply of raw materials, respectively ("Subject Contracts").

Pursuant to the OSP Agreement and Subject Contracts, PT&T was to

---

[32] For a criticism that the Court's ratio here is rather vague, *see* Young-ae Kwon, *Chae-mu-myun-tal-mok-juk-eu-ro-sul-rip-dwen dae-chae-hwe-sae-euh bup-in-kyuk-bu-in* [*Veil Piercing of Alternate Companies Established for Liability Evasion*] 8 COMMERCIAL CASE LAW REVIEW 1, 14 (Mar. 2005).

[33] Judgment of 21 Aug., 2008, 2006 Da 24438 (Supreme Court of Korea).

[34] *2004 D 26119,* at 1602.

pay 20 percent of the total contract price directly to the plaintiff. As for the remaining portions, PT&T was obliged to pay KTPI by installed repayment over seven years with a three-year grace period, and KTPI, in turn, was to pay the plaintiff in installments spread over two years with a grace period of three years.

The size of KTPI's capital was approximately KRW 1.6 billion, whereas the total volume of the OSP Agreement amounted to $ 87 million (later increased to $ 95 million through contractual amendments). For financing purposes, KTPI signed off a credit agreement with Chase Manhattan Bank ("CMB") on 24 July, 1996 with its credit ceiling capped at $40 million ("Credit Agreement").[35]

Prior to the Credit Agreement, the defendant entered into a guarantee agreement with CMB in relation to the financing to be provided under the Credit Agreement (the "Chase Loan") following an affirmative resolution of the defendant's management advisory committee. Under the Credit Agreement, KTPI took out the Chase Loan on demand and paid the plaintiff contract monies and interests thereon in accord with the Subject Contracts.

In the meanwhile, in the wake of an Asian financial crisis in 1997, PT&T declared a debt moratorium around 30 June, 1998. In response, the defendant directed KTPI to minimize withdrawal of what was left of the Chase Loan and to consult in advance with the defendant thereby blocking in effect further drawing out by KTPI of the Chase Loan. KTPI, in turn, stopped payments to the plaintiff under the Subject Contracts. The plaintiff also halted what remained outstanding of their material supplies to PT&T.

On or about 26 October, 2000, the plaintiff and KTPI confirmed the balance of account payables under the Subject Contracts at $ 20978488.23. Subsequently, on or about March 6, 2001, KTPI paid out to the plaintiff $ 1956998.44 in partial fulfillment of said account payables. The plaintiff instituted a suit on 12 September, 2001 for the purpose of claiming the balance.

B. Court Rulings

1. Judgment of 30 April, 2004, 2003 Na 11891 (Seoul High Court)[36]

In general, when a company takes on the appearance of a corporation but such appearance is but a façade, and the company, in essence, amounts to

---

[35] Id. at 1603.

[36] At the high court level, the plaintiff specifically alleged that: (1) KTPI lacked independent payment and overall fiscal abilities; (2) the defendant exerted com-

a sole proprietorship of the equity holder behind the corporate veil or to a tool for circumventing contractual obligations, exempting the principal from the liability of what is ostensibly an act of the company, under the pretext of the company's distinct legal persona, would dispel not only the principle of good faith, but justice and equity.[37] In such a context, therefore, both the company and the principal alike ought to be rendered answerable to the corporate act in question (in this regard, refer to *97 Da 21604*[38]).[39]

In particular, in order for veil piercing to apply in a parent–subsidiary relationship, the following criteria must be found present:

(1) a mere fact of the parent company holding sway over the subsidiary by virtue of wholly owning the subsidiary with attendant power to appoint directors and officers by exercise of shareholder rights, will not pass muster. It is necessary that the subsidiary has lost independent volition or existence, with the parent exerting complete control to the point of operating the subsidiary as part of a parental business clan; (2) there should be commingling of assets, business operation, and/or external corporate transactions between the parent and the subsidiary; (3) consolidation of accounts ought to be put in place between the two entities in tandem with disregard by the subsidiary of corporate formalities and protocols; (4) the size of the subsidiary's capital must be conspicuously small for the overall tenor and volume of business it carries on; (5) the corporate entity of the subsidiary must have been misused as an instrument to evade liability at the end of the parent.[40]

In addition, the high court added the catch that, as an exception to limited liability, the remedy of veil piercing will be granted only when the corporate personality in question is put to use for illicit objectives, or in violation of public policy, or as an instrument for rationalizing what is otherwise illegal, or to perpetrate fraud or aid and abet a crime, with the aim of stalling or making good such wrongs in line with the principles of

plete dominion over KTPI by way of shareholders' meetings and board of directors' meetings, with authority to issue business-related directions, plan budgets, pay out salaries and implement human resources policies; (3) the defendant's direction caused KTPI to stop drawing out the Chase Loan; and (4) since KTPI had been dissolved and hence rendered insolvent, absolving the defendant of contractual liabilities under the Subject Contracts on account of KTPI being a separate legal entity would be at odds with the principle of good faith.

37 *2003 Na 11891*, at 3, Da, (1), (Ga).

38 *See supra* II.C.

39 *2003 Na 11891*, at 3, Da, (1), (Ga).

40 *Id.* at 3, Da, (1), (Na).

equity.[41] As such, courts will not lift the corporate veil when: (1) the other party in a transaction could distinguish the parent from the subsidiary and was clearly aware of which entity it was dealing with; or (2) such other party was cognizant of the subsidiary being undercapitalized and still proceeded with the transaction without reasonable precautionary measures; or (3) there is no clear and convincing proof of illegality in the underlying transaction.

In the case at hand, the Seoul High Court found that:

(1) there were clear divides in organization, assets, accounting, and details of business flow between the defendant, a domestic Korean corporation, and KTPI, an offshore Philippines corporation; (2) the size of KTPI's capital was approximately KRW 1.6 billion, which might have been a bit small in light of KTPI's obligations under the Subject Contracts. Yet given the fact that KTPI had taken the role of an intermediary between PT&T and the plaintiff, rather than the ultimate payer, to lubricate the flow of credit, the size of KTPI's capital was not deemed markedly diminutive; (3) based on its full ownership of KTPI, the defendant held strong leverage over KTPI in a broad spectrum of areas including convening of shareholders and board of directors' meetings, as well as matters pertaining to human resources, business-related decisions, and remuneration policy. The directors of KTPI were all on secondment from the defendant, and KPTI underwent thorough advance consultation with the defendant before proceeding with each transaction. In the eyes of the court, such working relationship between the defendant and KTPI was not atypical for an overseas subsidiary, and taking on orders or directives from the sole shareholder, as in the case of KTPI, was in proper alignment with the quintessence of limited liability corporation. In the meanwhile, KTPI crafted on its own accord the planning, contract execution and performance of each underlying transaction. KTPI also requested the defendant to guaranty the drawing out of project funds while endorsing a debt restructuring plan following the autonomous resolution of KTPI's own Board of Directors despite the defendant's objection. In light of the foregoing, the court was unable to ascertain complete domination over KPTI by the defendant to the point of divesting KPTI of independent volition or corporate existence; (4) further, as noted previously, at the time of executing the Subject Contracts, the plaintiff was clearly aware that KTPI was privy to the Subject Contracts, not the plaintiff itself; (5) the defendant authorized KTPI to make independent calls on withdrawal of the Chase Loan in consideration of KTPI's own pecuniary resources; (6) above all,

---

41 *Id.* at 3, Da, (1), (Da).

the high court was unable to spot elements of unfairness in the Subject Contracts to pierce the corporate veil for any abuse of corporate entity. Nor could the court be certain that the defendant had put KTPI to use for illicit objectives, or against the public good or as an instrument for justifying what is otherwise prohibited at law, and/or to perpetrate fraud or aid and abet a crime.[42] Accordingly, the high court dismissed with prejudice the plaintiff's claim that the defendant's refusal to pay out contract monies by virtue of the distinct legal entity of KTPI would bring the principle of good faith into disrepute.[43]

2. Supreme Court Decision 2004 Da 26119

At the outset, the Supreme Court noted that it would be natural for certain degrees of labor and financial interplay to be in place between a parent company and its subsidiaries.[44] As such, the facts that: (1) certain officers or employees of the subsidiary are dually employed by the parent; (2) the parent holds sway over the subsidiary through entire ownership of the subsidiary with appurtenant rights to appoint directors, executives or officers; and (3) in spite of an upward spiral in the overall magnitude of the subsidiary's corporate operation, there was no proportional hike in the subsidiary's capital, will be, in and of themselves, insufficient to render the parent's assertion of the subsidiary's own legal persona an abuse of corporate personality vis-à-vis creditors of the subsidiary. To trigger threshold, the Court will require a showing of the parent company's complete domination over the subsidiary to the point of stripping independent volition or existence so that the subsidiary is made part of the parent's corporate clan.[45] Specifically, there should be objective indicia of assets, businesses and external transactional activities not being clearly distinguished between the parent and the subsidiary but mixed with each other. Above all, the court should be able to pinpoint the subjective motive or purpose with which the parent company arbitrarily abused the subsidiary's independent legal entity for dodging legal or pecuniary obligations.[46]

In this regard, the court below noted that: (1) at the time of entering into the Subject Contracts, the defendant was a public corporation, and KTPI, a company incorporated under the law of the Philippines, was carrying on telecommunications business in the Philippines subject to periodic external audits; (2) as an overseas subsidiary of the defendant,

---

42 *Id.* at 3, Da, (2), (Ga).
43 *Id.* at 3, Da, (3).
44 *2004 Da 26119*, at 1606.
45 *Id.* at 1606-1607.
46 *Id.* at 1607.

KTPI was capable of mapping out independent management objectives and corresponding budgets; and (3) in light of the universe of facts mused on by the high court including KTPI's independent assessment and performance of the Subject Contracts on its own accord and KTPI's request for a guarantee on the bank credit provision, the Supreme Court upheld the Seoul High Court finding that there were clear divides between KTPI and the defendant when it comes to the particulars of organization, assets, accounting, and management. Moreover, the Court was unable to deduce any element of illegality from the defendant's use of KTPI relative to the Subject Contracts. In the final analysis, the Court affirmed the high court holding that the defendant could rightfully assert the separate legal entity of KTPI in denying the defendant's contractual liabilities under the Subject Contracts vis-à-vis the plaintiff.[47]

IV. COMMENTARY[48]

A. The Criterion of Subjective Intent/Purpose

As the objective indicia for applying veil piercing in a parent company-subsidiary setting, *2004 Da 26119* required complete parental control of the subsidiary, coupled with intermingling of assets, business and external corporate activities between the two entities.[49] The Court also mandated a showing of the subjective motive or purpose with which the parent had

---

47 *Id.* at 1607-1608.

48 In respect of *2004 Da 26119*, a commentator noted that since the case involved a plea for lifting the corporate veil of an offshore (i.e. Pilipino) subsidiary of the defendant, a Korean corporation, the Supreme Court should have ascertained the appropriate governing law by applying conflicts of law principles in determining whether to lift the veil of such overseas subsidiary or not, and resolved the case in light of the governing law. Yet the Court erred in failing to consider this governing law issue at all. This observation is with merit, but beyond the scope of this piece. *See* Kwang-Hyun Suk, *Wae-guk-hwe-sa-eu-bub-in-kyuk-bu-in* [*Piercing the Corporate Veil of an Offshore Corporation*], LEGAL TIMES, 8 Sep., 2008. For further details in this regard, *see* Tae-Jin Kim, *Bub-in-kyuk-bu-in-eh-kwan-han-guk-je-sa-bub-juk-gum-to* [*Review of Veil Piercing from a Private International Law Perspective*], Presentation before the Korean Society of Private International Law (29 Aug., 2008).

49 The high court required as the objective criteria such factors as the absence of separate accounting machination between a mother company and her subsidiary, disregard of corporate protocols, undercapitalization of the subsidiary, and misuse of the subsidiary's legal entity.

abused the legal entity of the subsidiary for pursuit of illicit objectives such as dodging contractual obligations.

In this regard, the Supreme Court's decision is in line with the jurisprudence on the doctrine of *aemulatio vicini* or abuse of rights in that both require proof on the element of subjective motive or purpose.[50] Under said doctrine, which is codified in Article 2.2 of *Min Bup* [the Civil Code],[51] abuse of rights can be sustained on a showing of, inter alia, conscious exercise by the right holder of what is otherwise a lawful right for the sole purpose of inflicting affliction on a neighbor even in the absence of any lawful gain to be derived from such act.

Also, *2004 Da 26119* appears to be in line with a prevailing theory among Japanese jurists on the requirements of veil piercing. In Japan, the majority of jurists hold the position that extending the application of veil piercing in an indiscriminate manner will run counter to the maintenance of legal certainty.[52] As such, the element of illicit or unjust purpose is usually required before any disregard of corporate entity is attempted.[53]

In the meanwhile, the majority of Korean academics take the view that difficulties in substantiating the parental purpose or motive may dampen the overall efficacy of veil piercing.[54] In addition, there may be situations where foisting personal liability on the sole shareholder, despite lack of any mala fides on such person's part, would be consistent with the mandates of justice (for instance, when the subsidiary is all but solvent), hence rendering the criterion of subjective purpose/intent dubious at best.

In particular, the Court in *2004 Da 26119* refused to read or otherwise infer an illegal or unjust motive of the parent from a pre-determined set of facts.[55] This set of facts mostly pertained to the counterparty to the underlying transaction(s). However, the logical outworking of this deci-

---

50 For instance, in the Judgment of 14 Feb., 2003, 2002 Da 62319&62326 (Supreme Court of Korea), the Court required as prima facie proof of an abuse of right that the right holder exercise its right solely for the subjective purpose of inflicting pain and suffering on another party.

51 Article 2.2 provides: "Rights shall not be abused."

52 For a similar view in Korea, *see* Sang-Hyun Song, *Bo-jeung-chae-mu-gum-dung (Seoul-go-dung-bup-won-74-na-pan-gyul-pyung-suk)* [*Guarantee Liability, etc, Case Commentary on Judgment of Seoul High Court, 74 Na 2582*] LEGAL TIMES, 8, 27 May, 1974.

53 *See* Chang-Woo Nam, *Hwe-sa-bub-in-kyuk-mu-si-eu- bub-li* [Legal Theory of Corporate Veil Piercing] (1995), (unpublished Ph.D. dissertation, Korea University) (on file with Korea University).

54 *See Id.*; *see also* Chul-Song Lee, *Hwe-sa-bup-gang-yi* (*Lectures on Corporate Law*) 51-52, (Bak-young-sa 16th ed. 2009).

55 *See supra* III.B.2.

sion leaves open the possibility that knowledge or (in)action of such other party may well override or obviate the illicit purpose, if any, of the parent. By way of example, there may be situations where the other party in a transaction proceeded with the transaction without cautionary measures despite his or her awareness of the subsidiary being undercapitalized compared to the risk intrinsic in the transaction, while, all along, the parent did harbor an illicit motive in its transactions with the subsidiary. In such situation, the other party would be barred from asserting abuse of corporate entity by the parent based on an assumption of risk theory, rather than a piercing theory involving any parental purpose or motive.

Needless to say, lifting the corporate veil should be understood and carved out as an infrequent exception to limited liability. However, this normative issue will be more efficiently dealt with by raising the bar on the "objective indicia" without necessarily importing the murky element of parental motive or intent into the overall conceptual schema.

Even assuming *arguendo* that the need for parental motive or intent is indeed legitimate, courts will still need to rely on certain fact patterns of recurrence or with general applicability for sorting out such motive or intent. In this regard, it will be a desirable move for the Court to describe what such factual elements are in concrete terms so that the inordinate evidentiary burden on the plaintiff in proving the parental purpose/motive may be eased somewhat. It is anticipated that the criteria set forth in *2006 Da 24438*[56] will serve as a useful guidepost in ongoing judicial endeavors in this respect.

B. The Criteria for Disregarding the Corporate Entity in a Parent-subsidiary Corporate Group

Corporate law, which provides for the separate personality of a legal person, has been traditionally premised on autonomous corporate management accompanied by individual assumption of liability arising therefrom. Yet with the advance of capitalism, a sizable number of corporations have set up subsidiaries that operate under their control. These corporate groups often act as a single economic unit and evade liability by tinkering with the legal fiction of corporate person. As a product of this trend, the likelihood for minority stockholders or creditors of the subsidiary to suffer detriment is ever increasing. This state of affairs, in turn, heightens the need for proactive recourse to veil piercing for these stakeholders' protection.

---

56 *See supra* note 33.

Apart from the foregoing, albeit varying in degree, a subsidiary is in general under control of the parent with substantial ties in respect of, among others, labor and finance. As such, readily lifting the corporate veil on such nexus alone may well enervate the very backbone of corporate law as encapsulated in limited liability. In case of Korean conglomerates, it is the norm that the parent exerts dominant control over the subsidiary only in relation to significant matters with day-to-day business largely entrusted to the subsidiary. In this type of business milieu, just because the parent exerts certain degrees of control should not allow the corporate veil of the subsidiary to be readily pierced through. While a circle of legal scholars and commentators endorses the view that when veil piercing is applied to *Konzern* or a corporate group, it should be within the overall framework of dominance and control with no regard to abuse or formalization of the corporate entity,[57] such view is vulnerable to the criticism that disregarding corporate entity on control alone may lead to abuse of veil piercing in that a chain of command subsists in any given *Konzern*.

2004 Da 26119 took for granted the presence of ties between the parent and the subsidiary in human resources and finance. As such, the Supreme Court found it insufficient to infer an abuse of corporate personality from facts evincing some semblance of parental control. This judicial pronouncement is welcome in that it limits the likelihood of lifting the corporate veil for the reason of parental control alone.

In the meanwhile, the existence of complete parent control, which the Court listed as a quid pro quo to veil piercing, may be ascertained in each case by such objective indicia as commingling of assets, business, and/or external corporate activities,[58] and this requirement of objectivity appears reasonable. It is hoped that indicia and specifically when they can be found present will flesh out through evolution of jurisprudence down the road.

V. CONCLUSION

2004 Da 26119 was a landmark laying out the criteria for veil piercing in a parent company-subsidiary setting. The Court's holding in this case was balanced in that the facts of the case did not warrant lifting the corporate veil as evidenced by distinct divides between the defendant and its

---

57 Dae-Youn Kim, Ji-bae-jong-sok-hwe-sa-eh-dae-han-youn-gu(2) Gyul-hap-gi-up-eh-su-eh-bup-in-kyuk-bu-in-ron [*Second Study on the Parent-Subsidiary Corporation – Veil Piercing in the Context of Merged Corporations*] 44-1 Busan U. L. R. 347, 367 (2003).

58 *See supra* note 46.

subsidiary KTPI in respect of organization, assets, accounting, and business practices. On the other hand, the aspect of the decision mandating the subjective motive of the parent as a pre-condition for veil piercing is a cause for concern in that such proposition would in effect bring the doctrine of veil piercing to a standstill on account of the evidentiary difficulties it will invariably present in practice.

Since *2004 Da 26119*, the number of judicial decisions in Korea probing the constitutive prongs of veil piercing has been on an incremental increase.[59] Even though it may be ardent to systemize such criteria due to their general nature and applicability, the remedy of veil piercing will remain at the active disposal of claimants provided that the judiciary continues to hand down more trailblazing cases supplemented by enriching inputs from the legal academia.

---

59 *See, e.g.*, Judgment of 13 Jul. 2006, 2004 Da 36130 (Supreme Court) and Judgment of 21 Aug., 2008, 2006 Da 24438 (Supreme Court).

6. The range and scope of accounting books and records

Tony DongWook Kang

I. INTRODUCTION

While the right of a shareholder to inspect account books and records does not seem to be recognized in all countries, it is common to be an issue only during a control dispute. This is because the company's management has no reason to reject a shareholder's demand for inspection of company records if the shareholder has a good relationship and communicates well with the management. The former part of Section 7 "Accounting of Company" of Chapter IV "Stock Company" of the Korean Commercial Act provides for the shareholder's right to inspect the balance sheet, income statements or business reports that may be easily accessed by the shareholder, whereas the latter part of Section 7, i.e., Article 466 provides for the "Shareholder's Right to Inspect Account Books" which immediately precedes Article 467 (Inspection on Affairs and Status of Company's Property) that provides for the shareholder's right to apply for the appointment of an inspector to investigate the affairs of the company and the status of its property. Given the above structure of the Korean Commercial Act, our legislators are presumed to have prepared these latter provisions having taken into account a control dispute.

As in the case of Japan, Korea appears to have introduced the provisions concerning the shareholder's right to inspect account books and records similar to those adopted by the laws of the United States.[1] In the United States, such right is recognized under common law. The same common law, under which the English courts granted to shareholders access to corporate books and records in the early 1700s, was codified by corporate law statutes in the early 1800s.[2] Since Korea adopts the Continental legal

---

1 ByoungHoon Kwak, "The Shareholder's Right to Inspect Account Books and Records" [1999] 25 SahBubYunGooJahLyo 55, 60.

2 Randall S. Thomas, "Improving Shareholder Monitoring and Corporate

system based on civil law and there is no discovery process in Korean litigation procedures, the interpretation theory applicable to U.S. laws is not fully applicable in Korea.[3] Yet, the legislative intent appears to be the same (while a stock company is in essence a physical company that has an independent personality, its economic entity comprises shareholders who invested capital in return for shares, and the management is nothing but a nominee appointed at a general meeting of shareholders, and thus a conflict between the management and shareholders is philosophically excluded), and the two laws are similar in the respect that the same provisions apply to both listed companies and unlisted companies.

One thing that may be an issue in relation to the Korean Commercial Act is that "accounting-related documents" pursuant to Article 466(1) are not specifically defined therein. In this connection, the range and scope thereof vary depending on whether they are broadly or narrowly interpreted. However, since the provisions of Article 466(2) furnish the management with grounds to refuse the shareholder's right when the cause is proven unjust, there is no need to interpret "accounting-related documents" narrowly. Furthermore, it must be noted that the shareholder's right to inspect account books and records appears, as mentioned above, only in the event of a control dispute.

In addition, standing defenses of the company, records of the affiliate, choice of procedure, procedural requirements, indirect compulsory enforcements, etc. also may be relevant issues warranting discussion. However, the discussion will be limited to the range and scope of "accounting-related documents".

II. PROVISIONS OF THE COMMERCIAL ACT

A. Shareholder's Right of Accounting Inspection

Article 466(1) of the Korean Commercial Act provides that "any shareholder who holds shares representing no less than 3/100 of the total issued and outstanding shares may demand, in writing with the reasons thereof specified, the inspection or copying of the books of account and related documents," thereby granting to a minority shareholder having a certain

---

Management by Expanding Statutory Access to Information" [1996] 38 Arizona Law Review 331, 336; JaeYun Lim, *US Corporate Law* [PakYoungSa, 2004] 127.

3 GunShik Kim, "The American Shareholders' Right to Inspect Account Books and Records" [2000] 4 PanLyeShilMooYunGooHweh 344.

level of shares the right to inspect account books and records, whereas Article 466(2) provides that "a company shall not refuse the shareholder's demand mentioned in paragraph (1) unless it proves that such demand is improper," i.e., in certain cases, the company may refuse the demand.

On the other hand, paragraph (1) of Article 448 (Keeping and Public Inspection of Financial Statements, etc.) provides that "directors shall keep the documents set forth in Articles 447 and 447-2 as well as the audit report at the principal office of the company for five years and shall keep copies thereof at the branch offices for three years starting one week prior to the date of the ordinary general meeting," and paragraph (2) of Article 448 provides that "any shareholder or creditor of the company may, at any time during business hours, inspect the documents set forth in paragraph (1) and may demand the copying of such documents or an abstract thereof, by paying fees fixed by the company," thereby granting to all shareholders the right to inspect and demand the copying of the above documents including the bond register, minutes of meetings of the board of directors, business reports and audit reports.

In addition, paragraph (1) of Article 467 (Inspection on Affairs and Status of Company's Property) provides that "if there is any reason to suspect of a dishonest act or of a material fact in contravention of any Acts, subordinate statutes or the articles of incorporation in connection with the management of affairs, any shareholder who holds shares representing no less than 3/100 of the total issued and outstanding shares may apply to the court for the appointment of an inspector to investigate the affairs of the company and the status of its property," granting to a minority shareholder having a certain level of shares the right to apply to the court for the appointment of an inspector.

Comparing the shareholder's above rights of accounting inspection under the Commercial Act, i.e., the right to inspect financial statements, the right to demand the inspection and copying of accounting books, and the right to apply for the appointment of an inspector, they gradually develop in the order as described above from indirect to direct subject materials, from simple to detailed inspection, from voluntary inspection to inspection conducted by public power, and from a right easily granted to a right difficult to obtain, with a view to coordinate the rights of shareholders and the interest of a company. The shareholder's right to inspect account books and records is positioned in the middle of such rights.

B. Means for Shareholders to Oversee Directors

A shareholder of a stock company may, as an investor and beneficial owner of the company, participate in decisions on important matters of the company by attending a general meeting of shareholders and exercising its voting rights at the meeting in order to protect its interests (Article 361, Article 368 and Article 369 of the Commercial Act), demand the removal of a director (Article 385), apply for a preliminary injunction suspending the exercise of duties (Article 407), demand the cessation of an unlawful act (Article 402), and file a derivative suit (Article 403) in an effort to supervise and correct the performance by directors of their duties, and if it needs to recover its investment amount due to difficult management conditions of the company, the shareholder may prevent losses in advance by assigning its shares to a third party. After all, the reasons for which the Commercial Act ensures a minority shareholder's right to inspect account books and records is to ensure that the shareholder may exercise the above rights in a timely manner. Thus, among other things, the means to find out the management conditions, i.e., the accounting status of the company in advance are required most of all.

The shareholder's right to inspect account books and records is a means to effectively exercise various rights to supervise management that may be available to a shareholder and cannot be a purpose in itself. In other words, the shareholder's right to inspect account books and records is a starting point of various rights of a shareholder.

III. DEFINITIONS IN THE COMMERCIAL ACT

Comprehensively considering the relevant provisions of the Commercial Act, "Account Books" mean "books that record transactions and other particulars having effect on property in business" based on which financial statements and supplementary schedules thereto are prepared.

"Accounting Related Documents" mean documents used as materials to prepare account books such as slips and receipts.[4] However, there are no provisions defining the accurate meaning thereof in contrast to "Account Book".

On the other hand, as Article 447 through Article 448 of the Commercial Act specifically provide for the method for a shareholder to inspect and/or copy the balance sheet, income statement, statements of appropriation of retained earnings or statements of disposition of deficit, business report, audit report, etc., whether or not they are included in "accounting

---

4 DongWon Chung and MyungJo Yang, *Commercial Law* [4th edn, 2003] 361; KiWon Choi, *Commercial Law* [15th edn, 2008] 141, 147, 1076; ChanHyung Chung, *Lecture on Commercial Law* [10th edn, 2007] vol 1, 1035.

related documents" is not separately discussed. In fact, in the event that the contents of the balance sheet that must be kept and made public by directors are unreliable, the shareholder's right to inspect account books and records emerges, and thus they are discussed based on different assumptions.

Table 6.1 shows the relevant provisions in the Commercial Act.

IV. THE ACCOUNTING CYCLE

The accounting process is a series of activities an accountant must follow to analyze and record business transactions, prepare financial statements, and prepare for the next accounting period. This process commences with a transaction and ends with the closing of the books. Since this process is repeated every accounting period, it is referred to as an *accounting cycle*,[5] and includes the following steps.[6]

A. Journal Entry

The bookkeeping process begins by determining the relevant information regarding each transaction and analyzing/classifying what happened and why. The accountant should prepare the transaction's source document such as a purchase order or invoice.

Then the bookkeeper, using the original documents, makes the first original entry into the appropriate journal such as the sales journal, purchase journal, cash receipt or disbursement journal or the general journal, in a chronological order.

B. Post to the General Ledger

The journal entries are reorganized as they are posted to the general ledger. No matter how many journals a company has, all the journal entries will feed into one general ledger. The general ledger contains all of the accounts maintained by the company, such as cash, accounts receivable, inventory, prepaid insurance, equipment, accounts payable, notes payable, contributed capital, retained earnings, sales revenue, and

---

5 Oxford Dictionary of Accounting [4th edn, 2010] 7.

6 Jane L. Reimers, *Financial Accounting* [2007 Pearson Education] 108; "The Accounting Process (The Accounting Cycle)" (2011) NetMBA <http://www.netmba.com/accounting/fin/process> accessed 17 Jul 2011.

Table 6.1 Full text of relevant provisions

Article 29 (Kinds of and Principles for Making Trade Books)	(1) In order to make clear the situation of property, profit and loss in the business, the merchant shall prepare an account book and balance sheet.
Article 30 (Method for Making Trade Books)	(1) In an account book, there shall be entered transactions and other particulars having effect on the property in business. (2) A merchant shall, at the time of commencement of his/her business and thereafter at a fixed time, at least once a year, prepare a balance sheet based on the account books and a person who prepared it shall write his/her name and affix his/her seal or sign thereon, and a company shall prepare such a balance sheet in the same manner as a merchant at the time of its incorporation and at the end of each period for the settlement of accounts.
Article 396 (Obligation to Keep Articles of Incorporation, etc. and Open to Public Access)	(1) Directors shall keep the articles of incorporation and the minutes of the general shareholders' meetings at the principal office and each branch office, and shall keep the register of shareholders and the register of bonds at the principal office. In this case, if there is a transfer agent, the register of shareholders or the register of bonds or the duplicates thereof may be kept in the business office of the transfer agent. (2) Any shareholder or any creditor of the company may demand, at any time during business hours, the inspection or the copying of the documents set forth in paragraph (1).
Article 447 (Preparation of Financial Statements)	Directors shall prepare, at each period for the settlement of accounts, the following documents and supplementary schedules and obtain the approval of the board of directors: 1. Balance sheet; 2. Income statement; and 3. Statements of appropriation of retained earnings or statements of disposition of deficit.
Article 447-2 (Preparation of Business Report)	(1) Directors shall prepare, at each period for the settlement of accounts, a business report and shall obtain the approval of the board of directors.
Article 447-4 (Audit Report)	(1) Auditors shall submit to directors an audit report within four weeks from the date on which he or she receives the documents under Article 447-3.

Table 6.1 (continued)

Article 448 (Keeping and Public Inspection of Financial Statements, etc.)	(1) Directors shall keep the documents set forth in Articles 447 and 447-2 as well as the audit report at the principal office of the company for five years and shall keep copies thereof at the branch offices for three years starting one week prior to the date of the ordinary general meeting. (2) Any shareholder or creditor of the company may, at any time during business hours, inspect the documents set forth in paragraph (1) and may demand the copying of such documents or an abstract thereof, by paying fees fixed by the company.
Article 466 (Shareholder's Right to Inspect Account Books)	(1) Any shareholder who holds shares representing no less than 3/100 of the total issued and outstanding shares may demand, in writing with the reasons thereof specified, the inspection or copying of the account books and related documents.
Article 542-6 (Minority Shareholder's Rights)	(4) Any person who has continued to hold stocks equivalent to not less than 10/10000 (5/10000 in cases of listed companies determined by Presidential Decree) of the total number of shares issued by listed companies for more than six months may exercise the right as a shareholder under Article 466 (including cases where applied *mutatis mutandis* in Article 542).

operating expenses. All of a company's accounts can be found on the company's chart of accounts.

C. Prepare (unadjusted) Trial Balance

The trial balance is prepared to ensure that debits equal credits. It has a listing of all of the ledger accounts with debits in the left column and credits in the right column. Due to accounting computer softwares, trial balance is rarely created nowadays.

D. Prepare an Adjusted Trial Balance

The accountant then must correct any discrepancies in the trial balance and identify accounts that are not up-to-date and make adjustments to these accounts. The adjustments are called adjusting (journal) entries. After adjusting entries to record accrued, deferred, and estimated amounts, the adjusted entries are posted to the ledger accounts. This step will finally create a complete listing of all accounts, which is called the adjusted trial balance.

E. Prepare the Financial Statements

Now the bookkeeper takes the adjusted trial balance and prepares financial statements compiling similar accounts into one summary amount that is reported in a financial report. These financial statements include the balance sheet, income statement, statements of appropriation of retained earnings or statements of disposition of deficit, and the statement of changes in shareholders' equity. Finally, the cash flow statement is prepared from reviewing every transaction posted to the cash account.

F. Close the Books/Post-closing Trial Balance

Closing journal entries are prepared in order to close the temporary accounts such as revenues, expenses, gains and losses, and then those are posted to the general ledger. Now by preparing the after-closing trial balance to make sure debits equal credits, one cycle of accounting is finalized.

V. COURT PRECEDENTS

Since Korea adopts the civil law system, the principle of *stare decisis* is not applicable, but the de facto influence of precedents is substantial.

To date there have been only three Supreme Court precedents pertaining to the shareholder's right to inspect account books and records.[7] This is because most cases were proceeded with as injunction cases, and appeals thereto were rarely made.

In contrast, there are numerous precedents of lower courts, and the rulings on the range and scope of the shareholder's right to inspect account books and records vary. Many inspection requests were denied due to an ongoing hostile takeover or M&A or the conduct of competitive business, and thus the reasoning had nothing to do with the range and scope of the

---

[7] Supreme Court Judgment 99Da137 dated December 21, 1999; Supreme Court Judgment 99Da58051 dated October 26, 2001; Supreme Court Decision 2003Ma1575 dated December 24, 2004.

shareholder's right. However, occasionally among the remaining cases, it appears that the lawyers or judges handling the shareholder's right to inspect account books and records did not understand how account books and records of a stock company were actually prepared and thus such discrepancies arose.

Meanwhile, the Supreme Court of Korea did not present the specific interpretation of the range and scope thereof, but only determined upon (1) whether detailed reasons for the exercise of the right of demand were specified, and (2) whether the company had reasons to reject the demand. Since the Commercial Act expressly permits the company to exercise the right to reject an improper demand, even if the range and scope thereof is not limited based on sophisticated and artificial reasoning, this system may be operated harmoniously. Hence, the position of the Supreme Court of Korea resolving the issues without mentioning the range and scope thereof, is reasonable.

VI. DETAILED ANALYSES

While lower courts' precedents contain different conclusions, the shareholder's right to inspect account books and records is broadly recognized. Of course, the recognition may be deemed narrow when compared to inspection rights under common law which are available in respect of "all books and records of the corporation" or under statutory law which are mostly granted "when necessary to ascertain the value of one's stock".

The materials that may be an issue include (1) passbooks (2) contracts (3) minutes of a meeting of the board of directors and (4) statements of tax adjustment.

A. Passbooks

In reality, during a control dispute, one thing that most frustrates the parties (whether plaintiff or defendant) in a lawsuit involving the shareholder's right to inspect account books and records may be a passbook opened under the name of the company. This is because, while to examine the cash flow and compare it with financial statements is an efficient way to verify any breach of trust of the management, it may be inappropriate to disclose the statement of all remittances and all withdrawals including those not directly related to the control dispute.

Some completely exclude the passbook from the materials subject to the shareholder's right to inspect account books and records, asserting that only slips (journals) are materials directly used to prepare account books, and the passbook may be used as materials to prepare the slips, excluding it from the range and scope of accounting-related documents. However, this is superficial logic. Furthermore, since the deposit slips or withdrawal slips may be more easily forged than in the case of a passbook, and given the legislative intent or purpose expressly recognizing the shareholder's right to inspect account books and records, it would be reasonable to grant an opportunity to verify whether the contents of the slips are consistent with the actual remittances and withdrawals.

Nonetheless, it would be problematic to allow any and all passbooks without restrictions. Fortunately, as the Commercial Act expressly requires that demands be made "in writing with the reasons thereof," the demand can be properly controlled by checking whether the reasons are specific or related to the cause. Furthermore, since the company has an opportunity to prove that the demand is unjust, even if a shareholder demands the inspection of "all passbooks of the company for the last 20 years," the company may properly adjust the scope of inspection by demonstrating that given the reasons for which the shareholder intends to inspect account books, it is sufficient to inspect the account books for a certain period and that the account books for the remaining period are not relevant.

While lower courts' precedents contain both affirmative and negative positions, no clear criteria are found therein.

B. Contracts

What about contracts? In construing the scope of accounting-related documents, the narrow view is that contracts are included in such scope only if the contracts are directly used as underlying materials to prepare account books. However, contracts are important grounds based on which a company pays or receives funds, i.e., important bases for the "occurrence of transactions," and the purpose of "accounting" is to easily understand the effect of each transaction on the company's finances by describing the transactions. Thus, it is not reasonable to exclude contracts from the materials subject to the shareholder's right to inspect account books in all cases.

As the existence or details of the transactions under contracts are supported by original supporting documents including tax invoices and remittance receipts, and slips are prepared based on such original supporting documents, a shareholder has sufficient need to determine whether transactions have been properly made by comparing and analyzing whether the slips and original supporting documents have been prepared based on the contracts, or in accordance with the terms and conditions of the contracts. Of course, whether to allow a shareholder to inspect or copy "all contracts prepared by the company" can be (or has to be) sufficiently and properly controlled through examination of whether the reasons for demand are specific or the demand is unjust.

Nevertheless, according to lower courts' precedents, there are substantial cases where the inspection of "all contracts" is permitted. It is reasonable to restrict the scope based on the amount of transactions or counterparties, e.g., to allow the inspection of "all contracts entered into by and between the company and its officers or employees with the value of at least a certain amount." Given the purpose of the shareholder's right to inspect account books that may be exercised in writing with the reasons thereof specified, the purpose of a transaction (e.g., "all proposals and contracts related to treasury stocks") can also be the basis for restriction.

C. Minutes of Meeting of the Board of Directors

In practice, there are also different views on the minutes of a meeting of the board of directors. The reason is that the inspection or copying of the minutes of a meeting of the board of directors is based on Article 391-3(3) and (4) of the Commercial Act, and the request for the inspection or copying of the minutes of a meeting of the board of directors is not practically classified as a litigation case such as preliminary injunctions, but is deemed a non-contentious case subject to the Non-Contentious Case Litigation Procedure Act. After all, this issue should be discussed in relation to whether parties (shareholder/company) may add an agenda subject to a non-contentious case to the same litigation case to claim it through litigation. Yet, as this issue is beyond the scope hereof, it should simply be noted that there are contradictory lower court decisions. Since the judges in reality strongly recommend the shareholder (plaintiff) to partially withdraw the request for the minutes, it is not shown often in court decisions.

D. Statements of Tax Adjustment

Lastly, a statement of tax adjustment is of course included in accounting-related documents and its inspection or copying must be allowed.

For reference, Tokyo District Court Decision dated June 22, 1989 held to the effect that a final corporate tax return is not subject to the shareholder's right to inspect account books on the grounds that the final corporate tax return is a document prepared ex post facto by using account books including an income statement as materials. But since "corporate tax expenses" shown on an income statement are not simply calculated by applying a tax rate to "net income before corporate tax," this decision is logically incorrect.

In fact, if Form 3 of the Enforcement Rule of the Corporate Tax Act, "Corporate Tax Base and Tax Adjustment Statement," which is based on Article 60(2)2 of the Corporate Tax Act and Article 97(3) of the Enforcement Decree of the Corporate Tax Act (which corresponds to the final corporate tax return in the above Decision, and the Corporate Tax Act of Korea expresses it as the "statement of tax adjustment") is examined, any doubt is resolved.

Since Financial Accounting Standards and the Corporate Tax Act have different purposes and concepts, there are inevitable differences between them, and the adjustment of the net income – calculated under the accounting standards (No. 101 of Form 3) to the income under the Corporate Tax Act, i.e., the income amount for each fiscal year (Nos. 107 and 108 of Form 3) through the inclusion or non-inclusion in calculation of gross income or deductible expenses – must be done, and this we call a "tax adjustment." For instance, if the maximum amount of entertainment expenses under the Corporate Tax Act is KRW 20 million, even if the amount of entertainment expenses reflected on an income statement is KRW 30 million, the expenses are to be adjusted by not including the entertainment expenses of KRW 10 million in excess of the maximum amount in calculating deductible expenses, and such process can never be shown on an income statement.

In sum, since "corporate tax expenses" shown on an income statement cannot be finally determined without going through the process of tax adjustment, it is logically incorrect to prepare a corporate tax base and tax adjustment statement by making use of an "income statement." Rather, a shareholder has sufficient need to inspect the corporate tax base and tax adjustment statement in order to verify whether "corporate tax expenses" indicated on an income statement have been accurately calculated.[8]

Likewise, even though notes to an audit report show details of calculation of corporate tax, a shareholder needs to inspect the basis for calculation based on a statement of tax adjustment to find out whether or not the notes have been correctly described.

---

[8] In JaeBum Kim, "Requirement to Exercise Inspection Rights of Accounting Books and Records" [2000], 561 GyungYoungBubLyool 73, the author asserts that tax adjustment statements have no reason to be included as an accounting-related document, but this analysis is based on misunderstanding of the function of a tax adjustment statement. Also the author seems to have misinterpreted the underlying meanings of the Supreme Court Judgment 99Da137 dated December 21, 1999.

VII. SUMMARY OF PRECEDENTS

For reference, courts' positions for some major or notable cases are summarized in the table below. In general, the courts seem to broadly recognize the scope of inspection.[9] Since accounting-related documents became an issue in relation to the scope in most cases, they are not distinguished from account books in Table 6.2.

VIII. CONCLUSION

While the determination of the scope of "account books" and "accounting-related documents" is a sensitive and important issue in actual specific disputes, in practice, there has only been a consensus on the generally defined concepts that "account books mean books that record transactions and other particulars having effect on property in business based on which financial statements and supplementary schedules thereto are prepared" and "accounting-related documents" mean documents used as materials to prepare account books." There has been little effort to find a consistent answer as to the question of whether the individual materials of which inspection and copying are demanded by a shareholder should be regarded as account books and accounting-related documents.

There still exist contradictory practical cases with respect to the inclusion of certain documents in "accounting-related documents." However, given the general definition of the concept thereof as mentioned above, and considering the legislative intent of applicable laws to enhance the minority shareholder's rights and to practically guarantee the minority shareholder's power to monitor management as well as the current trend, there is no need to strictly restrict the scope of "accounting-related documents." With respect to the company books and documents of which inspection is demanded by a shareholder for the purpose of monitoring management in writing with considerably specific and reasonable reasons therefore specified, separate filtering can be made in the stage of examining the justification for the demand and the necessity of the inspection.

---

9 In this regard, the illustration, "There are many different views as to what should be counted as accounting books and records. However, the predominant view is that it is limited to the accounting books and accounting documents, such as receipts and slips used for drafting accounting books" in Jasper Kim, *Korean Business Law – The Legal Landscape and Beyond*, [Carolina Academic Press 2010] 208, is incorrect.

Table 6.2 Summary of notable precedents

No.	Inspection or copying allowed	Disapproved
1	Supreme Court Judgment 99Da137 dated December 21, 1999 (Seoul High Court Judgment 98Na21597 dated December 9, 1998	
	Contracts and proposals for sale of assets including Remicon trucks / statement of tax adjustment / extraordinary profit and loss books / fixed assets books / statement of non-operating expenses / cash book / notes and checks ledger [comments] *In the first instance, only the contracts and proposals were recognized.*	
2	Supreme Court Judgment 99Da58051 dated October 26, 2001 (Seoul High Court Judgment 99Ka187 dated September 3, 1999)	
	Report on acquisition of foreign currency securities / financial statements of a subsidiary / proposals / all documents relating to the open bidding for construction of a new company building / documents relating to the share sale and purchase agreement / share subscription agreement / criteria for valuation of shares and all supporting documents	
3	Supreme Court Decision 2003Ma1575 dated December 24, 2004 (Busan High Court Decision 2002La97 dated August 29, 2003)	
		A claim made by a shareholder in competition with a company during a hostile M&A process was dismissed in its entirety

4	Seoul Central District Court Decision 2004KaHap123 dated February 23, 2004	
	Closing financial statements and statement of tax adjustment / slips and original supporting documents / major contracts and proposals / copy of passbook / statement of entertainment expenses paid / audit report of overseas subsidiary / payroll by person and statement of suspended payment / statement of bad debt expenses for each customer / statement of impairment of intangible assets / statement of loss on disposition of trade receivables / statement of loss on disposition of tangible assets / statement of impairment loss on long-term investment securities / statement of short-term loans for each person / statement of advance payment for each customer [comments] *As the company refused to comply with the above decision with respect to inspection and copying, upon request of the shareholder in a subsequent case, the court rendered a decision of indirect compulsory enforcement permitting the inspection and copying for at least 10 additional days and ordering the company to pay a penalty of KRW 200 million (approximately USD 200000) per day for additional refusals (Decision 2004TaGi548 dated March 8, 2004).*	
5	Seoul Central District Court Decision 2003KaHap4043 dated March 9, 2004	
	Statement showing the current cash on hand and deposits / statement of securities currently held / statement of trade receivables / various tax invoices, receipts, contracts, and statements of delivery / statement of long-term and short-term loans to shareholders and officers	Cash flow plan for the next 5 years / prospectus, contracts and other documents relating to the issuance of overseas depositary receipts / documents showing the necessity of issuance of overseas depositary receipts, etc. / documents relating to business plan and investment plan

Table 6.2 (continued)

6	Seoul Central District Court Judgment 2003GaHap21495 dated March 19, 2004	
	Cash book / diaries / journals / ledgers / slips and supplementary schedules thereto	
7	Seoul Central District Court Decision 2004KaHap229 dated July 12, 2004	
	Books relating to salaries and bonuses for officers	Books relating to entertainment expenses concerning trade secrets, advertisement and promotion expenses, ordinary research and development expenses, etc.
8	Seoul Eastern District Court Decision Recommending Compromise 2005KaHap2876 dated December 21, 2005	
	Cash book / account book for deposit and note transactions and account book for purchase and sale	
9	Suwon District Court Decision 2005KaHap932 dated February 9, 2006	
	Closing financial statements / statement of tax adjustment / various slips / all contracts between the company and its major shareholder and the statement of all remittances and withdrawals between them / all documents relating to guarantees and security provided by the company to a third party for the benefit of the major shareholder	
10	Seoul Central District Court Decision 2006KaHap1377 dated July 11, 2006	
	Register of bonds / slips, supporting document file and tax invoice file	Passbooks (for all accounts opened under the name of the company at financial institutions)

11	Seoul Central District Court Decision 2006KaHap1602 dated July 19, 2006	
	Statement of traveling expenses / daily account (for daily financial plan and payment) / other supporting documents showing transaction activities / statement of major transactions including transactions with a specially-related person during a certain period / statement of various fund transactions, loan transactions and provision of security during a certain period / statement of rental income	
12	Seoul Central District Court Decision 2006KaHap2550 dated September 20, 2006	
	All service agreements entered into between the company and a third party company (A), statement of calculation of service fees and relevant supporting documents, and documents related to joining and resignation of officers and employees of company A / various contracts between the company and its subsidiary in the United States, and various documents exchanged between them, articles of incorporation, list of directors and auditors and their term of office, list of employees, minutes of general meetings of members, minutes of meetings of the board of directors, payroll and documents supporting expenses including traveling expenses of company A, and other relevant supporting documents	
13	Seoul Central District Court Decision 2006KaHap3137 dated October 25, 2006	
	Minutes of general meetings of shareholders for the last 3 years	Copy of passbook showing the statement of deposit transactions for the last 3 years, receipts, relevant contracts, and other supporting documents

Table 6.2 (continued)

14	Seongnam Branch Court Decision 2006KaHap584 dated November 6, 2006	
	Supporting materials relating to sale and purchase of LED-traffic-promotion electronic-display-board facilities / supporting materials relating to housing loans to employees	Cash book and statement of cash flow / books and documents relating to wages and service periods of officers and employees / slips and journals / books and documents relating to related party transactions / books and documents relating to monthly selling and administrative expenses / books and documents relating to the list of trading banks and bank transactions
15	Suwon District Court Decision 2006KaHap398 dated November 21, 2006	
	Minutes of general meetings of shareholders relating to treasury stock transactions, monetary transactions, real property sale and purchase transactions, lease agreements, construction contracts or similar transactions with related companies or specially-related persons	Register of shareholders / all documents relating to the composition and appointment of board members / minutes of a meeting of the board of directors relating to the approval of an urban planning implementation plan for Champion Hole 11 and other relevant documents / documents relating to approval of specific business, ledger of construction cost, etc. / all contracts and the statement of cash flow for electric cart equipment lease business / all contracts and relevant documents concerning split-off and merger with a third party

16	Seongnam Branch Court Decision 2006KaHap637 dated November 29, 2006	
	List of related companies, register of shareholders, the statement of investment amounts and transactions, and investment proposals, etc. / the company's equity method application policy, financial statements of the investee accounted for by applying the investment stock using the equity method / schedule of inventory, statement of manufacturing cost / internal proposals and contracts relating to treasury stocks / deposits and savings, status of operation of long-term and short-term loans, financial plan, daily report of funds / monthly statement of manufacturing cost / monthly statement of selling and administrative expenses / statement of ordinary development expenses and commissions paid	① Statement of transactions including the sales of related companies to a third party / amount of purchase and sale of each item of a subsidiary in the United States, statement of selling and administrative expenses, pay slips, statement of welfare expenses, schedule of inventory, and statement of trade payables and trade receivables for each customer / ② product cost statement, and the net realizable value of inventory for which an inventory valuation reserve is set aside
	[comments] *The inspection of the materials referred to in ① was rejected because such materials are not the account books or documents of the company. Given the ongoing dispute between the applicant and the respondent involving the attempt to acquire control, the inspection or copying of the materials referred to in ② constituting trade secrets cannot be permitted.*	
17	Seosan Branch Court Decision 2006KaHap327 dated January 10, 2007	
	Cash book / suspense payment and suspense receipt ledger / pay slips for directors / books or ledgers describing the statement of corporate credit cards used by directors	

Table 6.2 (continued)

18	Seoul High Court Decision 2006La1064 dated May 2, 2007	
	Contracts with a specific third party and invoices, slips, receipts and ledgers under or relating to the contracts / sales ledger, ledger for each bank / statement of compensation for directors, and expediency funds and expenses paid, and corporate credit cards used by directors / monthly closing financial statements / purchase ledger / tax return file / inspection report of audit committee and attachments thereto* / contracts or memoranda of understanding (specifying the terms and conditions)	Stock valuation report prepared in the stage for acquiring a third party company (A), financial statements of company A, specific contracts by and between company A and other companies / documents relating to the participation in shares in the fund other than contracts** / individual income tax returns of directors
	[comments] * *The court held to the following effect: Unless it is proved that there are special circumstances where the disclosure of the documents to a shareholder may cause material damage to the company, the documents describing the results of inspection of accounting are included in accounting-related documents subject to the right to inspect account books regardless of the names or titles of the documents.* ** *The court further ruled to the following effect: Internal proposals or minutes for the implementation or conclusion of a certain contract, letters exchanged in the course of executing the contract, etc. are documents showing the reasons for or the progress of the transaction rather than those describing the transaction itself and are not included in accounting-related documents, in principle, provided that upon submission of evidence supporting the existence of doubt regarding the forgery of documents, inspection or copying is allowed.*	

19	Seoul Central District Court Decision 2007KaHap762 dated May 15, 2007	
	Documents showing the statement of transactions with a subsidiary / all contracts executed with a specially-related person, and all documents showing the statement of transactions with a specially-related person / sale and purchase agreements for certain investments, consulting service agreements, and evidence of service deliverables	① Minutes of a meeting of the board of directors / ② list of specially-related persons, grounds for calculation of prices in sale and purchase transactions with a specially-related person, list of the largest shareholder of a specially-related person / ③, ④, ⑤
	[comments] *The reasons for disapproval by category are as follows: ① they are not subject to preliminary injunction proceedings; ② they cannot be deemed account books or accounting-related documents; ③ it is not proved that they are kept by the company; ④ they are not the account books prepared by the company; and ⑤ they are not related to the reasons for the inspection or copying as asserted by the applicant.*	
20	Mokpo Branch Court Decision 2007KaHap49 dated July 5, 2007	
	Customer ledger of a certain company (A), statement of relevant transactions, tax invoices, sales slips, slips concerning recovery of accounts receivable / contracts and slips concerning borrowing transactions with company A, report on the status of collection of withholding tax (interest) / subsidiary ledger for salaries, bonuses and severance pay for directors, regulations on payment of bonuses, and payroll / sale and purchase agreements for acquisition of assets not in use, relevant statement of transactions, description of assets not in use, and depreciation cost ledger	Copy of passbook of the account to which the borrowing was remitted / internal proposals for purchase of machinery and equipment / photos of assets not in use (the inspection of the foregoing documents is not permitted because they are not deemed account books or accounting-related documents or are not specific, or their scope is too broad)
21	Seoul Central District Court Decision 2007KaHap2025 dated August 9, 2007	
	All documents showing the statement of transactions with a subsidiary / all contracts executed with a specially-related person, and all documents showing the statement of such transactions	

Table 6.2 (continued)

22	Seoul Central District Court Decision 2007KaHap2370 September 20, 2007	
		Since the company disputes the status of the applicant as a shareholder even though the applicant is formally deemed a shareholder, the applicant must first be recognized as a shareholder in litigation on the merits
	[comments] *The above Decision was rendered on the assumption that the applicant has the burden of proof. But considering the effect of awarding capacity or the effect of presuming rights of the register of shareholders, the underlying logic of the above Decision is wrong.*	
23	Seosan Branch Court Decision 2007KaHap199 dated October 17, 2007	
		Bank transaction passbook and loan passbook – only the slips are materials directly used to prepare account books; the bank transaction passbook may be used to prepare slips but is not included in accounting-related documents
24	Seoul High Court Decision 2006Ra1752 dated March 13, 2008	
	Appeal made against the case No. 15 above (Suwon District Court Decision 2006KaHap398 dated November 21, 2006) to the same effect (appeal dismissed)	
25	Seoul High Court Decision 2007Ra1730 dated May 14, 2008	
		Dismissed in part – there is no urgent necessity of preservation

26	Seongnam Branch Court Decision 2008KaHap233 dated June 25, 2008	
	Description of real properties owned by the company and relevant contracts and proposals / all contracts executed by and between the company and its officers and employees in the amount not less than KRW 10 million and relevant proposals / all contracts executed by the company in the amount not less than KRW 50 million, proposals / statement of payment of compensation for officers / statement of all transactions indicated in passbooks issued by financial institutions	
27	Uijeongbu District Court Decision 2008KaHap940 dated January 21, 2009	
		The fact that the company hindered the applicant (statutory auditor) in inspecting account books has not been sufficiently proven
28	Seoul Southern District Court Decision 2008KaHap1620 dated March 2, 2009	
		Although the applicant asserts that "according to the respondent's financial statements, the total investment assets out of total assets of KRW 17.3 billion amount to KRW 5.3 billion, the labor cost accounts for approximately 70% of the total operating expenses, and roughly KRW 900 million was paid as service fees which appears to be an excessive expenditure, and thus it needs to verify relevant financial matters," the reasons for the inspection are not deemed sufficiently specific
	[comments] *While the above Decision requires that the reasons be specific, citing Supreme Court Judgment 99Da137 dated December 21, 1999, it appears to have totally misunderstood the intent of the Supreme Court Judgment and criticism for lack of understanding of the fundamental reason for which the shareholder exercises the right to inspect account books cannot be avoided.*	

Table 6.2 (continued)

29	Bucheon District Court Decision 2008KaHap1501 dated April 8, 2009 Bucheon District Court Decision 2009KaHap489 dated May 27, 2009	
	All contracts with third party companies in a special relationship and individual specially-related persons, and a statement of all relevant fund remittances and withdrawals / statement of payment of compensation, expediency funds, car and housing allowances for directors, and other relevant materials including slips and a statement of corporate credit cards used	
30	Chungju Branch Court Decision 2009KaHap109 dated May 15, 2009	
	An audit report and financial statements of a subsidiary (A)	Register of shareholders, investment-related review documents, reports, proposals, and register of documents sent and received are not included in accounting-related documents / the description saying, "business status data of company A for the 1st quarter, the 1st half and the 3rd quarter of 2008," is not sufficiently specific to be immediately enforceable

31	Seongnam Branch Court Decision 2009KaHap469 dated August 27, 2009	
	Bond certificates relating to the acquisition of convertible bonds of a third party company (A), evidence of withdrawal relating to the acquisition, and statement of interest income and accrued interest / statement of trade receivables and inventory related to the transfer of trade receivables of company A, relevant contracts, etc, / statement of loans to a third party company (B), evidence of withdrawal, loan agreements, etc. / reports to directors, proposals, contracts (including side agreements), evidence of remittance of share transfer price, statement of investment stock using the equity method, etc. relating to the sale of shares of company B / other various contracts for transactions with specially-related persons, evidence of withdrawal of the asset transfer price, list and statement of assets, etc. / all contracts relating to sales for the last 3 years / statement of monetary transactions relating to sales for the last 3 years / reports to directors, proposals, and share subscription agreements (including side agreements) relating to the capital increase with consideration in 2008, and all supporting documents showing the remittance and use of the price of the new shares	

Table 6.2 (continued)

32	Seoul Central District Court Decision 2009KaHap3045 dated November 2, 2009	
		Violation of requirements for a holding company
33	Seoul Southern District Court Decision 2009KaHap1011 dated November 11, 2009	
	Broadly recognized – However, there is an agreement entered into by and between the applicant and the company stating that "the company shall, upon the request of the applicant, report major changes in assets and major changes in the business plan, or prepare and submit relevant materials, on a regular basis and from time to time" and that "the applicant may, if it is necessary for the management of the company, conduct an audit of accounting business and overall business or management analysis"	
34	Ansan Branch Court Decision 2009KaHap219 dated December 23, 2009	
	Statement of manufacturing cost, all contracts for sale and a statement of monetary transactions for a certain period, and pay slips for officers and employees / articles of incorporation of related companies including subsidiaries, minutes of general meetings of shareholders, minutes of meetings of the board of directors, all documents showing the statement of transactions with the respondent company, all documents showing payment and receipt of funds, and a list of dispatched personnel and information on their dispatch periods	

7. Review of Korean laws pertinent to Foreign Financial Institutions' Korean business: with emphasis on a few issues that are frequently raised in practice

Hyunjoo Oh

I. OVERVIEW

There are two ways in which foreign investment firms and foreign banks (each a "Foreign Financial Institution") do business in Korea – (1) establish a local operational base in Korea in the form of a subsidiary, branch, etc. and have that local operational base obtain relevant licenses and offer services onshore (the "Onshore Operation") and (2) offer services to Korean residents directly from an offshore base without having any local operational base (the "Offshore Operation").

In case of the Onshore Operation, the local operation base and its activities would be subject to the regulations that Korean financial institutions would be subject to regarding such activities except for those matters that statutes say otherwise. In the case of the Offshore Operation, a Foreign Financial Institution's activities are generally deemed to take place outside Korea, to have little effect on Korea and to be insufficient grounds for imposing license requirements on such Foreign Financial Institution. However, if such activities are deemed to have direct impacts on the Korean market, such Foreign Financial Institution would be subject to pertinent Korean regulations, such as license requirements (e.g. foreign non-discretionary investment advisors or discretionary investment advisors are required to obtain licenses before they can provide services to domestic residents from their offshore bases) and registration statement requirements (e.g. a public offering of foreign-currency denominated securities by a Foreign Financial Institution to domestic residents would require filing of a registration statement in Korea).

In the case of the Onshore Operation, it can be said that there is not much uncertainty on the scope of permissible activities and relevant regulations because the local operational base would be put under supervision by the Korean authorities and subject to the regulations that comparable Korean financial institutions are subject to. In contrast, in the case of the Offshore Operation, a Foreign Financial Institution that is not well-versed in Korean laws may expose itself to legal and regulatory risks from having to research and review different parts of Korean laws, including without limitation the Financial Investment Services and Capital Markets Act ("FSCMA"), the Banking Act and the Foreign Exchange Transactions Act ("FETA"), for different types of activities it seeks to engage in, in order to get comfort that it may legally engage in such activities. For example, as FSCMA has an extraterritorial jurisdiction provision stating that an activity that takes place offshore may still be subject to FSCMA if such activity affects the Korean market (Article 2), a Foreign Financial Institution may be in breach of the Korean law without any awareness on its part.

This article reviews a few issues that are frequently raised in practice in the case of (a) the Onshore Operation and (b) the Offshore Operation.

II. ONSHORE OPERATION

A. Licensing Requirements

(a) When a foreign investment firm seeks to provide financial investment services, through its Onshore Operation, it would need to choose the type of financial investment services to be provided, financial investment products to be handled and investors to be served and obtain relevant permit(s) or register with the Financial Services Commission ("FSC") as may be necessary.[1]

(b) When a foreign bank seeks to provide banking services through its Onshore Operation, it would need to satisfy requirements under the Banking Act and the regulations thereunder and obtain a permit from FSC.[2]

A local subsidiary would be treated as a domestic financial institution and be subject to the same licensing requirements that Korean financial institutions are subject to. A local branch ("Branch") differs from a subsidiary

[1] Articles 12 and 18 of FSCMA.

[2] Articles 8 and 58 of the Banking Act, Item 17 of the Banking Business Approval Guideline.

in that its legal form is not limited to corporation. A Branch would cause the Foreign Financial Institution's head office to become the subject of licensing requirements. This follows naturally from the fact that a Branch does not have a legal personality separate from the Foreign Financial Institution's head office.

Previously under the regime of the Securities and Exchange Act, a foreign investment firm that sought to provide dealing, brokerage, asset management or trust services through more than one Branch was required to get a license for each Branch. Currently under the regime of FSCMA, such foreign investment firm would only be required to file a report with certain supporting documents to FSC at least 7 days prior to opening any additional Branch.[3] However, FSCMA does not explicitly address the case where a foreign investment firm seeks to open an additional Branch to provide non-discretionary or discretionary investment advisory services. It seems prudent that FSCMA as it is currently worded should be interpreted as requiring a registration with FSC for each Branch. The financial authorities have not taken a clear stance on this issue.

A similar issue exists under the Banking Act. The statute stipulates that a foreign bank needs to receive an approval from FSC when it seeks to establish a Branch to provide banking services or to close an existing Branch (Article 58(1)). It is silent on whether a separate approval is required for each additional Branch. Again, it seems prudent that the Banking Act should be interpreted as requiring a separate approval from FSC for each Branch. In addition, given that the Banking Business Supervisory Regulation published by FSC lists items that need to be reviewed when a Branch is to be added, it appears that the regulatory authority is operating on the belief that a separate license is required whenever a foreign bank seeks to add a branch.[4]

B. Regulation on Assets held by Branch

1. Relevant statutory provisions

FSCMA imposes the following duties on each Branch of foreign investment firms – (a) the duty to settle its books independently from its head office, (b) the duty to hold assets inside Korea in an aggregate amount equal to the sum of its operating capital and liabilities and (c) in case of its

---

3 Article 16(1) of the Enforcement Decree of FSCMA, Article 2-10 of the Regulation on Financial Investment Business.

4 Appendix 2-5, Section I.2.

liquidation or bankruptcy, the duty to use its assets held in Korea to pay off the creditors who have an address or reside in Korea first (Article 65).

Likewise, the Banking Act requires each Branch of foreign banks to hold assets inside Korea in an aggregate amount equal to the sum of its operating capital and liabilities and, in the case of its liquidation or bankruptcy, use its assets held in Korea to pay off Korean creditors and the creditors having an address or residing in Korea first (Article 62).

Main purposes of the provisions described above are to protect creditors of each Branch of Foreign Financial Institutions by requiring each branch to hold a certain level of assets in Korea and to give additional protection to domestic creditors in the case of its liquidation or bankruptcy by requiring it to treat them more preferentially than overseas creditors ("Preferential Treatment"). Moreover, these provisions are understood as measures to increase Foreign Financial Institutions' creditworthiness by imposing these two restrictions on the disposition of their assets held in Korea.

2. Application of Preferential Treatment

To understand the significance of Preferential Treatment, it is necessary to recognize when a Branch begins to be deemed to be in liquidation or bankruptcy.

A Branch needs to commence the process of liquidating its assets in Korea when its license is cancelled by the Korean government or is deemed to have been cancelled by law.[5,6,7]

FSC may cancel a license held by a Branch in any of the following cases:

---

5 Articles 420 and 421 of FSCMA.

6 Articles 61 and 62 of the Banking Act.

7 In the case of voluntary closure of a Branch by a foreign bank, the duty to liquidate assets located in Korea is not triggered (Article 61(1) of the Banking Act). Nevertheless, it is required to get an approval from FSC for such closure (Article 58 of the Banking Act). Since a schedule for liquidation process is a required part of the application for Branch closure, it is argued that a Branch should be deemed to enter into liquidation even in the case of voluntary disclosure ("Suggestions for improving the Banking Act for Establishing Infrastructure for Advancement of Financial industry", Dong-won Ko, 2006. 6.).

In contrast, there is no statutory provision addressing voluntary closure of a Branch by a foreign investment firm. So, a Branch may be in liquidation only when there is a court order to do so. Thus, there is a possibility that a Branch of a foreign investment firm can transfer its assets overseas during the process of its voluntary disclosure without being in liquidation (absent a court order to do otherwise) and without having the statutory obligation to provide Preferential Treatment under FSCMA. To the best of our knowledge, there has not been any precedent in practice. While this may be a problem that may be solved by legislation, this Article will not delve into this matter any further.

(a) regarding a Branch of a foreign investment firm (1) when the foreign investment firm (a) is dissolved, bankrupt or terminated due to a merger or business transfer, (b) has its licenses for those financial services equivalent to those that its Branch is providing cancelled or suspends or discontinues such services or (c) violates any foreign law and thereby causes the Branch not to function properly or (2) when FSC cancels all licenses held by the Branch because of any violation of requirements for maintaining licenses or business suspension order or any non-compliance of a correction order; and

(b) regarding a Branch of a foreign bank (1) when the foreign bank ceases to exist due to a merger[8] or business transfer or it becomes subject to a disciplinary action by any financial supervisory agency or it suspends or ceases its business or (2) when FSC cancels all licenses held by the Branch because of any violation of requirements for maintaining licenses or business suspension order or any non-compliance of a correction order.

Upon the occurrence of (b)(1), the Branch's licenses are automatically deemed to be cancelled without any action on the part of FSC; provided that FSC may designate a separate date as the cancellation date when deemed necessary to protect bank customers. Branches of foreign investment firms are not subject to any such automatic cancellation feature.[9]

A Branch needs to commence the process of liquidation when it is voluntarily closed by the Foreign Financial Institution's head office and ordered by the court to go into liquidation or when FSC cancels its license for any of the reasons above. Such process of liquidation should comply with provisions of the Commercial Code that concern the liquidation process of a foreign company's domestic office.[10] (This is discussed in more detail in part 3 below.)

One important thing to note here is that even if the Foreign Financial Institution's head office enters bankruptcy proceedings, its Branch is not automatically subject to such proceedings. Instead, it would have

---

8 In practice, when a foreign bank ceases to exist due to a merger and has all of its rights and obligations succeed by a surviving foreign bank, such surviving bank is deemed to have succeeded to the license of the disappearing bank's Branch in Korea. Instead of going through the steps of cancelling the previous license and applying for a new one under the name of the surviving bank, it is sufficient to report a name change of the Foreign Financial Institution's head office. It seems necessary that a similar process should be applicable in cases of mergers of foreign investment firms.

9 Article 60 of the Banking Act.

10 Article 61(3) of the Banking Act, Article 24-4 of FSCMA and Article 620 of the Commercial Code.

its license cancelled by law or FSC and be ordered to go into liquidation. This is because the Debtor Rehabilitation and Bankruptcy Act ("Bankruptcy Act") does not give automatic effect in Korea to any bankruptcy or rehabilitation procedures overseen by a foreign court (collectively, "Foreign Bankruptcy Procedures"). Instead, the Bankruptcy Act allows the Korean court to decide whether to give effect to any Foreign Bankruptcy Procedures upon the application by the bankruptcy trustee.

Thus, it does not follow that a Branch goes into bankruptcy automatically when the Foreign Financial Institution's head office is bankrupt. Rather, the Branch's assets can be liquidated by the bankruptcy trustee upon the approval by the Korean court. Moreover, it is unthinkable that a Branch can go into bankruptcy independently of the Foreign Financial Institution's head office.

As mentioned before, Preferential Treatment is triggered when a Branch goes into liquidation or bankruptcy. It is unclear when a Branch "goes into bankruptcy." It could mean the moment when the Foreign Financial Institution's head office goes into bankruptcy or the moment when an application is made to the Korean court for acknowledgement of the Foreign Bankruptcy Procedures or the moment when such acknowledgement is given.

Considering that (1) even if Foreign Bankruptcy Procedures have commenced against the Foreign Financial Institution's head office, it is difficult to say that the assets held by its Branch are subject to the "bankruptcy proceeding" under either Korean laws or foreign laws, (2) in such case, FSC may cancel the Branch's license and lead to the Branch's assets to be liquidated separately from the Foreign Financial Institution's head office, and (3) Preferential Treatment is a feature designed to permanently settle a Branch's legal obligations, it is reasonable to interpret "goes into bankruptcy" as meaning the moment when the Korean court acknowledges under the Bankruptcy Act the Foreign Bankruptcy Procedures against a Foreign Financial Institution.[11]

When the Korean court acknowledges the Foreign Bankruptcy Procedures against a Foreign Financial Institution, would the bankruptcy trustee's actions regarding the assets of the Branch be subject to Preferential Treatment? According to the Bankruptcy Act, the bankruptcy trustee appointed by the Korean court in its decision to acknowledge the Foreign Bankruptcy Procedures has the authority to perform the debtor's

---

[11] For legislative clarity, it would be better to revise the statute to read "When a Branch goes into liquidation or when the Foreign Bankruptcy Procedures of the Foreign Financial Institution's head office [are] acknowledged by the Korean court."

business and manage and dispose of the debtor's assets. The bankruptcy trustee needs to obtain approval of the court when it seeks to dispose of, realize or distribute assets in Korea or transfer any of them overseas.[12]

Although there has not been any precedent, it appears reasonable to interpret that the bankruptcy trustee would be required to comply with Preferential Treatment when it manages and disposes of the Branch's assets. This is because of the following two reasons. (1) Even when bankruptcy procedures are commenced against a Branch under the Bankruptcy Act, it does not exclude application of any other domestic laws including Preferential Treatment under FSCMA and the Banking Act. (2) If Preferential Treatment is not applicable in the case of a Branch in bankruptcy proceedings, it would allow a bankrupt Foreign Financial Institution's head office to avoid Preferential Treatment by applying for bankruptcy proceedings under the Bankruptcy Act instead of applying for liquidation under the Commercial Code, which would run against the spirit of Preferential Treatment (i.e. protection of domestic creditors).

3. Commencement of liquidation process

Under Article 620 of the Commercial Code, when a foreign company closes its Korean office, it may be ordered to commence a liquidation process by the court. It is understood that the purpose of this provision is to protect the interests of domestic creditors by preventing foreign companies from siphoning assets out of the country when they close their Korean offices, and to require the assets held by such offices to be liquidated in an objective manner.

The court may grant a liquidation order regarding a Branch upon the application by any interested person or ex officio, where "interested person" includes creditors, the representative of such local office and the person having the authority to manage the liquidation of the local office under the laws of the jurisdiction where the Foreign Financial Institution's head office is located.

Here, there may be uncertainty as to the scope of "creditors." While it could be interpreted as including creditors of the Branch and the Foreign Financial Institution's head office who are located in Korea, it could also be interpreted as including only the creditors of the Branch. Considering the purpose of the provision above, the latter view appears to be more appropriate.

A similar question arises with regard to the scope of "domestic creditors" and Preferential Treatment. It is uncertain whether the scope is

12 Section 5 of the Bankruptcy Act.

to include foreign creditors, who reside in Korea, of a Branch only or foreign creditors, who reside in Korea, of a Branch as well as the Foreign Financial Institution's head office. Given that the main purpose of Preferential Treatment is to protect domestic creditors, it appears that the former view is more appropriate.

III. OFFSHORE OPERATION

A. Licensing Requirements

1. Foreign non-discretionary investment advisors and foreign discretionary investment advisors

When a foreign non-discretionary investment advisor or a foreign discretionary investment advisor provides services from its offshore base directly to domestic residents or provides a discretionary investment advisory service or non-discretionary investment advisory service through domestic communication channels, it needs to satisfy the requirements under FSCMA and obtain a license.

The applicant is required to:

(i) have a registered communication agent for investor protection,
(ii) state in the contracts to be entered into with its customers that such contracts will be governed by Korean laws and subject to the jurisdiction of Korean courts,
(iii) establish appropriate procedures and standards that its officers and employees are required to comply with in performing their duties, and review the current status of the management periodically in order to check the compliance with the provisions relating to the prohibition of unfair business practice under FSCMA (Article 98),
(iv) prepare business reports for the periods of three months, six months, nine months and twelve months from the date of the commencement of every business year in accordance with the standards prescribed and publicized by FSC and file such business reports with FSC within one month from the end of each reporting period. If the applicant is a foreign discretionary investment advisor, it is required to, in addition to the items above,
(v) refrain from providing discretionary investment advisory services to any person who does not fall under certain categories of professional investors (see footnote no. 26) and
(vi) keep the securities denominated in foreign currencies acquired using the assets under management with a foreign custodian designated

by the Korea Securities Depository ("KSD") or (if it is not possible under the relevant foreign law or market practice for KSD to designate a foreign custodian) a depository institution or clearing house similar to KSD in the list of foreign custodians published by FSC.[13]

When a foreign non-discretionary investment advisor or foreign discretionary investment advisor (1) is dissolved, bankrupt or terminated due to a merger or business transfer,(2) has its foreign license for the advisory services equivalent to those that it provides to Korean investors cancelled, (3) suspends or discontinues such services or (4) violates any foreign law and thereby becomes incapable of functioning properly, FSC may cancel such entity's registration as a financial investment business. A foreign non-discretionary investment advisor or foreign discretionary investment advisor is required to notify FSC immediately upon the occurrence of any of the above.[14]

2. Offshore operation not subject to the licensing requirements

Domestic laws generally govern activities taking place in Korea or performed by domestic residents. As actions taken abroad began affecting the domestic market with the integration of global financial markets, it became necessary to regulate such actions. Thus, Article 2 of FSCMA stipulates that a license is required even for activities done by a foreign company if the effects of such activities extend to the territory of Korea. This provision gives rise to the question as to whether engaging in any of the following activities from an offshore base without any license may be a violation of Korean laws – (1) arrange overseas securities issuance by a Korean entity, (2) underwrite securities issued by a Korean entity outside Korea, (3) sell financial investment products to Korean residents and (4) provide investment advisory services to Korean residents. This is about finding where a boundary lies between what can be considered purely offshore activities and what can be considered as purely onshore activities.

Article 7 of FSCMA tries to draw a boundary line by stipulating that certain acts of foreign investment firms fall outside the definition of "financial investment services" under FSCMA. But, even this clause is subject to varying interpretations and uncertainty in its application.

According to the Article 7 of FSCMA, the following services are deemed not to fall under the definition of "financial investment services"

---

13 Article 100 of FSCMA, Article 101 of the Enforcement Decree of FSCMA, Article 4-15(2) of the Regulation on Financial Investment Business.

14 Article 421 of FSCMA.

with the Items (2)(b) and (3) below creating a carve-out commonly called "reverse inquiry:"

(1) when a foreign dealer comes to Korea to enter into or finalize an underwriting agreement with a Korean resident who seeks to make a public offering or private placement overseas upon the approval of its application for such actions (submitted at least 7 days prior to such actions) by FSC;[15]
(2) where a foreign broker or dealer conducts any of the following activities from its offshore base (a) providing brokerage or dealing services to a domestic broker or dealer as counterparty or (b) receiving without any solicitation or advertisement on its part buy or sell orders from a Korean resident (except domestic dealers and brokers) and providing brokerage or dealing services to such customer; and
(3) where a foreign non-discretionary investment advisor or foreign discretionary investment advisor provides without any solicitation or advertisement on its part discretionary investment advisory services or non-discretionary investment advisory services outside Korea to any of the following: the Korean government, the Bank of Korea ("BOK"), the Korea Finance Corporation, pension or public funds (other than the Credit Guarantee Fund and the Technology Credit Guarantee Fund) and their managers (activities under (2)(b) and (3) collectively, "Reverse Inquiry Activities").

Conceptually, these activities should be included in the definition of "financial investment services." Nevertheless, their nominal effects to the Korean market led to a policy decision of excluding them from the sphere of FSCMA.

To get an exemption pursuant to (1) above, it is necessary to make written submissions describing operations of the investment bank applying for the exemption and its underwriting experiences outside Korea in the past year, and to meet other requirements. To the best of our knowledge, we are not aware of any case where FSC granted an exemption on this basis. In practice, a route that does not require FSC's involvement is preferred. Such route would entail, among others, having the execution

---

[15] Such submission and approval are deemed to have been obtained if the securities concerned are (1) government bonds or (2) debt securities guaranteed by the Korean government. (Article 7 of FSCMA, Article 7(3)(5)~(7) of the Enforcement Decree of FSCMA, Article 1-5(2) of the Regulation on Financial Investment Business.)

and document finalization take place outside Korea and thereby eliminating the need to apply for the exemption.

In practice, the scope of Reverse Inquiry Activities frequently raises questions. The statute requires activities to take place overseas. Such activities can include contacting Korean residents via email or telephone from an overseas base. But, coming to Korea and contacting Korean residents directly are not likely to qualify as such activities.

However, if a foreign investment firm's activities in Korea are nothing more than conducting market researches and do not develop into activities designed to support business activities that require licenses, such market researches are not likely to be illegal.[16]

To understand the exact scope of Reverse Inquiry Activities, it is necessary to find out what "solicitation" is. The regulatory authority views Reverse Inquiry Activities as being comprised of (1) a voluntary request or order from a Korean resident and (2) a foreign investment firm executing a contract in response to it. The regulatory authority appears to conclude that there has been a solicitation for the purposes of FSCMA if a foreign investment firm, through the means of telephone, fax, personal visit and others, induced a Korean resident to place an order or request.

According to these views of the regulatory authority, if a foreign investment firm does not passively execute a contract at the request of a Korean resident but actively induces such contract, such action has the risk of being interpreted as a prohibited solicitation.

3. Offshore operation by foreign banks

Unlike FSCMA, the Banking Act does not have an extraterritorial jurisdiction clause. And there is no existing case law or guidelines published by the relevant regulatory authority touching upon the question of when a cross-border banking service will be deemed as being rendered in Korea which would then be subject to the license requirement.

At least in practice, the Financial Supervisory Service ("FSS") appears to act on the basis of its unofficial view that the question of whether a cross-border banking service is an activity subject to the licensing requirements under the Banking Act should be determined on the basis of the geographic location where the relevant activity is performed by a foreign bank. In other words, if the relevant activity is performed by a

---

[16] If such market researches lead to frequent contacts with customers and ultimately to financial investment services requiring licenses (i.e. brokerage, dealing and investment advisory), it is possible to be subject to sanctions by the regulatory authority.

foreign bank outside of Korea, such activity would not be regulated by the Banking Act and, thus, no license would be required even if the activity concerns a customer residing in Korea. Here, an activity taking place "outside of Korea" means the banking businesses under the Banking Act – lending funds raised from accepting deposits, issuance of securities and any other activities incidental thereto – is taking place overseas. If any of those services takes place inside Korea (e.g. lending funds or raising funds), the whole activity would be deemed to take place in Korea.

Refer to Section B for any financial investment services provided to Korean residents by a foreign bank having relevant licenses under foreign laws.

4. Anticipated legal changes relating to derivative-linked securities

Under the current interpretation of and practice under the FSCMA, foreign financial institutions are required to obtain a financial investment business license in Korea before they can issue and sell derivative-linked securities to Korean investors, unlike in the case of issuing stocks or bonds.

To avoid excessive regulation with regard to issuing of derivative-linked securities, the Korean government is currently preparing for amendment of relevant laws and regulations in the direction of permitting an exemption for foreign issuers of derivative-linked securities on the condition that (1) the foreign issuer is adequately supervised by an overseas regulatory body from whom the Financial Services Commission is able to obtain certain information, (2) the derivative-linked securities are to be sold in Korea through underwriting or broking by domestic broker-dealers and (3) the derivative-linked securities are to be sold only to professional investors.

B. Activity-specific Regulation

In the following pages, this article will review activity-specific regulations for a few activities that are frequently carried out by Foreign Financial Institutions regarding Korean residents.

1. Arranging or underwriting overseas securities issuance by a Korean entity

(a) Relevant provisions Under Article 119(1) of FSCMA, for each public offering of new or existing securities, the issuer is required to file a registration statement with FSC. Anyone who solicits or offers securities in violation of this requirement may be punished by an imprisonment of 5

years or less or a fine not exceeding KRW 200 million.[17] Regardless of who solicits or offers securities, the issuer is the party that is always responsible for filing a registration statement under FSCMA.

FSCMA classifies securities into six types which are set out as follows:

(1) debt securities;
(2) equity securities;
(3) beneficiary certificates – these are instruments which bear the indication of a beneficial interest in a trust;
(4) investment contract securities – these are instruments which bear an indication of a contractual right under which an investor is entitled to profits earned or liable for losses sustained depending upon the results of a joint venture in which such investor makes an investment jointly with another person and which is to be managed mainly by such other person. FSC has not published or provided any detailed standards on what kind of contracts can be considered as investment contract securities;
(5) derivatives-linked securities – these are instruments which bear an indication of a right under which the amount payable or recoverable is determined according to a predetermined formula tied to fluctuation in the price of an underlying asset, interest rate, indicator, unit or index; and
(6) securities depositary receipts – these are instruments issued by a person with whom any of the securities mentioned in (1) to (5) above are deposited in a country other than the country where such underlying securities were issued and bear an indication of the relevant right on the deposited underlying securities.

The determination of whether an instrument is a security in Korea depends on the legal characteristics of the instrument. The following points need to be noted. The domicile of the issuer is not important. Under Korean law, exchange-traded warrants are a subset of equity securities but exchange-traded futures and/or options are not securities. Certificates of deposit denominated in KRW are not securities but certificates of deposit denominated in foreign currency are securities. Commercial paper, which is a subset of debt securities, is confined to promissory notes tendered by a bank that makes a payment on behalf of an applicant and produced in the form of a bill with the words "corporate commercial paper" printed thereon.

---

17 Article 444(12) of FSCMA.

The standard for determining whether an offering of securities is a "public offering" is the number of people to whom such offering is made. It would be considered a "public offering" if a solicitation to subscribe or purchase is made to 50 or more people. Even if an offering is made to fewer than 50 people, it may still be deemed to be a public offering if there is a possibility that the securities may be transferred so that 50 or more people may end up holding such securities within 1 year from their issuance date.[18]

Especially, for securities issued overseas by a Korean entity, it will be deemed a public offering if the securities, rights attached to the securities or securities which are issued as a result of exercising such rights (collectively, "Securities") are issued in such ways that Securities may be acquired by any Korean resident (other than any investment dealer or broker who acquires Securities as underwriters) on or within 1 year from the date of issuance.

If an offering is or is deemed a "public offering," the issuer is under the obligations to submit to FSC a securities registration statement, use a prospectus as the offering document and wait for a certain period for the securities registration statement to become effective before accepting offers to subscribe or purchase.[19] However, even if a "public offering" is made, the obligation to submit a securities registration statement may be waived if the total principal amount of the offer is less than KRW 1 billion.[20]

For certain overseas securities issuances, Article 2-2-2(2) of the Regulation on Securities Issuance and Public Disclosure ("Issuance Regulation") provides exceptions to the registration requirement by excluding them from the definition of "public offering."[21] This carve-out

---

[18] Article 9(7)~(9) of FSCMA, Article 11 of the Enforcement Decree of FSCMA and Article 2-2-2(1) of the Regulation on Securities Issuance and Public Disclosure.

[19] Articles 119, 120 and 123 of FSCMA.

[20] Article 120(1) of the Enforcement Decree of FSCMA.

[21] Under this Article, none of the following is deemed a public offering:

1. The restriction that Securities may not be transferred at the time of issuance or within 1 year from the date of issuance to any Korean resident is explicitly stated on the face of the Securities (if in a definitive form), the relevant underwriting agreement, subscription agreement and the offering circular, and the issuer or the underwriter issues or transfers such Securities only after (1) receiving the written consent containing the acknowledgement of such issuance condition and the signature from each acquirer and (2) putting in place a mechanism designed to secure the performance of such written consent.

2. After the issuance, Securities are deposited with the issuer's official depository

clause separates equity-linked securities, such as equity-linked bonds and depository receipts, from bonds (other than equity-linked bonds). Regarding the former, it requires a measure to strictly prevent migration into Korea within 1 year from the issuance date. Regarding the latter, migration into Korea is permitted on the condition, among others, that securities are transferred only among certain types of professional investors. These disparate treatments are based on the understanding that ordinary bonds have less impact on the domestic financial market than equities.

One of the four exceptions in the carve-out clause (the fourth exception in footnote 21 to be exact) states "where the issuance of securities is structured in a way that prevents Korean residents from acquiring such Securities on or within 1 year from the issuance date." While the Issuance Regulation does not specify the elements that would be required under this exception, the following measures are frequently taken in practice: securities to be issued on the conditions that;

(1) their aggregate principal amount is equal to or more than USD 100 million,
(2) they are in the form of straight bonds (fixed rate or floating rate),

institution and execute a depository agreement which has provisions stating that Securities may not be withdrawn until the first anniversary of the deposit date and that Securities may not be transferred to any Korean resident.

3. Where bonds other than equity-linked bonds, such as convertible bonds, bonds with warrants and exchangeable bonds (but with respect to exchangeable bonds, only those which are exchangeable into shares, convertible bonds or bonds with warrants) are issued and transferred to the account of or for the benefit of any Korean residents who fall within certain categories of professional investor as specified in Article 11(1)(1)(a) and (b) of the Enforcement Decree of FSCMA, provided that (a) the bonds are denominated, and the principal and interest payments thereunder are made, in a currency other than Korean Won, (b) the amount of the bonds acquired by such Korean professional investors in the primary market is limited to less than 20 percent of the aggregate issue amount of the bonds, (c) the bonds are listed on one of the major overseas securities exchanges recognized by FSS or certain procedures, such as filing a registration statement or report with a foreign financial regulator, have been completed for offering of the bonds in a major overseas securities exchange, (d) the one-year restriction on offering, delivering or selling of the bonds to a Korean resident is expressly stated on the face of the bonds (if in a definitive form), the relevant underwriting agreement, subscription agreement and the offering circular and (e) the issuer and the arranger individually or collectively keep the evidence of fulfillment of conditions (a) through (d) above after having taken necessary actions therefor.

4. Where the issuance of Securities is structured in a way that prevents Korean residents from acquiring such Securities on or within 1 year from the issuance date.

(3) they are denominated in foreign currency and payments thereunder are also made in foreign currency,
(4) they have a face value of USD 100 000 or more and are prohibited from being broken into smaller amounts,
(5) they are in registered form,
(6) the subscription agreement, certificates and other agreements explicitly state that Korean residents are not allowed to acquire them within 1 year from the issuance date,
(7) they are issued in an overseas market such as the Euromarket,
(8) they are settled through an international clearing house such as Euroclear and Clearstream, and
(9) the underwriter(s) undertake to the issuer to be responsible for appropriate selling restrictions.

If all of the foregoing is satisfied, it is not necessary to obtain the written consent from each primary acquirer which contains the acknowledgement of the 1-year restriction of domestic migration and his signature.

(b) Extraterritorial application of issuance regulation These regulations on inbound migration are applicable to the underwriters or arranger in addition to the issuer. In other words, according to Article 2(1), the issuer or underwriter bears the obligation to collect the written consent from each primary acquirer which contains the acknowledgement of the 1-year restriction of domestic migration and his signature. Moreover, under Article 2(3)(d) of the same regulation, the issuer and the underwriter must take necessary measures and keep records of them individually or collectively.

These provisions explicitly stipulate the extraterritoriality of domestic regulations. But, considering that the obligation to file a registration statement lies with the issuer, there is no clear ground in the Issuance Regulation's higher laws to extend the regulatory power of this clause to Foreign Financial Institutions. Although Article 2 of FSCMA provides grounds for FSCMA's extraterritorial reach, Article 2 of FSCMA only concerns "activities done by a foreign company." So, it is questionable whether preventive steps under the Issuance Regulation that concern activities to be done in the future can have extraterritorial reach.

On the surface, it is difficult to conclude that these provisions of the Issuance Regulation benefit from Article 2 of FSCMA, a body of law directly above the Issuance Regulation. Moreover, there are few practical measures that the domestic regulatory authority can take against Foreign Financial Institutions that violate these provisions. Currently, the only measure taken is notifying the regulatory authority of the home jurisdiction of a Foreign Financial Institution that committed such violation.[22]

It may be more reasonable to interpret the provisions as imposing on the Issuer the obligations to "procure the underwriter to obtain" the written consent from each acquirer and to "procure the underwriter to take necessary measures and keep records of them." This point may not carry much significance given that Foreign Financial Institutions which act as underwriters or arrangers generally comply with these regulations in practice without much protest.

It needs to be noted that the definition of "securities" under FSCMA includes financial investment products issued by a foreign issuer.[23] Likewise, the Issuance Regulation is drafted on the assumption that securities issued by foreign issuers are also subject to the registration statement requirement under FSCMA and specifies the types of information to be stated in a registration statement and supplementary documents that need to be submitted along with the registration statement by a foreign issuer.[24]

Given this inclusion of securities issued by foreign issuers, the following inconsistency may arise. There may be a view that the wording of Article 2-2-2 of the Issuance Regulation suggests that it is applicable to securities issued overseas by foreign issuers. However, according to Article 2-2-2(1), when an issuer issues securities overseas on the condition that Korean residents can acquire such securities on or within 1 year from the issuance date, such issuance is regarded as an offering. Since an overseas issuance of securities by a foreign entity which targets Korean residents assumes that Korean residents would acquire them at the issuance, if Article 2-2-2 is read as suggested above, it leads to an unreasonable conclusion that securities issued overseas by foreign issuers will always require a registration statement regardless of whether it is a public offering or private placement.

If one takes the above view that the carve-out is applicable, it would create inconsistency with Article 7-33 of the Foreign Exchange Transactions Regulation as domestic investors would not be able to acquire the securities that they subscribe for within 1 year from their issuance despite having subscribed for such securities in reliance on the carve-out.

However, it appears more reasonable to see Article 2-2-2 as a provision not relevant to and, thereby, also not applicable to foreign entities' overseas issuances. To eliminate the potential confusion described above,

---

22 FSS' public notice published on 2003. 12. 24. (Measure taken in response to violation of Issuance Regulation).

23 Article 4(1) of FSCMA.

24 Article 2-11 of the Issuance Regulation.

it appears necessary to improve provisions about deemed offerings and the carve-out.[25]

(c) What kind of communications to investors and publicity are permitted prior to the issuance of the securities? The kinds of permitted communications and publicity depend on whether the offering is a public or private offering.

In the case of private offerings, care must be taken not to fall under the classification of public offering (i.e. solicitation to 50 or more persons). There are no separate regulations in relation to the method of solicitation under a private offering. However, solicitation should not take place through means which would disseminate information on the offering to a wide group of unspecified people, such as newspapers.

In the case of public offerings, the kinds of permitted communications and publicity will depend on the following three phases:

(1) Prior to the submission of a securities registration statement: offers or acts of soliciting offers are prohibited.
(2) After the submission of the securities registration statement but prior to it becoming effective: offers and acts of soliciting offers can be made but only with a preliminary prospectus. However, the issuer, seller or their agents cannot accept any offer to subscribe / purchase from investors.
(3) After the securities registration statement becomes effective: offers and acts of soliciting offers can be made but only with a prospectus. The issuer, seller or their agents can accept offers to subscribe / purchase from investors.

A prospectus needs to be distributed to the investors. However, it is not necessary to distribute the prospectus to professional investors, related

---

[25] Considering that (1) equities or equity-linked securities issued overseas by foreign entities are likely to have little impact on the Korean market, (2) bonds issued overseas by foreign entities are likely to have less impact on the Korean market than in the case under (1), (3) the registration requirement under FSCMA is to protect ordinary investors from asymmetry of information and certain measures for protecting ordinary investors are provided as they are required to delegate execution of transactions regarding foreign currency-denominated securities to a broker (Article 7-33(4) of FETA) and such broker has certain obligations to protect investors (e.g. know-your-client rule under Article 46 of FSCMA and disclosure/explanation requirement under Article 47 of FSCMA), it is questionable whether the registration statement requirement needs to be applicable to securities issued overseas by foreign entities. In light of this, it appears necessary to broaden the migration carve-out for such securities.

persons or any persons who have in writing declined to receive the prospectus.

2. Sale of foreign collective investment securities to domestic residents

When a foreign asset manager seeks to offer interests in a foreign fund (e.g. foreign collective investment scheme, foreign investment trust and foreign anonymous investment association), such foreign fund needs to be registered with FSC. The purpose of this requirement is to protect domestic investors. Registration requirements vary depending on whether such interests are offered to retail investors or certain professional investors.[26,27] Both public and private funds can be registered. Interests in a private fund can only be offered to professional investors.[28] When offering interests in a fund publicly, a registration statement needs to be filed prior to such offering. Article 2-11(1)(3) of the Issuance Regulation specifies the types of information to be stated in a registration statement and supplementary documents that need to be submitted along with the registration statement.

Interests in a foreign fund can be sold to Korean residents only through

26 "Professional investors" mean those specified in Article 301(2) of the Enforcement Decree of FSCMA. The scope of "professional investors" under this provision is narrower than those under other provisions. While most financial institutions are included, non-financial entities (even the ones with much investment experience and assets under management) are rarely included. In other words, it includes the Korean government, the Bank of Korea, special banks established under the specific statutes, financial institutions under the Banking Act, the National Agricultural Cooperative Federation, the National Federation of Fisheries Cooperatives, insurance companies, financial investment banks, securities companies, merchant banks, credit brokerage companies, financial holding companies, credit companies, mutual savings banks and national federations thereof, the National Forestry Cooperatives Federation, the National Community Credit Federation, the National Credit Union Federation, the Korea Deposit Insurance Corporation, the Korea Asset Management Corporation, the Korea Housing Finance Corporation, the Korea Investment Corporation, the Korea Finance Corporation, the Korea Financial Investment Association, the Korea Securities Depository, the Korea Exchange, FSS, collective investment schemes (excluding collective investment schemes established under statutes other than FSCMA), the Credit Guarantee Fund, the Technology Credit Guarantee Fund, public or pension funds established in accordance with specific statutes and their managers, corporations carrying on mutual aid projects in accordance with specific acts and municipal governments.

27 Article 279 of FSCMA.

28 Table 19 in Article 7-53(3) of the Regulation on Financial Investment Business.

a domestic broker or dealer. If this requirement is violated, FSC may revoke the registration of the relevant fund.[29]

It is uncertain whether having to distribute through a domestic broker or dealer means that such intermediary has to underwrite the fund interests being offered or subscribe such interests in its name for the benefit of investors or simply bring together the foreign seller and investors ("Simple Brokerage").

Since the statutory wording "through a broker or dealer" does not explicitly exclude Simple Brokerage, there is a view that Simple Brokerage is allowed.[30] There is a conflicting view that the intermediary has to be a party to the distribution by standing in-between the foreign seller and domestic investors and, thus, Simple Brokerage is not permitted on the basis that Article 7-56(1) of the Regulations on Financial Investment Business (a subset of regulations below FSCMA) says "when a broker or dealer receives an order concerning interests in a foreign fund from an investor, such broker or dealer shall execute a contract with such investor relating to such transaction."

According to the main body of Article 7-56(2) of the Regulation on Financial Investment Business, transactions of foreign fund interests with ordinary investors should be entered into under the "Standard Terms on Transactions of Foreign Fund Interests" published by the Korea Financial Investment Association. The standard terms are written on the assumption that a domestic intermediary would enter into a transaction with the foreign seller on behalf of domestic investors and there is no privity between the foreign seller and domestic investors. So, it appears to exclude Simple Brokerage. Nonetheless, Article 7-56(2) says that the standard terms are not required when domestic investors are professional investors. Thus, it is far-fetched to conclude that Simple Brokerage is not permitted across the board.

While it is not clear, the financial authority appears to take the position that Simple Brokerage is not allowed and has established its practice on that basis. Such practice is likely to be based on the policy consideration that a domestic intermediary that offers Simple Brokerage does not give enough protection to investors.

---

[29] Articles 280(1) and 420(1)(7) of FSCMA and Article 373(1)(23) of the Enforcement Decree of FSCMA.

[30] *The Financial Investment Services and Capital Markets Act*, Je-ho Byun, et al., Jiwon Publishing p. 729.

3. Sales of OTC derivatives to Korean residents

(a) Sales of OTC derivatives as part of onshore operation When a Foreign Financial Institution enters into an OTC derivative through its local subsidiary or Branch, it needs to obtain a license for it. In addition, there are many regulations to abide by depending on the type of such Foreign Financial Institution, the type of counterparty (i.e. an ordinary investor vs. a professional investor) and the type of the OTC derivative. Examples of such regulations include the obligation to verify the hedging purpose for ordinary investors, the obligation to abide by the hedging ratio for corporate investors and the obligation to submit to a prior examination by the Korea Financial Investment Association for certain OTC derivative products.[31]

When a local subsidiary or Branch acts as transaction party for and on behalf of itself or the Foreign Financial Institution's head office, (1) any FX derivative transaction with a corporate investor or (2) any OTC derivative transaction (including any FX derivative transaction) with an ordinary investor must be for hedging purpose only.

Here, the term "FX derivative transaction" means OTC derivative transactions whose underlying is a foreign currency (e.g., currency outright forwards, currency options and currency swaps) and includes non-deliverable forwards but excludes currency swaps and currency futures. The term "corporate investor" refers to (1) any listed corporation that has notified the local subsidiary or Branch in writing of its intent to be treated as a professional investor, (2) any local corporation issuing stock certificates listed on a foreign securities market or (3) any local corporation that has obtained the status of professional investor under Article 10(3) 16 and 17 of the Enforcement Decree of FSCMA. The term "corporate investor" does not refer to any government-owned enterprises.

A transaction is for hedging purposes if, at the time of executing the transaction, (1) the counterparty owns or is scheduled to own underlying exposures and (2) the aggregate notional value of OTC derivatives entered into during the contract term does not exceed the notional value of the underlying exposures.

For a local subsidiary or Branch to act as a transaction party, each of the following types of OTC derivative transactions must, in principle, be reviewed in advance by the Korea Financial Investment Association (Article 166-2(1)(6) of the Enforcement Decree of FSCMA): (1) any OTC

---

[31] Article 166-2 of FSCMA, Table 15-2 in Article 41 of the Detailed Rules of Banking Business Supervision.

derivative whose underlying asset is not a financial investment instrument, currency or commodity (e.g., credit or environmental risks); or (2) any OTC derivative targeting ordinary investors. However, there is a relatively broad exception clause under Article 177-2 of the Enforcement Decree of FSCMA, which exempts certain types of the above OTC derivative transactions from the review requirement.

(b) Sales of OTC derivatives as part of offshore operation When a Foreign Financial Institution enters into an OTC derivative with a Korean resident which is a corporate investor or an ordinary investor through its overseas base, without having any local presence in Korea, the regulations mentioned above would not be applicable. In other words, an OTC derivative transaction without involvement of a local subsidiary or Branch, in principle, does not have to be for hedging purposes only. Nevertheless, it needs to be noted that such transaction may require a prior report under FETA.[32]

In addition, the offshore office should check whether any restriction applies under the relevant Korean law pursuant to which the counterparty is established (e.g., in the case of the Korea Development Bank, the Korea Development Bank Act). Also, the offshore office should review the articles of incorporation and bylaws of the counterparty for any restriction on speculative transactions.

To elaborate on this point of checking corporate authority, the articles of incorporation of a Korean company lists the types of activities that it can engage in. It is generally understood that any action by a company that falls outside the scope of corporate purposes set forth in its articles of incorporation is null and void (i.e. ultra vires). Thus, when entering into an OTC derivative transaction with a Korean corporation as counterparty, it is necessary to check whether it is authorized to enter into such OTC derivative.

One thing to keep in mind is that the Korean court, while acknowledging the principle of ultra vires, interprets the scope of corporate purposes set forth in an articles of incorporation quite broadly as including "those activities that are necessary for or incidental to achieving any of the foregoing purposes." Under this case law, there arises the question whether transacting in OTC derivatives is "an activity that is necessary for or incidental to achieving the foregoing purposes" when the counterparty's articles of incorporation does not explicitly state such activity as a permitted activity.

---

[32] While there may be other laws and regulations that may be applicable to the counterparty, they are not covered in this article.

There is no case law or established view on this issue and it appears reasonable that OTC derivative transactions entered into for hedging purposes should generally be seen as such ancillary activity. This is because it can be generally acknowledged that there may be needs for hedging various risks that arise while pursuing corporate purposes through OTC derivative transactions.

However, there may be a controversy in case of OTC derivative transactions entered into for speculative purposes. There is no precedent on this point. Even in the famous suits lodged by Korean companies (including both ordinary investors and professional investors) against domestic banks concerning losses from knock-in and knock-out options ("KIKO Transactions"), the defendants (i.e. the banks) did not raise the issue of the Korean companies' authority to enter into such OTC derivative transactions.

Given the lack of precedent, it is difficult to predict how the court would rule on this issue, if it is raised. For now, it is prudent for a Foreign Financial Institution that seeks to enter into an OTC derivative transaction with a Korean counterparty whose purpose is speculation to check the counterparty's articles of incorporation to see whether it lists "transacting in OTC derivatives."

Each OTC derivative transaction between a Foreign Financial Institution and a Korean resident needs to be reported to BOK unless the resident is a foreign exchange agency regarding OTC derivatives under FETA. Generally, foreign exchange banks, dealers and collective investment managers are foreign exchange agencies regarding OTC derivatives. Even so, the scope of OTC derivatives that can be handled by each foreign exchange agency may vary.

Even if the counterparty to an OTC derivative transaction is a foreign exchange agency, it is necessary to submit written evidence proving such transaction's appropriateness to BOK in any of the following cases – (1) 20 percent or more of the notional amount is paid as an upfront fee (e.g. in the form of an option premium), (2) the price of such transaction incorporates loss under another OTC derivative transaction that is being amended, cancelled or terminated and (3) such transaction is entered into for the purpose of circumventing reporting requirements under FETA.[33]

Both sides to an OTC derivative transaction are jointly responsible for complying with the reporting obligations as described above. So, only one side needs to file a report. In practice, the domestic counterparty which is close to BOK generally files a report but the counterparty that is a Foreign

33 Article 7-40 of the Foreign Exchange Transactions Regulations.

Financial Institution needs to keep in mind that it remains responsible for the reporting obligations and that if such obligations under FETA are not complied with it may be subject to criminal liability.

An ISDA documentation practice regarding OTC derivative transactions that needs to be touched upon is the use of multi-party set-off. There have been many cases where a Foreign Financial Institution, when entering into the ISDA with a Korean counterparty for OTC derivatives, would insert a provision in the Schedule to revise Section 6(f) of the ISDA Master Agreement, which concerns set-off. The revision typically expands the scope of set-off to include not just the receivables and payables under the ISDA Master Agreement but also under other agreements between the parties and their affiliates, or allows the Foreign Financial Institution to include its affiliates as a party to the set-off against the Korean counterparty. The purpose of it appears to be to manage the counterparty risk on a group-wide basis.

However, under Korean law, a set-off is valid and enforceable only between the parties that agreed to that set-off. If such set-off is to include any third party, such party should be a party to the agreement. Thus, the revised set-off, including affiliates which are not parties to the agreement, as described above is unlikely to be valid and enforceable. Since this approach is unlikely to be effective in managing risks in a group-wide fashion, there appears to be a need to look for another way.

4. Conversion of a Branch into a local subsidiary

There are cases when a Foreign Financial institution seeks to convert its Branch into a local subsidiary to expand its business. This chapter concludes by describing the pros and cons of such conversion.

The main advantages of pursuing such conversion are that (1) a local subsidiary can issue securities solely on the basis of its balance sheet and such securities can take the form of, inter alia, equities, bonds and derivative-linked securities, (2) its liabilities would be contained within itself and will not reach its parent company and (3) it may seek offshore borrowings, including subordinated borrowings, subject to certain restrictions. In sum, the conversion would allow the Foreign Financial Institution to manage the contagion risk and provide it with a broader range of financing and product options.

The main disadvantages are that (1) all licenses currently held by the Branch will be extinguished upon the conversion and the new local subsidiary will have to apply for them again and may be subject to a different set of requirements, which would include qualifications on the part of its parent company, (2) the local subsidiary would be subject to requirements under the Korean Commercial Code and (3) various tax issues may arise in connection with the conversion, including dividend tax, transfer pricing and capital gains tax on the "sale" of the Branch's business to the newly formed local subsidiary. While this is not a strictly legal issue, an important operational consideration for Foreign Financial Institutions is that all major IT systems of their local subsidiaries are required to be maintained in Korea.

8. Recent regulatory developments regarding ABS in Korea

Kyung Hwa Moon

I. INTRODUCTION

Korea enacted the Asset-Backed Securitization Act (the "ABS Act") on September 16, 1998 in the wake of the Asian financial crisis that hit the country in 1997. Even before the enactment of the ABS Act, there were attempts to securitize assets held by Korean companies, especially merchant banks and other financial institutions. However, not only were such attempts frustrated by the financial crisis, but also there proved to be many legal obstacles that made it practically impossible for securitization transactions to take place in Korea. The ABS Act was enacted to address such problems, especially by providing for special methods of perfection, minimization of insolvency risk, and tax and other benefits.[1]

Since the enactment of the ABS Act, the securitization market in Korea has grown rapidly and has become an important source of funding. In 2010, a total of over KRW 28 trillion asset-backed securities were issued.[2] In terms of the proportion of asset-backed securities in the direct financing market in Korea, KRW 11.1 trillion asset-backed securities were publicly offered in Korea in 2010 out of a total of around KRW 112.9 trillion corporate bonds issued.[3] In the initial stages after the enactment of the ABS Act, the securitized assets were mostly non-performing loans held by financial institutions and securitization was used to dispose of such non-

[1] For a detailed background on the enactment of the ABS Act, *see* Society for Research on Practices of Asset Securitization, KumYoongHyukMyung ABS [Financial Innovation ABS] at 291-295 (1999).

[2] Financial Supervisory Service, Press Release on Issuance of Asset-Backed Securities in 2010 (Feb. 7, 2011), available at http://www.fss.or.kr/fss/kr/promo/bodobbs_view.jsp?seqno=14946.

[3] Financial Supervisory Service, Press Release on Direct Financing by Corporations in 2010 (Jan. 17, 2011), available at http://www.fss.or.kr/fss/kr/promo/bodobbs_view.jsp?seqno=14886.

performing loans. The securitization market in Korea has since evolved to include credit card receivables, auto loans and other consumer loans, mortgage loans, sales receivables and project-financing loans, among others.[4]

However, the ABS Act has not changed much since its enactment. There were several attempts made to amend the ABS Act to reflect the needs of the market in 2005 and 2007, but they failed to be consummated due to the surrounding circumstances such as the outbreak of the global financial crisis. The government took up the task of amending the ABS Act again reflecting the market demand and the international discussion on securitization after the global financial crisis. The government submitted its proposal for amendments to the ABS Act to the National Assembly of Korea on December 29, 2010 (the "Proposed Amendments"), where it is currently being reviewed and pending approval.[5]

This chapter will take an overview of the current ABS Act, discuss the contents of the Proposed Amendments to review whether they adequately reflect the changes necessary, and lastly consider whether any further amendments are necessary, especially considering the international regulatory development surrounding securitization after the global financial crisis.

II. OVERVIEW OF THE CURRENT ABS ACT

The ABS Act was enacted not to regulate securitization, but to promote and enable securitization transactions to take place more easily in Korea. Therefore, securitization transactions can take place outside of the ABS Act.[6] However, due to certain legal restrictions as discussed more fully below, in some cases it is not possible to conduct securitization transactions in Korea without the benefit of the ABS Act. In order to take the benefit of the ABS Act and issue asset-backed securities under the ABS Act, the requirements under the ABS Act must be met. Set forth below is an overview of the basic terms and requirements of the ABS Act.

---

4 For an overview on the development of the securitization market in Korea, *see* Symposium, *JaSan YuDongHwa SypNyunUi HoiGoWa JeonMang (Reflection on Securitization over the past 10 Years and its Prospect]*, 31 BFL at 7-9 (2008).

5 The full text of the Proposed Amendments can be found at http://likms.assembly.go.kr/bill/jsp/BillDetail.jsp?bill_id=ARC_J1L0C1X2A2N9C1R6O1N1G3O7O0W2Q3.

6 In fact, due to the limitations of the ABS Act, there is a growing number of securitization transactions taking place outside of the ABS Act. For a detailed discussion on such transactions, *see* Kim, Yong Ho, Lee Seon Ji and Yoo Ie Hwan, *BeDeungRok YouDongHwaGeoRaeUi ShilTaeWa BubJeok MoonJae [Status and Problems Surrounding Securitization Transactions Outside the ABS Act]* 31 BFL (2008).

A. Certain Defined Terms

1. Originator

The ABS Act restricts entities that can transfer the securitized assets and carry out a securitization transaction pursuant to the ABS Act. Entities that are eligible to become an originator under the ABS Act ("Originator") are mostly financial institutions such as banks, securities companies, asset management companies, insurance companies and other public enterprises such as the Korea Asset Management Corporation. Other corporations can also be Originators, but they are required to have a credit rating of investment grade or higher, or must have listed shares on the Korea Exchange or KOSDAQ in order to qualify as an Originator under the ABS Act.[7]

The reasoning behind such restriction is that since the ABS Act provides tax and other benefits for those using the ABS Act, these benefits may be subject to abuse if general corporations were allowed to use the ABS Act as Originators. Therefore, in order to minimize any negative side-effects, the scope of entities eligible to become Originators was limited to financial institutions and the like, with plans to expand the scope depending on the use of the ABS Act and other circumstances in the future.[8]

2. Securitized Assets

The ABS Act defines assets that can be securitized under the ABS Act ("Securitized Assets") as receivables, real estate and other property rights that are the subject of securitization.[9] The ABS Act restricts entities that can become Originators, but as can be seen from the definition of Securitized Assets, there is practically no limit on what an Originator can securitize under the ABS Act. Of course, by nature of securitization, only assets that are transferable and can generate future cashflow would actually be used as Securitized Assets.

3. Asset-Backed Securities

The ABS Act defines asset-backed securities issued under the ABS Act ("Asset-Backed Securities") as equity securities, bonds, beneficial certificates and other securities or certificates that are based on Securitized Assets and issued pursuant to a securitization plan filed pursuant to the

---

7 ABS Act, art. 2, item 2.

8 Society for Research on Practices of Asset Securitization, *supra* note 1, at 302-303.

9 ABS Act, art. 2, item 3.

ABS Act.[10] The term is broadly defined, so there is virtually no limit to the type of securities that can be issued as Asset-Backed Securities.

4. Securitization SPC

Securitization Specialty Companies ("Securitization SPCs") are special-purpose companies set up pursuant to the ABS Act for the purpose of carrying out securitization transactions under the ABS Act.[11] The ABS Act requires a Securitization SPC to be established as a limited liability company,[12] prohibits a Securitization SPC from opening branches or having employees,[13] and requires it to delegate servicing of Securitized Assets to qualified servicers and other administrative matters to Originators or third parties.[14]

The business of a Securitization SPC is restricted to (1) buying, transferring or entrusting Securitized Assets, (2) administration, management and disposal of Securitized Assets, (3) issuance and redemption of Asset-Backed Securities, (4) execution of agreements required for carrying out the securitization plan filed by it, (5) temporary borrowing of funds necessary for the repayment of Asset-Backed Securities, (6) investment of surplus funds and (7) other business activities incidental to the above (1) through (6).[15] A Securitization SPC cannot carry out any other business.

5. Securitization

The ABS Act allows for four types of securtization structures by defining "Securitization" as one of the following transactions.[16] Therefore, in order to carry out securitization transactions under the ABS Act, the transaction structure must fall under one of the following;

(1) Originator transfers Securitized Assets to a Securitization SPC (or a foreign company engaging in only securitization), the Securitization SPC issues Asset-Backed Securities based on such assets, and makes payment of principal and interest or dividends on such securities from borrowed money or profits generated by administrating, managing or disposing of the Securitized Assets;

---

10 *Id.*, art. 2, item 4.
11 *Id.*, art. 2, item 5.
12 *Id.*, art. 17.
13 *Id.*, art. 20.
14 *Id.*, art. 10, 23.
15 *Id.*, art. 22(1).
16 *Id.*, art. 2, item 1.

(2) Originator entrusts Securitized Assets to a trustee company ("Trustee Company") licensed under the Capital Market and Financial Investment Business Act ("Capital Markets Act"), the Trustee Company issues Asset-Backed Securities based on such assets, and pays distributions on such securities from borrowed money or profits generated by administrating, managing or disposing of the Securitized Assets;

(3) Investors of Asset-Backed Securities issued by a Trustee Company entrust money to the Trustee Company, the Trustee Company buys Securitized Assets from the Originator with such money, and pays distributions on the Asset-Backed Securities from borrowed money or profits generated by administrating, managing or disposing of the Securitized Assets; or

(4) A 2-tiered structure where a Securization SPC or Trustee Company transfers Securitized Assets or Asset-Backed Securities based on such Securitized Assets to another Securitization SPC or Trustee Company, the transferee issues Asset-Backed Securities based on such assets or securities, and makes payment of principal and interest, dividends or distributions on such securities from borrowed money or profits generated by administrating, managing or disposing of the Securitized Assets.

B. Procedure of Securitization under the ABS Act

1. Filing of the securitization plan

In order to carry out securitization transactions under the ABS Act, the relevant Securitization SPC, the foreign company engaged only in securitization business or the Trustee Company ("SPVs") must file a securitization plan in a designated form with the Financial Services Commission ("FSC"), which has delegated its duties in this respect to the Financial Supervisory Service ("FSS"), its executory arm.[17] A Securitization SPC can only file one securitization plan.[18]

Since the ABS Act provides many benefits for carrying out a securitization transaction as discussed in more detail in Section II.C below, this provision of a mandatory requirement to file a securitization plan was instated to act as a supervisory tool to prevent any misuse of such benefits and ensure soundness in securitization transactions carried out under the ABS Act. The securitization plan also serves as a tool for providing

---

[17] *Id.*, art. 3.

[18] *Id.*, art. 3(2).

disclosure to investors, as the plan is registered and made available to the public through the electronic disclosure system of the FSS.[19] The relevant servicing agreement and the administration agreement are required to be attached to the securitization plan, and as such, documentation for the relevant securitization transaction is usually finalized before filing of the securitization plan.

The securitization plan must contain information on:

(1) the Securitization SPC, the foreign company engaged only in securitization business or the Trustee Company, as relevant, including the details on the officer, delegation of its business to the servicer and administrator and accounting method
(2) the Originator and its business, financials and officers and employees
(3) the type, total amount, valuation, method of transfer and other relevant information on the Securitized Assets
(4) details on the Securitization structure, the type, total amount, terms and conditions and redemption plans regarding the Asset-Backed Securities, method of servicing the Securitized Assets and plans for borrowing and management of funds, and
(5) other matters necessary for the protection of investors of Asset-Backed Securities.[20]

If there is any amendment to the information filed in the securitization plan, an amended filing must be made.

The FSS may refuse registration of the securitization plan or require amendments to it if (1) there is any false statement or requisite information that is omitted, (2) there is any item in the securitization plan that is in violation of law or (3) there is any violation of law regarding the establishment of the relevant Securitization SPC.[21] The FSS has 10 business days after a securitization plan has been submitted to decide whether to refuse registration or require amendments to such securitization plan. If the FSS does not refuse registration or require amendment within the 10 business-day period, the securitization plan is deemed to have been registered on the date of the filing.[22]

In practice, a draft securitization plan is submitted to the FSS or

19 Society for Research on Practices of Asset Securitization, *supra* note 1, at 307-308.
20 Supervisory Regulation on Asset-Backed Securitization Business, art. 4.
21 ABS Act, art. 5.
22 Supervisory Regulation on Asset-Backed Securitization Business, art. 7.

discussions with the FSS are held regarding the securitization structure before making a formal filing of the securitization plan in order to minimize the risk of refusal of registration or request for amendment by the FSS. The FSS exercises supervision over securitization transactions through this review process of the securitization plan.

2. Filing of the asset transfer registration

After a securitization plan is filed and accepted by the FSS and the Securitized Assets are transferred or entrusted pursuant to the securitization plan, the Originator must make an asset transfer registration as soon as the transfer or entrustment is made. An asset transfer registration must also be made by the SPVs as relevant, when there is a transfer or return of the Securitized Assets to the Originator, the SPV transfers or is returned the relevant Securitized Asset to or from another SPV, or the Securitized Assets are pledged or mortgaged or such pledge or mortgages are terminated, all pursuant to the relevant securitization plan.[23]

The asset transfer registration must be in the designated form and must contain information on (1) the Securitized Asset that is the subject of the relevant transfer, etc., (2) method of transfer, including timing and payment method, (3) special provisions in the relevant transfer agreement such as cancellation terms of transfer, right of first refusal of the Originator regarding the Securitized Assets, bearing of risk and asset warranty regarding the Securitized Assets, (4) whether the transfer is perfected against the obligors, (5) whether any special provisions of the ABS Act regarding transfer of Securitized Assets are applicable, (6) disclosure of relevant evidentiary documents to transfer and (7) other matters necessary for the protection of investors of Asset-Backed Securities.[24]

Unlike the securitization plan, there is no review process regarding asset transfer registrations. Once an asset transfer registration is made, there are some special benefits given regarding perfection, as more fully described in Section II.C below.

3. Issuance of Asset-Backed Securities

The Asset-Backed Securities can be issued after the asset transfer registration is made. However, if a public offering is to be made, a separate registration statement must be filed pursuant to the Capital Markets Act before the Asset-Backed Securities can be issued. The total amount of

---

[23] ABS Act, art. 6.

[24] Supervisory Regulation on Asset-Backed Securitization Business, art. 9.

Asset-Backed Securities that can be issued is limited to the sales price or valuation price of the Securitized Assets transferred or entrusted.[25]

C. Special Provisions in the ABS Act

1. Special provisions regarding perfection

In principle, in order to perfect transfer of receivables against the obligors, the Civil Code of Korea requires the transferor to send a notice to, or receive consent from, the relevant obligor. In order to perfect such transfer against third parties, such notice or consent must be fixed-date stamped. Such a perfection method would be very burdensome and virtually impossible to achieve in securitization transactions where there are thousands and in some cases, millions of obligors. In order to facilitate securitization, the ABS Act provides for some simplified rules of perfection.

First, perfection against third parties is deemed to have been made at the time asset transfer registration is made. Second, with respect to perfection against the obligor, not only the transferor but the transferee can also send the perfection notice to the obligor. Also, in the event the transferor or the transferee has sent perfection notices by content-proof mail twice but such notices have been returned, then the perfection notice will be deemed to have been made if a public notice of the transfer is made in two or more daily newspapers circulated in the area of the address of the obligor.[26]

In essence, the ABS Act still requires perfection notices to be sent to the obligors in order for perfection to occur against obligors (but relaxing the relevant requirements), while providing for a much simplified form of perfection against third parties. In practice, since the Originators usually act as the servicers of the Securitized Assets, there is not much need for perfection against the obligors, and perfection notices are only sent to obligors once the Originator is terminated as the servicer or early amortization events occur. The special provisions of the ABS Act on perfection serve as a useful tool in securitization transactions by ensuring perfection against third parties.

2. Fixation of claims secured by keun-mortgages

Keun-mortgage is a type of mortgage under the Civil Code which secures multiple unspecified fluctuating receivables that occur from a continuing contractual relationship, up to a registered maximum amount. Keun-mortgage is often used by banks in giving mortgage loans to customers. In

---

25 ABS Act, art. 33.
26 *Id.*, art. 7.

order to transfer a keun-mortgage, the Supreme Court of Korea is of the position that the amount of claims secured under the keun-mortgage has to be fixed. In order to fix the secured claims before the termination of the underlying contractual relationship, a consent from the obligor is needed. It would be practically impossible to carry out a mortgage-backed securitization if consents from the thousands and sometimes millions of obligors need to be obtained.

In order to solve this problem, the ABS Act provides that if the Originator sends a notice by content-proof mail to the obligor notifying the amount of claims secured by the keun-mortgage and the intent to not create any new claims secured by the keun-mortgage but transfer such fixed claims, the claims shall be deemed to have been fixed on the day after the date such notice is sent; provided that, if the obligor raises objections within 10 days, then the foregoing shall not apply.[27] By providing for fixation through notice instead of obtaining consent, the ABS Act greatly eased the process for mortgaged-backed securitization in Korea.

3. Acquisition of mortgages, etc.

The ABS Act also provides that if the receivables transferred pursuant to the securitization plan are secured by mortgages or pledges, the SPV acquires the mortgages or pledges at the time of asset transfer registration.[28] Under the Civil Code, in order to acquire a receivable secured by a mortgage, the transfer of the mortgage must be registered in the real estate registry.[29] In order to acquire a receivable secured by a pledge, there needs to be a transfer of the pledged property (if the pledged property is a movable asset) or a notice with a fixed-date stamp sent to the obligor (if the pledged property is a receivable). The ABS Act gets rid of these requirements.

This special provision of the ABS Act is especially helpful with respect to mortgages since most of the loan receivables held by financial institutions are secured by mortgages, and under the current real estate registry system, in order to make a registration one would need to apply for registration at the real estate registry office located in the area where the real estate is located. Therefore, without the above special provision, the Originator would have to file for registration of transfer of mortgages

---

27 *Id.*, art. 7-2.

28 *Id.*, art. 8.

29 The Civil Code requires all transfers of real rights (jus in rem) regarding real estate to be registered in the real estate registry for such transfers to be effective. An exception to such requirement is when the acquisition of such real rights is made pursuant to a provision in law. Article 8 of the ABS Act falls under such provision of law.

in all the real estate registry offices where the mortgaged properties are located, which may be thousand or millions in number, which would take a tremendous amount of effort and money. The ABS Act gets rid of this requirement thereby facilitating securitization of receivables secured by mortgages.

4. True sale

The essence of securitization is making securitized assets bankruptcy-remote from the originator, so that the investors of asset-backed securities are only exposed to the credit risk of the securitized assets and not the credit risk of the originator. In order to achieve this, the transfer of securitized assets from the originator to the transferee must be a true sale, and not an establishment of security interest.

In order to provide for legal certainty regarding true sale, the ABS Act requires the transfer of the Securitized Assets to meet the following requirements, in which case it shall be deemed that the transfer is not for the establishment of security interest;

(1) the transfer shall be by way of sale or exchange;
(2) the transferee must be entitled to the profit derived from the Securitized Assets and may dispose of the Securitized Assets at its discretion (this will not be negated even if the transferor has a first right of refusal in the event the transferee decides to dispose of the Securitized Assets);
(3) the transferor must not have the right to require return of the Securitized Assets, and the transferee must not have the right to require return of the consideration paid for the Securitized Assets; and
(4) the transferee must assume the risk regarding the Securitized Assets (in this regard, it is allowed for the transferor to bear the risk for a certain period or provide warranty for defect of the Securitized Assets (including where the transferor has warranted the repayment abilities of the obligors)).[30]

As mentioned in Section I, even before the enactment of the ABS Act, there were several attempts to carry out cross-border securitization transactions. One of the hurdles to successful consummation of the transactions was the lack of trust of overseas investors in achieving a true sale between the originator and the special-purpose company to whom the originator

30 ABS Act, art. 13.

would transfer the securitized assets, as there was no explicit rules or regulations or court precedent on point. The above provision on true sale was instated to act as a kind of a safe harbor provision to provide legal clarity on true sale and thereby induce investments from the bankruptcy risk sensitive foreign investors and to overall promote securitization transactions. However, as the provision requires all transactions carried out under the ABS Act to follow its requirements for true sale, it is not a true "safe harbor clause."[31]

Because the fulfillment of the above requirements is mandatory, in practice, a true sale opinion from the transaction legal counsel confirming that the transaction meets the above requirements is provided and the contents of such opinion are disclosed in the securitization plan. However, because the language of the above provision is broad and ambiguous in many respects, the interpretation of the above provision is sometimes challenging, especially regarding the fourth requirement requiring transfer of risk. The guideline of the FSS on this point is that all types of risk borne by the Originator regarding the Securitized Assets, whether in the form of subordinated Asset-Backed Securities, credit support, warranty liability regarding collectibility or otherwise, must be below 50 percent of the total risk regarding the Securitized Assets.

5. Tax benefits

The ABS Act and the related tax laws provide tax benefits for securitization transactions carried out under the ABS Act. Among such benefits, Securitized Assets transferred, entrusted or mortgaged pursuant to the securitization plan filed under the ABS Act are exempt from the requirement to purchase national housing bonds.[32] Pursuant to the Special Tax Treatment Control Law, acquisition tax and registration tax regarding Securitized Assets is reduced and withholding tax on interest income from Securitized Assets is exempt. Also, if a Securitization SPC distributes 90 percent or more of its distributable profit as dividends, then these dividends will be deducted from its taxable income.

D. Disclosure

The FSS must make available to the public the securitization plans, asset transfer registrations and any amendments thereto that are registered

---

[31] For a detailed discussion on the background for enactment of Article 13, *see* Society for Research on Practices of Asset Securitization, *supra* note 1, at 384.

[32] ABS Act, art. 36-2.

with the FSS.[33] In practice, these documents are loaded on the electronic disclosure system of the FSS (DART) and are accessible by the general public.

There is no explicit provision regarding ongoing disclosure. However, if there is any change in the securitization plan filed with the FSS, an amendment filing must be made. Also, If there is any additional transfer of Securitized Assets, then an asset transfer registration must be additionally filed, so to such limited extent there is some ongoing disclosure. The SPVs are also required to report to the FSS immediately upon the occurrence of the following events:

(1) a dissolution event occurs with respect to the SPV;
(2) Originator, servicer or administrator is unable to carry out its duties due to the insolvency or other similar event regarding such entity;
(3) there has been a termination or amendment to the servicing agreement, administration agreement or other important agreement, or the performance of the terms and conditions of such agreements are rendered impossible;
(4) with respect to transfer of Securitized Assets, the performance of agreement with respect to such transfer is rendered impossible or serious problems occur with respect to the exercise of rights with respect to such assets due to litigation or otherwise; or
(5) there occurs any serious problem with respect to the issuance, redemption or transfer of Asset-Backed Securities.[34]

The SPVs report the above events through the electronic disclosure system of the FSS, so to that extent, these reports conduct ongoing disclosure regarding Securitization transactions carried out under the ABS Act.

In addition, for public offerings of Asset-Backed Securities, the Capital Markets Act applies with respect to the issuance of such securities. Under the Capital Markets Act, an issuer of Asset-Backed Securities must file a registration statement with the FSC.[35] It must also prepare an investment prospectus and submit it to the FSC on the day the relevant registration statement becomes effective.[36] The contents of the registration statements and investment prospectus are tailored to reflect the different nature of the Asset-Backed Securities from other securities.

---

33 *Id.*, art. 9.
34 Supervisory Regulation on Asset-Backed Securitization Business, art. 19.
35 Capital Markets Act, art. 119(1).
36 *Id.*, art. 123(1).

There are ongoing reporting requirements under the Capital Markets Act for issuers of publicly offered Asset-Backed Securities. Such issuers are required to submit to the FSC and the Korea Exchange an annual report within 90 days of the end of the fiscal year, and quarterly and semi-annual reports within 45 days of the end of the relevant period.[37] Such reports must contain information on the issuer, the servicer and the method of servicing, status of the securitization transaction and other information necessary for the protection of investors.[38] However, in practice, the contents disclosed in these reports merely follow formality and do not provide substantive information regarding the status of the securitization transaction, such as the performance of the Securitized Assets, etc.[39]

III. PROPOSED AMENDMENTS TO THE ABS ACT

A. Expansion of Scope of Originator

The Proposed Amendments seek to expand the scope of entities eligible to become Originators by getting rid of the "good credit" requirement for corporations. Instead, the Proposed Amendments list corporations that were audited by an independent auditor for the latest financial year and that satisfy the standards prescribed by the FSC (which take into consideration credit worthiness or asset size) as eligible entities that can become Originators.

The reasoning put forth by the government behind the above proposal is that since the redemption of asset-backed securities depends on the value of the securitized asset sold or entrusted to the ABS, SPC, etc. and not on the Originator, there is a need to allow access to securitization under the ABS Act to corporations with qualifying assets even if their credit worthiness is somewhat low in order to provide for easier funding for such corporations.

As seen in Section II above, the current ABS Act and the relevant regulations thereunder restrict the scope of entities eligible to become Originators to mostly financial institutions and other public enterprises

---

37 *Id.*, art. 159(1), 160.

38 Regulation on Financial Investment Business, art. 4-3(4).

39 For a detailed discussion concerning the limits of the current disclosure system surrounding securitization, *see* Kim, Yeon Mi, *YuDongHwaJeungKwonAe ItSuh GaeSokJukIn GongSiAe KwanHan YeonGu [A Study on Ongoing Disclosure Regarding Asset-Backed Securities]*, The Korean Journal of Securities Law (June, 2007).

such as the Korea Asset Management Corporation. Other corporations are required to have a credit rating of investment grade or higher, or must be a listed company in order to qualify as an Originator. The reasoning behind such restriction is to minimize any misuse of the benefits provided by the ABS Act by restricting the entities that can carry out securitization transactions under the ABS Act. However, such an approach of limiting the scope of Originators under the current ABS Act has been under criticism as not being in line with the purpose of the ABS Act and giving excessive favor to financial institutions.[40]

One of the main benefits of securitization is that it allows originators to obtain lower cost funding by separating the high-credit securitized assets from the credit risk of the originator and issuing securities based on the credit risk of the securitized assets only. Companies whose debt securities are rated investment grade can usually issue securities in the capital markets at interest rates competitive with, or even lower than, other generally available sources of funds, such as bank loans and as such, may not have much need for securitization. On the other hand, securitization transactions can provide cost savings to originators whose debt securities are rated less than investment grade or whose securities are unrated, by enabling them to obtain funding through a special purpose vehicle whose debt securities have an investment grade rating.[41] However, since the current ABS Act allows only companies with investment grade ratings or listed companies as Originators eligible to conduct securitization pursuant the ABS Act, companies who most need to conduct securitization transactions under the benefit of the ABS Act are cut off from access.

Therefore, the Proposed Amendments seem to be in the right direction of getting rid of the entry barrier to use the ABS Act. However, since the FSC standards are yet to be announced, it remains to be seen by how much the barrier has been actually reduced.

---

40 Kim, Jae Hyung, *JaSanYuDongHwaAe GwanHan BubRyulUi HyunHwangGwa MoonJaeJum [Current Status and Problems of ABS Act]*, Human Rights and Justice, Vol. 293, 90 (Jan. 2001) (*criticizing* the ABS Act giving excessive favor to financial institutions); Hwang, In Seok, *JaSanYuDongHwaJaeDoUi MoonJaeJum Mit GaeSunBangAnAe GwanHan GoChal [A Study on Problems regarding the ABS System and Measures for Reform]*, Korea Legal Research, 239 (2005) (pointing out that companies with credit ratings of below investment grade may be in more need of funding through securitization).

41 Steven L. Schwarcz, The Alchemy of Asset Securitization, Stanford Journal of Law, Business & Finance, Vol 1:113 at 137 (1994).

B. Multiple Registration of Securitization Plans by Securitization SPCs

The Proposed Amendments allow a Securitization SPC to file more than one securitization plan if it is acquiring Securitized Assets from the same Originator. As a condition to such additional filing, the Securitization SPC must state in its initial securitization plan its intention to file additional securitization plans. Also, the period during which a Securtization SPC can file additional securitization plans is limited to a period set forth by the presidential decree to the ABS Act, which period shall be within 5 years from the date of the filing of the initial securitization plan. A Securitization SPC which has filed additional securitization plans must separately entrust the Securitized Assets for each securitization plan to a Trustee Company.

As mentioned in Section II.B above, the current ABS Act allows a Securitization SPC to file only one securitization plan. The reasoning put forth by the government behind the Proposed Amendments is that because of the above restriction, even Originators who carry out Securitization transactions on a repetitive basis with similar Securitized Assets need to establish a Securitized SPC every time it carries out a Securitization transaction, which requires additional time and costs. By enabling Originators to use the same Securtization SPC, it is expected that the Proposed Amendments will save time and costs from repetitive establishments of Securitization SPCs. The time limitation within which a Securtization SPC has to file additional securitization plans and the requirement for separate entrustment of Securitized Assets for each securitization plan are measures to protect investors.

The reason for restricting a Securitization SPC to file only one securitization plan in the first place was because if Securitization SPCs were allowed to file several securitization plans and carry out several securitization transactions, complex legal problems may arise such as segregation of Securitized Assets belonging to different securization transactions, and the legislators decided to simplify as much as possible considering that Korea was only in the initial stages of securitization.[42,43] However, as the securitization market developed, the requirement of setting up a new Securitization SPC each time an Originator conducted a securitization transaction proved to be costly and cumbersome, and there has been

---

[42] Society for Research on Practices of Asset Securitization, *supra* note 1, at 309.

[43] However, with respect to Trustee Companies, since the Trust Law of Korea and Capital Markets Act requires segregation of assets for each trust account, a Trustee Company is allowed under the current ABS Act to register multiple securitization plans for each trust account.

market demand to allow for Securitization SPCs to carry out multiple securitization transactions.[44]

The Proposed Amendments address this market demand. However, the Proposed Amendments require the Securitization SPC carrying out multiple securitization transactions to separately entrust the Securitized Assets for each transaction to a Trustee Company, thereby prohibiting commingling and sharing of Securitized Assets among each series of Securitization transactions. This requirement is aimed at protecting investors, but such rigid restriction may work against efficiency and require additional transaction cost, which undermines the purpose of allowing for multiple securitization plans in the first place. It may be more efficient for the investors to decide whether they want strict separation between different series of Securitized Assets or not. Providing for adequate disclosure, especially ongoing disclosure, could address the issue of investor protection in case of commingling of Securitized Assets. Also, the Proposed Amendments limit the period within which a Securitization SPC can file for additional securitization plans to 5 years. This period is very short compared to the market practice in the U.S. and Europe,[45] and so it may not be worth the effort of Originators to set up multiple series securitization programs. It is understandable that the government may want to take a more cautious approach since the master trust/master programme type structure is not fully developed in Korea, but depending on market development, re-examination of the adequacy of requiring separation of Securitized Assets and 5-year limitation period could be required.

C. Amendments to Provision regarding Acquisition of Mortgages, etc.

As mentioned in Section II.C(3) above, the ABS Act has a special provision enabling Securitization SPCs to acquire mortgages securing the receivables being securitized simply by making an asset transfer registration with the FSS, without having to register the transfer of mortgages in the real estate registry. However, since such special provision only

---

44 Master trust structure has been introduced in the Korean market and credit card companies have used the master trust structure to issue asset-backed securities starting from 2004. However, under the current ABS Act, a new Securitization SPC needs to be set up to acquire each series of the beneficial interest certificates issued by the Trustee Company in the master trust structure.

45 Master trust structures used in developed markets normally require an assignment of future receivables to be generated for up to 20 years after the structure is set up. *See* Tim Lester, Mohammed Asaria and Udo van der Linden, *Korea and Taiwan Follow Japanese Securitization Path*, IFLR at 42 (Nov. 2002).

provides for acquisition of mortgages by the Securitization SPC, in the event the Securitization SPC retransfers such Securitized Assets to the Originator,[46] under the Civil Code, the Securitization SPC would first need to register the transfer from the Originator to the Securitization SPC and then register the transfer from the Securitization SPC to the Originator.[47] This would greatly undercut the benefit provided by the special provision regarding the acquisition of mortgages.

In order to solve this problem, the Proposed Amendments provides that the Originator may also acquire mortgages or pledges that are securing receivables included as Securitized Assets by way of asset transfer registration. In practice, this problem is solved by structuring the retransfer from the Securitization SPC to the Originator as an agreed cancellation of the original transfer from the Originator to the Securitization SPC. In this way, it could be construed that registration of mortgages for such retransfer is not required under the Civil Code.[48] However, there was some legal uncertainty regarding such interpretation, and the Proposed Amendments take away the ambiguity by making it clear that any acquisition of mortgages by the Originator does not need to be registered in the real estate registry.

D. Strengthening of Disclosure

The Proposed Amendments require SPVs to make disclosure as soon as possible after the occurrence of the following matters;

(1) SPVs establish or terminate pledge or mortgage over Securitized Assets;
(2) a dissolution event occurs with respect to the SPV;
(3) the servicer, administrator or the Trustee Company who is entrusted with the Securitized Assets for multiple securitization plans by the

---

[46] Such need for retransfer may arise at the end of a securitization transaction where the Securitization SPC has repaid all of the Asset-Backed Securities and the Originator wishes to acquire the remaining Securitized Assets, or in a case where there is a breach of asset warranty given by the Originator regarding a Securitized Asset and the Securitized SPC receives the indemnity payments from the Originator regarding the breach and needs to retransfer such Securitized Asset to the Originator.

[47] This is because under the Civil Code, even if acquisition of real rights regarding real estate was made pursuant to provision of law and thereby became effective without the registration in the real estate registry, in order to make any further transfers, registration in the real estate registry is required.

[48] Under the Civil Code, in the event of cancellation of a transfer, the related real rights are interpreted to return to the transferor as a matter of course and registration in the real estate registry is not required for such change to be effective.

relevant SPV is unable to carry out its duties and obligations due to its dissolution, bankruptcy, cancellation of license, suspension of business or other analogous events; or

(4) other events necessary for the protection of investors of Asset-Backed Securities as set out in the Presidential Decree to the ABS Act.

These amendments have been proposed to strengthen investor protection by requiring disclosure of events that may affect the management and administration of Securitized Assets, performance of agreements regarding the relevant Securitization transaction and redemption of Asset-Backed Securities. While it is good that the ABS Act is strengthening ongoing disclosure through the Proposed Amendments above, there seems to be room for improvement in this area, as further discussed in Section IV below.

E. Others

The current ABS Act restricts entities eligible to become servicers of Securitization SPCs to (1) Originators, (2) entities licensed under the Act on Use and Protection of Credit Information with all of the credit inquiry business license, credit investigation business license and claims collection license, and (3) other entities that meet specific requirements as set out in the Presidential Decree. The Proposed Amendments seek to broaden the scope of entities eligible to become servicers by only requiring the claims collection license instead of all of the above three licenses under the Act on the Use and Protection of Credit Information.

Also, the Proposed Amendments seeks to get rid of the minimum capital requirement applicable to Securitization SPCs under the Commercial Code, and to exempt the Securitization SPCs from the obligation to make legal reserves required under the Commercial Code.

IV. FURTHER CONSIDERATIONS

A. Improvements to Disclosure

On a worldwide basis, one of the key areas of reform regarding securitization after the recent global financial crisis has been the improvement of disclosure regarding securitization transactions. The International Organization of Securities Commissions ("IOSCO") reports a wide consensus on the need to improve disclosure to investors so that they have the necessary information that would allow them to perform robust due diligence. Especially, improvements have been called for in regard to (1) initial and ongoing information about the underlying asset pool performance, as well as on the creditworthiness of any person with direct or indirect liability to the issuer, and (2) representations and warranties to be provided by the originator to ensure, among others, the buy-back of the underlying assets under certain conditions.[49]

In this regard, the Dodd–Frank Wall Street Reform and Consumer Protection Act (the "Dodd–Frank Act") enacted by the U.S. to address the problems raised by the global financial crisis, requires the U.S. Securities Exchange Commission ("SEC") to, among others, (1) adopt regulations requiring each issuer of an asset-backed security to disclose, for each tranche or class of security, information regarding the assets backing that security, which shall require issuers of asset-backed securities, at a minimum, to disclose asset-level or loan-level data, if such data are necessary for investors to independently perform due diligence, and (2) prescribe regulations on the use of representations and warranties in the market for asset-backed securities that require, among others, any securitizer to disclose fulfilled and unfulfilled repurchase requests across all trusts, aggregated by the securitizer, so that investors may identify asset originators with clear underwriting deficiencies.[50]

Pursuant to the Dodd–Frank Act, the SEC has adopted, among others, Rule 15Ga-1 requiring a securitizer to disclose, on an ongoing basis, any repurchase activity relating to applicable outstanding asset-backed securities, including (1) the assets that were subject to a repurchase demand, including investor repurchase demands upon a trustee; (2) the assets that were repurchased or replaced; (3) the assets that were not repurchased or replaced because the demand was withdrawn or rejected; and (4) the assets that are pending repurchase or replacement due to a cure period or dispute.[51]

The SEC has also proposed rules[52] requiring issuers of asset-backed

---

[49] Emerging Markets Committee of the International Organization of Securities Commissions, Securitization and Securitized Debt Instruments in Emerging Markets, Final Report (Oct. 2010), which can be found at http://www.iosco.org/library/pubdocs/pdf/IOSCOPD334.pdf.

[50] Dodd–Frank Act, Sec. 942(c), Sec. 943.

[51] SEC Rel. Nos 33-9175 and 34-63741, Disclosure for Asset-Backed Securities Required by Section 943 of the Dodd–Frank Wall Street Reform and Consumer Protection Act available at www.sec.gov/rules/final/2011/33-9175.pdf.

[52] SEC Release No. 33-9244, Re-proposal of Shelf Eligibility Conditions for Asset-Backed Securities, available at http://www.sec.gov/rules/proposed/2011/33-9244.pdf and SEC Release No. 33-9117, Asset-Backed Securities, available at http://www.sec.gov/rules/proposed/2010/33-9117fr.pdf.

securities to provide detailed, ongoing, asset-level or grouped account data regarding both the characteristics of the pool assets and related obligors and collateral, and the performance of the pool assets. The proposal sets forth general data requirements for assets underlying all SEC-registered asset-backed securities and specific data requirements for 10 asset classes; residential mortgage loans, commercial mortgage loans, auto loans, auto leases, equipment loans, equipment leases, student loans, floorplan financings, corporate debt and resecuritizations. Issuers of credit card and charge card asset-backed securities are exempt from the asset-level disclosure requirements, but instead would be required to provide grouped account data, which would be created by compressing the asset-level data into groups organized by combinations of account characteristics.

As seen in Section II above, the ABS Act requires a securitization plan and asset transfer registration to be filed with the FSS in order to conduct a securitization transaction, whether private or public, under the ABS Act. The securitization plan and asset transfer registration contains detailed information regarding the transaction, including specific information on the type, size, valuation and transfer method of Securitized Assets. As such, there currently seems to be an adequate system of disclosure at the initial stage of a securitization transaction. The Proposed Amendments seek to address the issue of ongoing disclosure by requiring disclosure of important events that occur after the issuance of asset-backed securities that may impact investors.

However, the Proposed Amendments do not provide for disclosure regarding the performance of Securitized Assets after the issuance of asset-backed securities nor on the creditworthiness of any person with direct or indirect liability to the issuer. It also does not cover repurchase activities by the Originator during the term of the securitization transaction. The global financial crisis has proved the importance of adequate ongoing disclosure, as well as initial disclosure for securitization transactions. It is desirable for the ABS Act to also provide for ongoing disclosure regarding the above matters for the better protection of investors, especially as the market develops and more complex securitization structures emerge. Very detailed disclosure rules released by the SEC can serve as a reference point in addressing this issue in the ABS Act.

B. Risk Retention

Another key area of reform regarding securitization after the global financial crisis has been the alignment of incentives through risk-retention practices. The IOSCO reports a wide recognition on the need to better align incentives of different participants in the securitization chain to the longer-term performance of securitized assets. The G-20 has recommended that originators be required to retain a portion of the asset-backed securities issued as a key element to align their incentives with the longer-term performance of the securitized assets.[53]

The Dodd–Frank Act also requires the relevant regulators including the SEC to adopt regulations to require any securitizer to retain in principle at least 5 percent of the credit risk for any asset that the securitizer, through the issuance of an asset-backed security, transfers, sells or conveys to a third party.[54] In accordance therewith, the SEC and the relevant regulators have proposed rules[55] which require a sponsor to retain an economic interest equal to at least 5 percent of the credit risk of the assets collateralizing an issuance of asset-backed securities. The proposed rules permit a sponsor to choose from a menu of risk-retention options, which were designed to provide appropriate flexibility, while also ensuring that the sponsors actually retain risks designed to align incentives.[56]

In Korea, it is market practice for Originators to retain a portion of the asset-backed securities issued in a securitization transaction.[57] Of course there are cases where the Originator does not retain any credit risk, but usually the Originator holds a portion of the subordinated bonds issued by a Securitization SPC or the subordinated beneficial interest issued by a Trustee Company, and provides a warranty regarding the Securitized Assets. Indeed, it has been an issue as to what extent the Originator can take on the risk associated with the Securitized Assets without compromising true sale, and the guideline of the FSS on this matter is that the total risk exposure of the Originator with respect to the Securitized Assets should not exceed 50 percent of the total risk related to the Securitized Assets. In calculating 50 percent, all forms of risk retention are included, such as subscription of subordinated Asset-Backed Securities issued, provision of warranties regarding collectibility and retention of cash reserves. This prevalent market practice of risk retention by Originators is perhaps

---

[53] Emerging Markets Committee of the International Organization of Securities Commissions. *supra* note 49 at 13.

[54] Dodd–Frank Act, Sec 941.

[55] SEC Rel. No. 34-64148, Credit Risk Retention, available at http://www.sec.gov/rules/proposed/2011/33-64148.pdf.

[56] Testimony on Understanding the Implications and Consequences of the Proposed Rule on Risk Retention given by Meredith Cross, director of Division Corporation Finance of SEC before the Subcommittee on Capital Markets and Government Sponsored Enterprises of the United States House of Representatives, available at http://www.sec.gov/news/testimony/2011/ts041411mc.htm.

[57] Emerging Markets Committee of the International Organization of Securities Commissions, *supra* note 49 at 23.

due to the fact that the securitization market is not yet matured in Korea and there is still reliance on the Originator to provide credit enhancement in the form of risk retention. Also, the requirement of filing securitization plans and the review process of such securitzation plan by the FSS act as a screening mechanism to protect investors.

As such, it does not seem to be a pressing point at this time for the ABS Act to require risk retention. However, there is a limit to the extent the government can protect investors through the review of the securitization plan, and misalignment of interest is an inherent problem of securitization. Originators create and have the most information about the securitized assets, but unless they have some stake in the transaction after the issuance of asset-backed securities, after they transfer the securitized assets and the risk associated with such assets, they are not affected by the performance of the assets transferred. As such, they have no incentive to maximize returns for investors who do not have direct access to information on the securitized assets. Therefore consideration needs also to be given to requiring mandatory retention of risk by the Originators in the ABS Act to address this issue, especially as the market develops and credit enhancement by Originators is not as prevalent.

C. Synthetic Securitization

One of the amendments to the ABS Act that was anticipated but was not included in the Proposed Amendments is the amendment to allow synthetic securtization transactions under the ABS Act. There has actually been one case of synthetic CDOs issued under the ABS Act, which was consummated in May, 2005. The purpose of that transaction was for the Industrial Bank of Korea to transfer its credit exposure from a credit support agreement that it entered into with respect to the senior Asset-Backed Securities issued in another securitization transaction. The transaction structure was not the same as that of a typical synthetic CDO. The Industrial Bank of Korea did not enter into a credit default swap directly with the Securitization SPC nor did the Securitization SPC directly purchase the collateral with the proceeds from the securities it issued, as would be the case in a typical synthetic CDO transaction.[58] Instead, the Industrial Bank of Korea first entered into a credit default swap with a bridge financial institution, Samsung Securities Co., Ltd., who also bought collateral

---

[58] For a detailed discussion on the structures of typical synthetic securitization, *see* Ian Bell and Petrina Dawson, *Synthetic Securitization: Use of Derivative Technology for Credit Transfer*, 12 Duke J. Comp. & Int'l L. at 557-560 (2002).

assets with its own proprietary assets. Samsung Securities Co., Ltd., acting as the Originator then transferred the collateral assets and the credit default swap agreement to FNfine Securitization Specialty Co., Ltd., the Securitization SPC established for that securitization transaction.[59]

The reason for such a unique structure was because of the requirements of the ABS Act. The ABS Act requires transactions to be carried out pursuant to the ABS Act to fall under one of the structures defined as "Securitization," and under such definition there has to be a transfer of Securitized Assets from the Originator to the Securitization SPC. As such, in the above transaction, the collateral assets acted as Securitized Assets and Samsung Securities Co., Ltd. acted as the Originator. The FSS also required the Originator to negotiate and execute the credit default swap and then transfer such agreement to the Securitization SPC, as it felt that it would be inadequate for a Securitization SPC to negotiate such agreement.[60]

However, after the above transaction, FSS changed its position and has since been of the position that synthetic securitization transactions are not allowed under the current ABS Act because there is no funding through asset sale in such transaction but only transfer of risk, which is outside the scope of the ABS Act. Since the FSS has taken such a stance, there have been requests from the industry to amend the ABS Act to include synthetic ABS transactions as Securitization transactions that can be carried out under the ABS Act.[61] The inclusion of synthetic securitization transactions as part of Securitization was one of the draft proposed amendments to the ABS Act in 2007, but it was not included in the Proposed Amendments presumably due to the global financial crisis to which synthetic CDOs were believed to have contributed.

But keeping synthetic securitization transactions out of the ABS Act does not seem to be the right way forward. Synthetic securitization enables financial institutions to pass their unwanted credit risks onto the capital markets in a very flexible way.[62] True, the global financial crisis

---

59 The details of the securitization structure carried out by FNfine Securitization Specialty Co., Ltd. can be found in the securitization plan filed by it which is available on http://dart.fss.or.kr.

60 Symposium, *supra* note 4, at 25-26.

61 As a result of FSS's prohibition of synthetic CDO transactions under the ABS Act, a number of synthetic ABS transactions were carried out outside the ABS Act in the form of ABCPs.

62 For a detailed discussion on the benefits of synthetic securitization, *see* Ian Bell and Petrina Dawson, *supra* note 58 at 550, and Frank Partnoy and David A. Skeel, Jr., *The Promise and Perils of Credit Derivatives,* 75 U. Cin. L. Re. at 1022-1031, (2006-2007).

has highlighted the downsides of synthetic securitization, such as complex structures difficult for investors to understand and transfer of risk creating misalignment of interest. But adequate disclosure and proper alignment of incentives could alleviate such downsides. Simply banning synthetic securitization under the ABS Act to avoid such downsides also has the potential of banning beneficial transactions that may take place. Admittedly, it is not the best time to include synthetic securitization in the ABS Act considering the global financial crisis and the fact that demand for synthetic securitization is not high at the moment in the Korean market. But, as the market develops, it may become beneficial to include synthetic securitization within the scope of the ABS Act. Of course, in allowing for synthetic securitization transactions under the ABS Act, measures to address the potential problems that may arise with respect to such transactions should also be taken, such as requiring adequate disclosure and risk retention.

V. CONCLUSION

Since the enactment of the ABS Act, the securitization market in Korea has grown tremendously, and the ABS Act no doubt has played an important role in bringing about such growth. The ABS Act has provided the legal framework to enable securitization to take place under the Korean legal system in a much more efficient manner, and has provided legal clarity and assurance necessary for the market to grow.

However, the securitization market has evolved in Korea while the ABS Act has not changed much since its enactment, and some revisions are needed to bring the ABS Act up to the market. The Proposed Amendments address some of the long awaited revisions to the ABS Act, such as expanding the scope of entities eligible to become Originators, and allowing for a single Securitization SPC to carry out multiple securitization transactions. But as the Proposed Amendments were made in the wake of the global financial crisis, the government seems to have taken a more cautious approach in meeting the market demand. Allowing for synthetic securitization to take place under the ABS Act while strengthening ongoing disclosure and requiring risk retention would be a good next step forward.

Securitization in Korea is currently facing some tough challenges. The global financial crisis has reduced the market size. One of the main purposes of securitization is to improve the financial structure of a corporation through off-balance sheet funding, but Korea adopted the International Financial Reporting Standards in 2011, which now makes obtaining off-balance sheet treatment very difficult. It is hoped that the Proposed Amendments will encourage further growth of the securitization market and provide the foundation for the securitization market to more fully develop and mature in Korea.

9. Private equity in Korea: history, industry and policy

Hwa-Jin Kim and Alice Z. Chen

I. INTRODUCTION

When the Korean economy first opened its doors to the world in 1996 as a condition of its acceptance into the Organization for Economic Cooperation and Development ("OECD"),[1] the country's policies, regulations, and social and political mindsets were not ready for financial globalization. This plunged Korea into the Asian financial crisis, which resulted in a forced conciliation to the International Monetary Fund for loans and a hasty embrace of foreign capital without a proper understanding of the underlying risks or policies required.

Korea initially welcomed investments from foreign private equity funds ("PEFs"). Such funds typically raise capital from institutions and individuals such as pension funds and university endowments. Buyout PEFs invest this capital in companies that are on the brink of bankruptcy, laden with distressed assets, or undervalued by the market. The buyout funds then restructure these companies using different business strategies to make improvements, and usually make an exit within two to four years by selling the improved company to a strategic buyer or taking their shares to the public market through an initial public offering.[2]

Initially viewed as white knights in the years immediately following the Asian financial crisis, public sentiment toward foreign PEFs gradually

1 Hye-Sun Hwang, The Impact and Implication of Capital Globalization on Korea after 1997: From the Perspective of Foreign Private Equity Funds 12 (Feb. 2008) (unpublished M.A. thesis, Korea University Graduate School of International Studies) (on file with author).

2 Jiyeon Shin and Wonseok Woo, *An Analysis of Private Equity Funds in Korea and Their Role in the Korean Economy in the Post-Crisis Period*, 9 INT'L STUD. REV. 54 (2008). *See generally*, Josh Lerner et al., VENTURE CAPITAL AND PRIVATE EQUITY: A CASEBOOK, 4th ed. (2009); Brian Cheffins and John Armour, *The Eclipse of Private Equity*, 33 DEL. J. CORP. L. 1 (2008).

shifted as Koreans watched these funds "grip and flip" Korean companies, essentially making enormous profits without paying taxes to Korea. Foreign PEFs were recast as corporate raiders and Korea proceeded to have a knee-jerk reaction to punish them via lawsuits, investigations, and the introduction of a capital gains tax on foreign funds that built their headquarters in tax-exempt areas and invested in Korea.

In response to the uncertainty caused by this backlash, deal activity flattened in 2006. However, a second wave of private equity has emerged in Korea due to a more welcoming government position toward foreign investment, the emergence of attractive targets caused by the depression of the Korean won ("KRW"), the sale of assets by family-owned conglomerates (known as *chaebols*) burdened by debt, and new strategies for investment.

The current PEF landscape is dramatically different from 2006. The government has further relaxed the rules governing the PEF industry, and domestic resistance to foreign investment has abated. A nascent domestic PEF industry has developed, with the most successful firms employing a business model comprised of domestic and foreign elements. What follows is an examination of the PEF industry and the various roles it has played in Korean history, from white knight to corporate raider, and culminating in the hybrid funds existing today that are a testament to Korea's acceptance and adoption of global financial models.

II. SETTING THE STAGE: THE ASIAN FINANCIAL CRISIS

From the 1960s to the 1990s, Korea enjoyed remarkable economic growth without significant international investment.[3] While other Asian nations such as Singapore and Malaysia invited in multinational companies, Korea created its own enterprises and aggressively marketed its products around the world. Korea recognized that continued growth and integration in the global markets would require some degree of liberalization, but having seen what happened in the United States where deregulation had culminated in the 1980s savings-and-loan debacle, Korea decided to take it slow.[4] However, Wall Street saw profitable opportunities and did not want to wait. Under pressure from the United States and as a condition

---

3 Until the mid-1990s, Korea recorded a high growth rate of 7 percent annually. Hwang, *supra* note 1, at 40.

4 Joseph E. Stiglitz, Globalization and Its Discontents 102 (2003).

to joining the OECD in 1996, Korea relinquished its tight control over its financial markets and permitted domestic firms to borrow abroad.[5]

In 1997, following the collapse of the Thai baht, Korea became one of many nations embroiled in the Asian financial crisis. At that time, the crisis came from the sudden increase in overseas short-term loans, large foreign exchange liabilities, a lack of reserves, a vulnerable financial industry, weak financial supervision, and capital outflow of foreign funds as foreign banks who had been so eager to lend money to Korean firms decided not to roll over their loans.[6] To make matters worse, the pre-1996 centralized economy provided preferential treatment to family-owned *chaebols* with political ties, leaving the nation with high expenses, low efficiency, weakening export competency and a deficit in current accounts.[7]

Korea did not realize how risky foreign capital was until it had to purchase U.S. dollars to stopgap the shortage in its foreign reserve, causing the value of the Korean won to plunge. Companies went bankrupt continuously, and foreign investors withdrew their money from the Korean market based on the assumption that the crisis might affect the fragile economic fundamentals of the nation.[8]

All of this led Korea to ask the International Monetary Fund ("IMF") for financial aid. As a condition to providing aid, the IMF required Korea to satisfy certain conditions, including: immediate closure of insolvent financial institutions; increase interest rates; reform corporate governance structures and practices; improve management transparency and reporting procedures; and provide a flexible job market.[9] Korea also had to commit to liberalizing its financial market up to 55 percent by the end of 1998, making the country more open and friendly to foreign investment.[10]

As a result of these policies, the Korean economy's dependency on foreign capital increased even further and the door to the Korean market

---

[5] *Id.* at 94.

[6] Hwang, *supra* note 1, at 11; Hyeong-nam Pak, The 1997 Financial Crisis in Korea and the Role of the Private Equity Fund 1 (Feb. 2007) (unpublished M.A. thesis, Korea University Graduate School of International Studies) (on file with author).

[7] Hwang, *supra* note 1, at 11.

[8] *Id.* at 12.

[9] Charles Harvie and Hyun-Hoon Lee, Korea's Economic Miracle, Fading or Reviving? 85 (2003).

[10] Fair One Park, Corporate Governance and the Future of Foreign Private Equity Funds in Korea: The Case of Lone Star Funds in Korea Exchange Bank 14 (Feb. 2007) (unpublished M.A. thesis, Ewha Women's University Graduate School of International Studies) (on file with author).

was now much more accessible to foreign investors and businesses.[11] As of 2007, foreign capital controlled more than 43 percent of the stock market, 65 percent of the banks, and 50 percent of the blue-chip companies in Korea.[12] South Korean economists knew that the policies being pushed on their country by the IMF would be disastrous, but they were afraid to openly disagree. "The IMF could not only cut off its own funds, but could use its bully pulpit to discourage investments from private market funds by telling private sector financial institutions of the doubts the IMF had about Korea's economy."[13] Korea had no choice.

Korea felt that foreign PEFs were the solution. They hoped that such funds would provide Korea's financial institutions with a much needed transfusion of capital, introduce advanced financial techniques, create more jobs, and provide a broad overhaul of corporate governance with a resultant enhancement in efficient management skills and the transparency of domestic businesses, leading to higher market valuations.[14]

III. WHITE KNIGHTS: PRIVATE EQUITY'S FIRST FORAY INTO SOUTH KOREA

Private equity investors swarmed into Korea in the aftermath of the Asian financial crisis, with a particular interest in the country's ailing domestic banking industry. The foreign-owned equity ratio in Korean financial institutions and financial services firms increased from 14.6 percent in 1997 to 59.2 percent in 2004 in Korea, whereas in other East Asian countries, the ratio was generally less than 20 percent.[15] This was due to a number of reasons.

From the standpoint of the foreign PEFs, who were earning limited returns in advanced countries, the newly liberalized Korean market would enable them to generate profits by acquiring domestic banks, improve their value through restructuring, then sell them within a short period of time.[16] The theory was that the different ownership structure of a PEF would allow companies to make these restructuring decisions at pivotal moments, a luxury that is lacking in publicly held companies

---

[11] Hwa-Jin Kim, *The Case of Market for Corporate Control in Korea* (2009) Oxford U Comp. L Forum 2 at ouclf.iuscomp.org, text after note 15.

[12] Pak, *supra* note 6, at 22.

[13] STIGLITZ, *supra* note 4, at 42.

[14] Hwang, *supra* note 1, at 29.

[15] Pak, *supra* note 6, at 7.

[16] *Id.* at 5-6.

with their quarterly earnings pressures and accountability to diverse shareholders.[17]

From Korea's perspective, it made sense to relax its regulations regarding the acquisition of domestic firms by foreign capital in order to facilitate transactions that would help the nation's financially troubled banks and improve efficiency in the banking industry.[18]

A. Benefits of PEF Involvement in Korea

Foreign PEF involvement in Korea did indeed bring about many of the benefits the Korean government had anticipated. These PEFs were seen as white knights, speeding up Korea's economic recovery by stabilizing the Korean banking industry, providing badly needed foreign exchange liquidity in the post-crisis period, facilitating financial reform, and introducing new advanced financial services and financial techniques to the then under-developed Korean financial market.[19]

Foreign PEFs also succeeded in creating a better model of corporate governance and challenging the traditional *chaebol* system. Many efforts to improve the corporate governance system of Korean companies have been undertaken since the 1997 Asian financial crisis,[20] and such improvements are particularly necessary in the domestic banking industry because banks work with the public, and need to conduct fair and transparent transactions and operations in order to gain trust and attract potential customers.[21] At the same time, borrowers must establish a reliable background in order to become potential candidates to receive the financing, so banks should not only practice good corporate governance themselves but are also responsible for ensuring that corporations improve their corporate governance practices.[22]

Finally, although PEFs certainly reaped a reward for their successful restructuring strategies, so too did the companies they invested in, as is evidenced below:

---

17 Justin Robertson, *Private Equity and Asian Political Economy: "Domestic" Private Equity Funds as New Actors*, 50 ASIAN SURV. 359 (2010).

18 Pak, *supra* note 6, at 5-6.

19 *Id.* at 8.

20 Hwa-Jin Kim, *Living with the IMF: A New Approach to Corporate Governance and Regulation of Financial Institutions in Korea*, 17 BERKELEY J. INT'L L. 61 (1999).

21 Park, *supra* note 10, at 25.

22 *Id.*

B. Case 1: Newbridge Capital's Acquisition of Korea First Bank in 1999

In 1999, Newbridge Capital acquired a 51 percent stake in Korea First Bank for US$454 million. Newbridge Capital held the investment for six years, from 1999 until 2005, making a complete exit in early 2005. The exit value was US$3.3 billion, of which US$1.7 billion was paid to Newbridge.[23]

Korea First Bank went through dramatic changes after Newbridge assumed control in 1999. Newbridge identified the troubled bank's major problem as a costly institutional branch network. The new management streamlined branch operations with simpler layouts in high-traffic consumer locations, consolidating some branches and closing others. The new management focused on information technology to centralize back office processes, customer service, and risk management. The bank also introduced mortgage loans with maturities of more than 30 years and monthly fees on low-amount deposit accounts. It gradually reduced business with large conglomerates and focused on households and small- and medium-sized companies, which helped the bank reduce bad loans and maintain a high capital-adequacy ratio.[24]

C. Case 2: The Carlyle Group's Acquisition of KorAm Bank in 2000

The Carlyle Group has been very successful with past investment in South Korea. The Washington firm invested $40 million in South Korea's KorAm Bank in June 2000, and then co-invested with JPMorgan Corsair to pump US$395 million of equity into the bank. Four years later, it sold its stake to Citigroup for US$2.6 billion, generating an internal rate of return of around 25 percent.[25]

At the time of its exit in 2004, significant improvements had been made in the KorAm Bank's non-performing loan and capital adequacy ratios. Under Carlyle's management, KorAm Bank was able to cut costs and reduce its expense ratio from 58.4 percent to 32.1 percent, one of the lowest ratios in the banking industry.[26]

---

[23] Jiyeon Shin and Wonseok Woo, *An Analysis of Private Equity Funds in Korea and Their Role in the Korean Economy in the Post-Crisis Period*, 9 INT'L STUD. REV. 58 (2008).

[24] *Id.* at 61.

[25] Kelly Holman, *South Korea's New PE Age?*, IDDMAGAZINE.COM, June 5, 2009, http://www.pgpcapital.com/pages/pdfs/IDD_06052009.pdf.

[26] Shin, *supra* note 23, at 61.

IV. CORPORATE RAIDERS: THE BACKLASH AGAINST FOREIGN PRIVATE EQUITY FUNDS

Public sentiment toward foreign PEFs began to change as Koreans watched many such funds earn enormous returns without contributing anything to the economy in the way of taxes. This brought about controversy regarding "national wealth outflow" by foreign PEFs.[27] There were also concerns that the relatively short-term investments by some foreign PEFs would harm domestic corporations in other ways. The Korean media termed the activities of foreign PEFs as "eat and run," viewing their investments as more speculation than investment.[28]

A. Main Critiques of Foreign PEF Involvement in Korea

Foreign PEFs don't pay taxes: In the post crisis period, the Korean government was keen to make Korea more attractive for foreign investment. One way it did so was by creating tax-free incentives to foreign PEFs, which resulted in a backlash against these same PEFs when they turned profits without paying taxes to the Korean government.[29]

Foreign PEFs are greedy and socially irresponsible: The Korean public argued that foreign PEFs and the firms and banks they controlled didn't invest locally, didn't contribute to the local bailout, and didn't provide loans to businesses, choosing instead to remain risk averse and increase profits.[30]

Foreign PEFs maximize short-term profits to the detriment of long-term growth: Foreign PEFs engage in a policy of shareholder capitalism, seeking to maximize short-term profit instead of implementing long-term growth strategies. Until the mid-1990s, Korea recorded a high growth rate of 7 percent annually, but in the period from 2000 to 2006 after the IMF bailout the growth rate plunged to 4.5 percent. This can be attributed to a shift in management practices toward the seeking of financial soundness and to a reduction of investment in facilities.[31] The Korean public accused foreign PEFs of being speculative and encroaching on the public interest in the name of maximization of shareholder profits through massive lay-offs, bulky dividends and frequent share buybacks.[32] Since shareholders

27 Pak, *supra* note 6, at 2.
28 Shin, *supra* note 23, at 56.
29 Pak, *supra* note 6, at 10.
30 *Id.* at 9.
31 Hwang, *supra* note 1 at 40.
32 Pak, *supra* note 6 at 11, 22.

were only interested in retrieving their investments in the shortest time possible, the capital base needed for long-term investments began to dry up.[33] Korean institutions were also concerned that this focus on short-term investment might have a negative effect on corporate governance, as described below.[34]

B. Case: Lone Star's Acquisition of Korea Exchange Bank in 2003

Lone Star was established in 1991 in Dallas, Texas as a closed-end, private-equity limited partnership. Its principals began to invest globally in 1995, raising a US$13.3 billion fund that invested in non-performing loans and real estate in Asia, North America, and Europe. 75 percent of these invested assets were concentrated in Asia. Lone Star began to invest in Korean real estate after the financial crisis, but was determined to expand its business into the Korean financial market to generate larger returns. After making unsuccessful bids on two Korean domestic banks, Seoul Bank and Cho Hung Bank, Lone Star successfully acquired 51 percent of Korea Exchange Bank's ("KEB") shares for KRW 1.084 trillion in October 2003.[35] Lone Star later tried to sell KEB to Commerzbank in 2005 for a return of over KRW 4 trillion, but its attempt was blocked.[36]

After a long investigation and much litigation, Lone Star finally reached an agreement to sell its 51 percent stake in KEB to Hana Financial Group for KRW 4.69 trillion or US$4.1 billion.[37] Initially, Hana Financial Group was supposed to complete the takeover by late May 2011, but the parties reached an agreement to extend the deal for six months due to the Korean FSC's decision to delay its review of whether Lone Star was an eligible shareholder of KEB.[38] In the negotiations to extend the deal deadline, Hana Financial Group reportedly tried to lower the takeover price by KRW 283 billion when KEB's board paid out a quarterly dividend of KRW 1510 per share, allowing Lone Star to rake in dividends of KRW 496.9 billion. Hana Financial Group also declared in a regulatory filing

---

33 *Id.*

34 Park, *supra* note 10, at iv.

35 *Id.* at 5-8.

36 Chang-Hee Yun, *Lone Star Must Return to Korea Exchange Bank*, JOONGANG DAILY, 19 June 2006, at E1.

37 Evelyn M. Rusli, *Lone Star Set for Korean Deal*, N.Y. TIMES, Nov. 24, 2010, http://dealbook.nytimes.com/2010/11/24/lone-star-set-for-korean-deal/.

38 Cynthia J. Kim, *Hana, Lone Star agree to extend KEB deal,* THE KOREA HERALD, July 8, 2011, http://www.koreaherald.com/business/Detail.jsp?newsMLId=20110708000589.

that Hana Bank would be lending KRW 1.5 trillion to Lone Star in loans backed by the U.S. company's 51 percent stake in KEB.[39]

In March 2011, the Supreme Court of Korea overturned a lower court's decision to acquit Lone Star's former head of Seoul operations and Lone Star's Belgium-based unit, which holds a majority stake in KEB, of rigging stock prices in relation to KEB's credit card unit, and ordered a new trial. A Seoul High Court Judge said the ruling would be made on October 6, 2011 after witnesses testified and prosecutors and defense lawyers wrapped up their cases in Lone Star's trial on September 8, 2011.[40] The FSC will look into whether Lone Star was an eligible buyer of KEB. If the court holds that Lone Star is an ineligible shareholder in KEB, the FSC can order the U.S. buyout fund to sell out its stake in KEB exceeding 10 percent within six months. These shares could be transferred to Hana Financial Group in the process, given the fact there is no rule designating the means of disposal.[41]

Lone Star's ownership of KEB did produce some positive effects on KEB's corporate governance. Robert E. Fallon was designated as President of KEB on January 29, 2004. Fallon's management team restructured and reorganized KEB. It wrote off nonperforming loans, sold unprofitable assets, and initiated services in the areas of e-banking and mobile telephone operation, increasing the efficiency of the bank. Fallon's team also restructured bank operations into a three-bank platform that was different from the centralized management strategy KEB had used in the past. In February 2004, a mere four months after the acquisition, Lone Star made paper marginal profits of KRW 972.6 billion, because the price per share of KEB rose from KRW 4000 to KRW 7230. KEB profits reached US$509 million in 2004, after a US$209 million loss in 2003.[42]

Despite earning such substantial operating profits, Lone Star was not paying taxes to the Korean government because Lone Star's headquarters were located in Belgium, a country with which Korea had established a mutual tax treaty prohibiting double taxation, and it operated through a subsidiary in Bermuda, a tax haven country. Lone Star was not responsible for paying any taxes to the Korean government, but the Korean

---

39 *Id.*

40 Ju-Min Park, *S. Korean Court Says to Rule on Lone Star Case Oct. 6*, Reuters, Sept. 8, 2011, http://www.reuters.com/article/2011/09/08/lonestar-keb-idUSL4E7K204I20110908.

41 Private Equity Korea, *Courts May Rule on Loan Star-KEB As Early As September*, Aug. 22, 2011, http://www.privateequitykorea.com/ma-news/courts-may-rule-on-lone-star-keb-as-early-as-september/.

42 Park, *supra* note 10, at 19, 26-27.

public believed that such tax exemption was unfair. Additionally, Lone Star was accused of fabricating the Bank for International Settlements capital adequacy ratio ("BIS rate") for KEB in 2003 by lowering the rate and acquiring KEB at a price below the fair market value of the business at that time.[43]

Finally, when Lone Star decided to sell KEB two years after its acquisition, there were concerns that such a short-term investment could bring negative effects to the growth and value of KEB and undermine corporate governance objectives. The argument is that when ownership changes at banks, banks often go through major changes in the composition of their board of directors, causing uncertainty for employees, depositors, and shareholders about the future direction of the bank. Lone Star's failed attempt to sell KEB in 2005 may affect the corporate governance of KEB and the future sale price of KEB in the long run.[44] Corporate governance is especially important in the banking sector because it enables banks to increase the efficiency of their activities and minimize risks, (which provides easier access to capital markets and decreases the cost of capital), increases growth rate, attracts strategic investors, improves the standards of lending, protects the rights of minority shareholders and other counterparts, strengthens their reputation, and raises the level of investors and clients' trust.[45]

As the Korean public's discontent with Lone Star grew, the Korean National Assembly passed an amendment on May 2, 2006 in response to the tax critique. This revision regarding international taxation stated that "The government of Korea can collect taxes from foreign funds that build their headquarters in tax exemption areas and invest in Korea."[46] This law seems to contradict the concept of tax exemption areas because companies build their headquarters in tax haven countries to avoid paying tax to the invested country. However, even if this law was to go into effect, taxes owed by Lone Star would be paid to Belgium, not to Korea, because Lone Star is registered in Belgium and there was an agreement between Korea and Belgium not to impose double taxation on firms.

Another amendment effective as of July 1, 2006 was aimed at imposing taxes on certain tax haven countries. Such an amendment could hinder investment by foreign investors that have their headquarters located in tax haven countries.[47] The only way for such a tax to be successful is to

---

43 *Id.* at iv.
44 *Id.* at 26, 29.
45 *Id.* at 31.
46 *Id.* at 13.
47 *Id.* at 23.

establish a pact with other East Asian countries in levying such a tax for their mutual benefit.[48] Otherwise, competition among states to attract foreign funds will lead to a race to the bottom, with countries providing incentives such as tax cuts which will result in an under-taxation of capital in general.[49] The Korean government was placed in the difficult position of balancing the interests of foreign investors, Korean business entities, and the Korean public.

In 2006, the Korean government also introduced a favorable tax regime for local private equity funds and directed government pension funds to invest in these domestic institutions, presumably convinced that domestic private equity is superior to foreign private equity. Other domestic elites have floated the proposal that *chaebol* assets could be diverted to these preferred domestic funds. The implication is that locally run private equity funds serve Korea's national economic interest, unlike private equity houses from abroad.[50]

The Korean government worried that the Lone Star case would cause foreign capital to dry up, and indeed it did trigger other foreign private equity funds to refrain from investing in Korea, decelerating the development of the Korean financial market.[51] Deal activity flattened in 2006, and average deal size slumped to US$73 million, less than half of what it had been a year earlier.[52]

V. THE SECOND WAVE: A RENEWAL OF PRIVATE EQUITY INVESTMENT

Following the scandal and controversy in the Korean PEF industry in 2006, a new wave of private equity investment emerged for a number of reasons, including motivated corporate sellers, a favorable foreign exchange environment, and the resolution of the Korean bank liquidity crisis. A number of PEFs that have spent time in China are finding it difficult to do deals in China, and are hence interested in investing in Korean firms with a high export rate to China. There are also many attractive

---

48 Pak, *supra* note 6, at 24-25.

49 *Id.* at 39.

50 Robertson, *supra* note 17, at 362.

51 Park, *supra* note 10, at 1.

52 Chul-Joon Park and Hugh MacArthur, *South Korean PE's Second Act*, Bain & Company, Apr. 10, 2007, http://bain.com/bainweb/publications/publications_detail.asp?id=25748&menu_url=publications_results.asp.

assets sitting inside some larger conglomerates as well as standalone public companies that present attractive investment opportunities.[53]

In 2009, Korea was the third most active M&A market in Asia after China and Japan, according to Dealogic. That year, the Korean M&A market was dominated by the sale of government stakes in private companies.[54] As the backlog of government sell-downs subsides, some deal flow is expected to come from South Korea's *chaebols*, or conglomerates like Samsung Group, SK Group and LG group that are over-leveraged from having gone on acquisition binges over the last few years and, hence, are expected to divest non-core divisions to pay down debt.[55]

Another reason for the renewed buyout firm interest in South Korea is the change in the Korean political climate since President Lee Myung-bak took office in February 2008. Unlike deceased President Roh Moo-hyun, who was known for his protectionist sentiment, President Lee wants to make South Korea a pro-business nation. Political sentiment has really changed in favor of inviting foreign investors back, with some heralding this as "the golden age of Korean private equity."[56]

Finally, in this second wave of investment, PEFs are pursuing new investment strategies. These include investing in the underperforming units of South Korea's giant *chaebols* and reinvigorating them, financing promising startups that were previously reluctant to cede control to private equity investors, and teaming up with strategic partners to achieve synergies. Further, Chul-Joon Park, a partner in Bain & Co.'s Seoul office, has noted that a generation of successful South Korean entrepreneurs who helped to launch the nation's dynamic economic growth in the 1970s and 1980s will soon be retiring, which may mean that a wave of management-led buyouts will be on the cards for PEFs in the near future.[57]

An example of a "Second Wave" transaction is Kohlberg Kravis Roberts' ("KKR") acquisition of Oriental Brewery in 2009. KKR purchased Oriental Brewery from Anheuser-Busch InBev in 2009 for US$1.8 billion. Financing was provided by a large syndicate of banks including HSBC, JPMorgan, Nomura and Standard Chartered.[58] This transaction

---

[53] Nisha Gopolan, *South Korea's Hot Deals Market Lukewarm for Bankers*, Wall St. J., Dec. 13, 2009, http://online.wsj.com/article/SB10001424052748704121504574593601273137882.html.

[54] *Id.*

[55] Holman, *supra* note 25.

[56] *Id.*

[57] Park and MacArthur, *supra* note 52.

[58] Holman, *supra* note 25.

gives KKR control of Korea's second largest beer maker and the right for Oriental Brewery to distribute Budweiser, Bud Ice and Hoegaarden beers in South Korea. Oriental Brewery was a strong, healthy, and efficiently run company with a good management team. This was basically a traditional leveraged buyout wherein the PEF tried to unlock capital locked in the conglomerate, as opposed to a restructuring buyout with profits based on turnaround gambles. Nat Zilkha, a director in KKR's Menlo Park, California office, says "Our thesis for OB is one of growth, as opposed to cost-cutting." Zilkha believes this transaction marks a shift in KKR's strategy, taking a position as a long-term investor with confidence in South Korea's future.[59]

VI. CURRENT LANDSCAPE OF THE KOREAN PRIVATE EQUITY INDUSTRY

In Korea today, there is generally a better awareness of what PEFs are, better financial regulation, and less political backlash from a more pro-business administration. PEFs, which had kept a low profile in South Korea in recent years amid fears of a backlash, are stepping up their hunt for bargains again as cash-strapped conglomerates look ready to sell assets.[60] The slumping won is also making South Korea more attractive to outside buyers, while local business groups, once strong competitors, have been obstructed by the country's financial troubles.[61]

Some debt-laden *chaebols* may have to abandon core assets very soon in order to survive. South Korea's top 30 conglomerates had a combined KRW 50 trillion in debt at the end of September 2008, a 59 percent increase from 2007, according to chaebul.com, which offers financial data on conglomerates. Out of the total, borrowings with less than one year of maturity soared 75 percent to KRW 29 trillion, indicating many firms would have to find cash soon to repay the debt.[62]

The backlash against Lone Star made foreign buyers wary, but the Seoul court in October 2008 rejected claims that Lone Star's KEB deal was

---

59 *Id.*

60 Kim Yeon-Hee, *Private Equity Firms Look to South Korea for Bargains*, N.Y. TIMES, Oct. 27, 2008, http://www.nytimes.com/2008/11/27/business/worldbusiness/27iht-equity.1.18197784.html.

61 Andrew Ross Sorkin, *Blackstone to Start South Korean Unit*, N.Y. TIMES, Jan. 20, 2009, http://dealbook.nytimes.com/2009/01/20/blackstone-to-launch--skorea-unit/.

62 Kim, *supra* note 60.

illegal, providing relief to foreign investors.[63] Further, Korea's Financial Services Commission ("FSC") is seeking to relax rules related to the setup and operation of private equity funds to attract more local and overseas investors.[64] Currently, PEFs in Korea account for approximately 34 percent of the country's KRW 306.6 trillion (US$266 billion) investment funds market, but operate under regulations that are more complex and restrictive than those in many other countries.[65]

Today's PEF deals in Korea are very different from the turnaround gambles of the late 1990s and early 2000s. These deals may fare better because the business environment is no longer one in which domestic institutions have no clear understanding of the risks involved in taking foreign money.

VII. FUTURE TRENDS IN PRIVATE EQUITY INVESTMENT

There are two schools of thought about the future of PEF investment in Korea. On the one hand, some scholars believe that there is a space for domestic and foreign PEFs to co-exist, but as distinct entities.[66] On the other, the argument is made that there is really only one model of private equity common to both foreign and domestic funds, the hybrid PEFs that operate in an in-between space.[67]

A. The Case for the Domestic PEF Industry

Since December 2006, the Korean government has encouraged banks and other institutions to set up PEFs to compete with foreign investors.[68] There are still those that speak ill of foreign funds, saying "they made easy money . . . they put in their money and waited for the situation to normalize: a lot of capital gains from them and no financial contribution to Korea."[69] An executive at Vogo, one of Korea's new domestic private

---

63 *Id.*

64 Yvette Choo, *South Korea to Loosen Private Equity Regulations*, PRIVATE EQUITY INT'L, Feb. 4, 2010, http://www.peimedia.com/Article.aspx?article=50364&hashID=C17D2CBD04FF21391CA6CD732C2B505D16D1DAC6.

65 *Id.*

66 Shin, *supra* note 23, at 48.

67 Robertson, *supra* note 17, at 367.

68 Shin, *supra* note 23, at 65.

69 Robertson, *supra* note 17, at 365.

equity funds, boasted of a transaction that "it was the local expertise, knowledge and relationships that enabled us to properly evaluate and execute the investment."[70] The head of MBK Partners, another Korean private equity fund, commented that "if you're investing in these countries, you are a guest and you have to follow cultural imperatives and respect the traditional values of Asia."[71] However, there are limitations to the growth of local buyout funds.

First of all, the domestic PEFs that exist are too small to compete with foreign PEFs.[72] Vogo Fund holds a little more than KRW 500 billion (US$435 million), which is too little money to take over big and competitive corporations, considering it would take between KRW 3.2 and 3.9 trillion to take over a 51 percent share of LG Group.[73] As a result, domestic PEFs have had no choice but to stick to M&As of small and mid-sized firms.

Further, domestic antitrust law also acts to block one domestic business from acquiring a competitor, which discourages the growth of domestic private equity funds. The "50 percent market share rule" has been discouraging domestic and foreign private equity finds alike from making deals because it would be harder for private equity funds to make an exit if there were not enough strategic buyers.[74]

Finally, potential investors in domestic PEFs are hesitant to put their assets into high-risk and long-term investment products since there are no track records or any other guarantee on domestic fund managers.[75] Analysts have said that homegrown PEFs should focus on enhancing specialty businesses by investing in specific industries to secure competitiveness at the early stage.[76]

B. The Case for Hybrid PEFs

In some senses it is certainly true that localness is a critical advantage, and the more you can convince a seller that you are like them, the more successful you are likely to be.[77] But an examination of the current state of

---

70 *Id.*
71 *Id.* at 368.
72 Shin, *supra* note 23, at 65.
73 Pak, *supra* note 6, at 18.
74 Shin, *supra* note 23, at 66.
75 *Id.* at 65.
76 Pak, *supra* note 6, at 19-21.
77 Robertson, *supra* note 17, at 368.

the Korean PEF industry suggests that there is really only one model of private equity common to both foreign and domestic funds.

In Korea today, hybrid funds have developed in the guise of domestic funds, financed by Western capital and run by Western managers, or in the form of Western funds funded by Korean capital. Headlines in the Lone Star era and beyond have focused on the tension between foreign and domestic interests, but fail to grapple with these complex issues in emerging markets and in the global political economy.[78]

Today's locally run PEFs wrap themselves in domestic colors so analysts refer to them as home-grown funds, but they actively solicit foreign capital, tout their global best practices, and are staffed by members of the global financial diaspora.[79] Furthermore, domestic PEFs also tend to invest for short-term gain. Once a PEF announces its intention to invest in a target company, the share price of the target company soars in light of the expectation of changes in management, which might lead to an increase in the value of an asset. In reality, some funds that have declared their intentions to participate in management have resold their stake back to the public market and realized capital gains in a short period of time.[80] This strategy, which is what the Korean public has accused foreign PEFs of doing in the past, adds instability to the Korean market.

The current state of the Korean PEF industry calls into question theoretical models that continue to draw sharp distinctions between domestic economic structures in the developing world and the rest of the world economy. There seems to be a need for theoretical frameworks that incorporate hybrid actors that are neither fully foreign nor fully domestic.[81] Yet little space has been left for these hybrid arrangements that are neither fully convergent nor fully divergent – Asian countries now operate "somewhere in between the old model of domestic protection of a small cadre of business and political elites on the one hand, and the liberal ideal of open markets on the other."[82]

By way of example, MBK Partners is incorporated and headquartered in Korea, where its investment team sits. It is led by a Korean-American who left the senior ranks of the American-owned Carlyle Group. MBK's operations are much more representative of global private equity funds than traditional Korean business practices. Several of its private equity funds are also registered outside Korea in jurisdictions such as the

---

78 *Id.* at 363.
79 *Id.* at 368-69.
80 Shin, *supra* note 23, at 66.
81 Robertson, *supra* note 17, at 360.
82 *Id.* at 362.

Cayman Islands and Hong Kong, for tax purposes. Finally, MBK attracts primarily global investment funds rather than financing from within the Korean economy.

C. Case: State Actors Going Global

Korea Development Bank: Korea Development Bank has established a private equity fund of over US$1 billion, meaning that a key state-run body has entered the world of private equity, which would have been unimaginable before the Asian financial crisis.

Korean Asset Management Corporation: The Korean Asset Management Corporation has demonstrated that it has mastered how to restructure distressed assets, venturing into the Chinese market with plans to buy non-performing loans from Chinese institutions.

Korean National Pension Service: South Korea's national pension fund, NPS, the world's fourth largest, is taking aggressive steps to broaden its portfolio this year. It plans to invest a total of US$10 billion overseas, of which US$6 billion will be in equities and fixed-income securities and US$4 billion in alternatives, including several possible investments in the United States. NPS is already the dominant investor in Korean markets and is growing faster than the capacity the local market can offer – thus it is looking for higher returns overseas. NPS partnered with KKR in a US$1 billion deal to buy a 23.4 percent stake in Colonial Pipeline, the largest refined-products pipeline in North America, from Chevron Corp.[83]

The strategies adopted by these state actors are arguably far more consistent with a liberal model of the economy than with a resistant image.

VIII. CONCLUSION

Korea was not prepared for the quick introduction of foreign capital in 1996 or the liberalization of its market as required by the IMF after the Asian financial crisis. However, the short history of the Korean PEF industry has provided Korea with some invaluable lessons. Korea now better understands the importance of financial capital, as well as the notion that the future of the Korean financial market and economy highly depends on finding the optimal balance between domestic and foreign

---

[83] Alastair Gale, *Korea Fund Is Looking Overseas*, Wall St. J., Feb. 18, 2011, http://online.wsj.com/article/SB10001424052748704171004576149391027645126.html.

interests.[84] Korea has also experienced a significant reduction in its bad debt loan ratio and the stabilization of its financial institutions, along with improved management and corporate governance practices. Finally, Korea has developed its own nascent domestic private equity industry that has taken on many of the characteristics of the Western private equity model.

The evolution of the private equity industry in Korea is a coming of age story. Despite a bit of a rough start, today there is less of a distinction between what is foreign and domestic, and South Korea has truly begun to embrace both global capital and global ideas. Anglo-American models of global finance appear to be spreading across emerging markets, even if the agents are not always Western in nationality. Perhaps this is an indication that traditional national labels have lost some of their meaning in the international economy, especially in the domain of private equity.

REFERENCES

Cheffins, Brian and John Armour, *The Eclipse of Private Equity*, 33 Del. J. Corp. L. 1 (2008).

Choo, Yvette, *South Korea to Loosen Private Equity Regulations*, PRIVATE EQUITY INT'L, Feb. 4, 2010, http://www.peimedia.com/Article.aspx?article=50364&hashID=C17D2CBD04FF21391CA6CD732C2B505D16D1DAC6.

Gale, Alastair, *Korea Fund Is Looking Overseas*, WALL ST. J., Feb. 18, 2011, http://online.wsj.com/ article/SB10001424052748704171004576149391027645126.html.

Gopolan, Nisha, *South Korea's Hot Deals Market Lukewarm for Bankers*, WALL ST. J., Dec. 13, 2009, http://online.wsj.com/article/SB10001424052748704121504574593601273137882.html.

Harvie, Charles and Hyun-Hoon Lee, KOREA'S ECONOMIC MIRACLE, FADING OR REVIVING? (2003).

Holman, Kelly, *South Korea's New PE Age?*, IDDMAGAZINE.COM, June 5, 2009, http://www.pgpcapital.com/ pages/pdfs/IDD_06052009.pdf.

Hwang, Hye-Sun, The Impact and Implication of Capital Globalization on Korea after 1997: From the Perspective of Foreign Private Equity Funds (Feb. 2008) (unpublished M.A. thesis, Korea University Graduate School of International Studies) (on file with author).

Kim, Cynthia J., *Hana, Lone Star agree to extend KEB deal,* THE KOREA HERALD, July 8, 2011, http://www.koreaherald.com/business/Detail.jsp?newsMLId=20110708000589.

Kim, Hwa-Jin, *Living with the IMF: A New Approach to Corporate Governance and Regulation of Financial Institutions in Korea*, 17 BERKELEY J. INT'L L. 61 (1999).

---

[84] Pak, *supra* note 6, at 39.

Kim, Hwa-Jin, *The Case of Market for Corporate Control in Korea* (2009) Oxford U Comp. L Forum 2 at ouclf.iuscomp.org.

Kim, Yeon-Hee, *Private Equity Firms Look to South Korea for Bargains*, N.Y. TIMES, Oct. 27, 2008, http://www.nytimes.com/2008/11/27/business/worldbusiness/27iht-equity.1.18197784.html.

Lerner, Josh et al., VENTURE CAPITAL AND PRIVATE EQUITY: A CASEBOOK, 4th ed. (2009).

Pak, Hyeong-nam, The 1997 Financial Crisis in Korea and the Role of the Private Equity Fund (Feb. 2007) (unpublished M.A. thesis, Korea University Graduate School of International Studies) (on file with author).

Park, Chul-Joon and Hugh MacArthur, *South Korean PE's Second Act*, Bain & Company, Apr. 10, 2007, http://bain.com/bainweb/publications/publications_detail.asp?id=25748&menu_url=publications_results.asp.

Park, Fair One, Corporate Governance and the Future of Foreign Private Equity Funds in Korea: The Case of Lone Star Funds in Korea Exchange Bank (Feb. 2007) (unpublished M.A. thesis, Ewha Women's University Graduate School of International Studies) (on file with author).

Park, Ju-Min, *S. Korean Court Says to Rule on Lone Star Case Oct. 6*, REUTERS, Sept. 8, 2011, http://www.reuters.com/article/2011/09/08/lonestar-keb-idUSL4E7K204I20110908.

Private Equity Korea, *Courts May Rule on Loan Star-KEB As Early As September*, Aug. 22, 2011, http://www.privateequitykorea.com/ma-news/courts-may-rule-on-lone-star-keb-as-early-as-september/.

Robertson, Justin, *Private Equity and Asian Political Economy: "Domestic" Private Equity Funds as New Actors*, 50 Asian Surv. 359 (2010).

Rusli, Evelyn M., *Lone Star Set for Korean Deal*, N.Y. TIMES, Nov. 24, 2010, http://dealbook. nytimes.com/2010/11/24/lone-star-set-for-korean-deal/.

Shin, Jiyeon and Wonseok Woo, *An Analysis of Private Equity Funds in Korea and Their Role in the Korean Economy in the Post-Crisis Period*, 9 INT'L STUD. REV. 54 (2008).

Sorkin, Andrew Ross, *Blackstone to Start South Korean Unit*, N.Y. TIMES, Jan. 20, 2009, http://dealbook.nytimes.com/2009/01/20/blackstone-to-launch-skorea-unit/.

Stiglitz, Joseph E., GLOBALIZATION AND ITS DISCONTENTS (2003).

Yun, Chang-Hee, *Lone Star Must Return to Korea Exchange Bank*, JOONGANG DAILY, June 19, 2006, at E1.

10. The present and future of private equity funds (PEF) in Korea

Hee Jeu Kang and Hyun Kim

I. INTRODUCTION

With the enactment of the Indirect Investment Asset Management Business Act (Asset Management Act) on January 5, 2004, asset management companies became able to form mutual funds and investment trusts to manage assets. Such types of funds could not play a significant role as investment tools for mergers and acquisitions (M&A), however, because they were subject to various regulatory restrictions. Notable restrictions included their inability to essentially function as limited liability partnerships despite being private funds; as well as their obligation to treat investors equally and their obligation to engage outside custodians and other outside service providers.

To promote corporate restructuring and M&A markets and be in line with global standards, amendments to the Asset Management Act were made on October 5, 2004 and went into effect on December 6, 2004. These amendments scaled back certain restrictions and introduced private equity funds (PEF) in Korea.

With its enactment on February 4, 2009, the Financial Investment Services and Capital Markets Act (FSCMA), designed to be the overarching body of law governing all aspects of capital markets, replaced and took over the functions of the Asset Management Act. Even under the FSCMA, PEFs are regulated separately from other types of collective investment schemes. Corporate restructuring funds and M&A funds, being organizational forms provided for under the Asset Management Act, were abolished under the FSCMA due to low utilization as a result of the restrictive regulatory framework that applied to them. In the aftermath of the global financial crisis, amendments were made to the FSCMA on March 12, 2010 (effective on June 13, 2010) to introduce a type of PEF designed to invest mainly in companies under distress or restructuring (called "corporate financial stability PEFs") and grant certain regulatory exceptions for 3 years to this type of PEF with the aim of facilitating fund sourcing and asset management.[1]

II. PEFS UNDER THE FSCMA

In the following pages, we will touch mainly upon distinct characteristics of PEFs, which are similar to those of limited partnerships existing in the US and English legal systems, and which no other form of collective investment scheme has under the FSCMA.

A. Concept

The PEF type of collective investment scheme under the FSCMA takes the form of an investment purpose limited company that issues its shares solely in private placement transactions and is established to make investments for the purpose of participating in the management, business or corporate governance restructuring of its investee companies. Even though PEFs are a type of collective investment scheme, the FSCMA has a separate section dedicated to distinctive provisions that are only applicable to PEFs.[2]

B. Legal Form

As an investment purpose limited company, each PEF takes the form of a limited company under the Korean Commercial Code. As required for all limited companies, each PEF is required to have one or more unlimited liability partners and fewer than 50 partners (including both unlimited liability partners and limited liability partners) in total. (Although equity stakeholders in such companies are often referred to as "partners" due to the organizational similarities with limited partnerships, they are sometimes also referred to as "members" or "shareholders.") Given the prevalent use of limited partnerships for PEFs in the international market, there was much discussion in Korea about introducing PEFs in the form of limited partnerships, which would have been similar to the standard form of partnership provided for under the Korean Civil Code. While the limited partnership form would have given PEFs more flexibility in shaping relationships among investors, for example with regard to

---

1 Refer to the announcement of the amendments to the FSCMA [Act No. 10063, as amended on March 12, 2010].

2 Article 268 through 278-2 of the FSCMA.

distributions, it would lack a separate legal personality which could bring the effectiveness of its actions *vis-à-vis* third parties into question. Because of this shortcoming, the FSCMA specifies the "limited partnership company" (*hapja hoesa* in Korean) as the prescribed legal form for PEFs, which is one of the corporate forms provided for in the Korean Civil Code and is structurally most similar to limited partnership.

C. Formation and Registration of PEFs

The legal formation of a PEF requires the completion of the registration of the PEF with the Commercial Registry after all of its members (equity stakeholders of the PEF) have executed the PEF's articles of incorporation. A PEF can be formed without any capital injection because its paid-in capital amount is not an item that needs to be registered with the Commercial Registry. After such formation and registration, the PEF's members make contributions in proportion to their commitment ratios when the managing partner of the PEF makes capital calls.

A PEF is required to apply for registration as a PEF with the Financial Services Commission (FSC) within 2 weeks from the date of its registration with the Commercial Registry. There is a standard application form that is required to be filled out and filed together with relevant supporting documents specified therein. Upon the receipt of an application, the FSC has 30 days to make a decision on whether to register the PEF and give written notice of its decision to the applicant. If the FSC finds any inadequacy in the application, it may make requests for additional information. When calculating the 30-day period mentioned above, the time taken for (1) requesting and receiving information from other institutions, which is to be used to determine whether the applicant has met the requirements for registration as a PEF and (2) processing any additional information request is excluded.

Certain information about the managing partner (e.g. registered name and address) needs to be registered with the Commercial Registry. But no private information about limited partners (LP) is required to be registered with the Commercial Registry. Moreover, the FSC application does not require any information specific to the LPs, including their commitment amounts. Such protection of the confidentiality of LPs functions to encourage investor participation in PEFs.

D. Term of PEF

No PEF may exist for more than 15 years from the date on which it is registered with the Commercial Registry. (Typically, the expiration date of a PEF's term triggers the commencement of liquidation and dissolution proceedings for the PEF.) Accordingly, a PEF is generally not a suitable vehicle for any investment requiring a timeframe of 15 years or more.

E. PEF Members

Each PEF requires at least one unlimited liability partner and at least one limited liability partner. At least one unlimited liability partner needs to serve as a managing partner (sometimes referred to as the "GP" based on the similar managing function of a general partner in an unincorporated limited partnership).

There are no particular qualifications for being a managing partner of a PEF. The FSCMA overrides the general restriction against a corporation being an unlimited liability partner of a limited partnership company. Thus, a corporation can be a managing partner of a PEF. While the FSCMA requires managers of collective investment schemes other than PEFs to have a relevant license, it does not impose any restriction on who may establish a PEF and serve as its managing partner. The FSCMA allows financial entities governed by other bodies of law to become managing partners of PEFs and carry out related duties in such capacity to the extent not in violation of such other laws.

The LPs of a PEF are prohibited from exercising any influence over voting rights of shares or equity interests owned by the PEF. As a financial investor, an LP's liability to creditors of the PEF is limited to its commitment amount less its cumulative contribution amount. In return for exempting PEFs from a number of investor-protection measures, the FSCMA sets forth minimum commitment amounts for LPs, i.e. Korean Won (KRW) 1 billion for LPs that are natural persons and KRW 2 billion for LPs that are corporations and other entities.

F. Partner Contributions

Under the Commercial Code, an unlimited liability partner of a limited partnership company may contribute credit, labor or cash while a limited liability partner may contribute cash only. However, in regard to PEFs, both unlimited liability partners and LPs may only contribute cash; provided that securities may be contributed to the PEF if they can be objectively valued and such contribution is not likely to harm the interests of other partners and all partners consent to such contribution. So far, all PEFs have received contributions in cash only. There have not yet been any cases where securities have been contributed to a PEF.

Accordingly, unlike ordinary limited partnership companies under the Commercial Code, it is not possible to contribute real estate to PEFs and contributions of securities are not made under current market practice.

G. Transfer of Partnership Interest

A managing partner (as well as any non-managing unlimited liability partner) is prohibited from transferring its interest to another person unless the PEF's articles of incorporation permits such transfer with the consent of all the other members. An LP may transfer its interest to another person with the consent of all. Any partial transfer of partnership interest is prohibited if such transfer results in the PEF having more than 49 partners.

It is typical for a PEF's articles of incorporation to grant rights of first refusal to the non-transferring partners in proportion to their shareholding ratios and to provide specific grounds and procedures for a partner's withdrawal and removal.

H. Management of PEF Assets

Management of PEF assets is subject to restrictions on types of eligible investment and methods of investment and disposition.

1. Investment to participate in corporate governance

Within 2 years from the receipt of contributions, a PEF must deploy 50 percent of such contributions for making (1) equity investment in another company that is not a fund and which shall amount to at least 10 percent of the investee company's total issued voting stock or shareholders equity, (2) investment that provides the PEF with direct or indirect control of the investee company by, for example, receipt of the right to appoint one or more directors, or (3) investment in SOC funds.

Given that a PEF is a collective investment scheme whose primary purpose is making equity investment in order to participate in the management of investee companies, it is not allowed to lend money. A PEF is required to be able to participate in the management of an investee company even if it is not such company's largest shareholder. There previously was an issue as to whether investments with option features should be characterized as investments for obtaining corporate control instead of as loans. In response to this uncertainty, the Financial Supervisory Service (FSS) has published a guideline for such investments that PEFs are required to comply with. A summary of the guideline is as follows:

(1) There shall be no agreement with an investee company for any call or put option.
(2) Option features shall have characteristics reasonably necessary to facilitate the PEF's goal of increasing the value of an investee company through corporate governance.
   a) Call options and put options shall not simultaneously exist between the parties to the option.
   b) Mere expiration of time shall not be a ground for exercising the option.
   c) The exercise price shall not exceed the relevant market price (if there is none, its inherent value); provided that a guaranty of principal may be made.
   d) No excessive demand for or provision of collateral (which is a characteristic of loan) shall be made.
   e) Details of the option shall be set forth in a contract and be immediately reported to the FSS.

2. Methods of investment and disposition

Once it makes an equity investment for the purpose of participating in corporate governance, the PEF may not dispose of such investment within the 6-month period immediately following the date of such investment.[3] This requirement is imposed to differentiate such investment from a simple equity investment.

If any of its equity investments do not satisfy the requirement for participation in the investee company's management within the 6-month period following the date of such investment, the PEF must dispose of the equity investment, in its entirety, to another party not related to members of the PEF within 1 month and immediately report such disposal to the FSC.[4]

3. PEFs and cross-holding restricted business groups

If a PEF or a GP of the PEF is an affiliate of a business group subject to the restriction on cross-holding under the Monopoly Regulation and Fair Trade Act and makes another company its affiliate ("additional affiliation"), the PEF must dispose of any equity holding in such other company to a person that is not an affiliate of the restricted business group and must

---

[3] In a limited number of situations, a disposition may be made before the expiration of the 6-month period with the approval of the FSC.

[4] In certain cases where making such disposition is difficult, it may be postponed with the approval of the FSC for a period determined by the FSC.

do so within 5 years from the date of the occurrence of the additional affiliation. Such PEF may not acquire equity shares issued by any affiliate of such restricted business group.

The Monopoly Regulation and Fair Trade Act determines how to define a business group and whether a business group is subject to the restriction on cross-holding. A "business group" is a group of companies that is under common control of one person, which may include persons related to him, through direct or indirect means by holding at least 30 percent of the voting shares issued by the company at the top of the group hierarchy. Any companies under direct or indirect control of the top company are deemed to be members of the same business group. Companies belonging to the same business group are deemed to be affiliates. A business group becomes subject to the restriction on cross-holding if the group companies' total assets as at the end of the previous fiscal year amount to KRW 5 trillion or more. As of July 1, 2011, there were 55 cross-holding restricted business groups. Their members numbered 1578.[5] Every month, the Korean Fair Trade Commission announces a list of cross-holding restricted business groups.

When a member of a cross-holding restricted business group becomes the largest LP of a PEF by acquiring 30 percent or more of the PEF, there is an issue as to whether such PEF should be regarded as an affiliate of such a business group. Given that LPs are not allowed under the FSCMA to exercise any influence with regard to voting rights the PEF has with its investee companies, the PEF is not deemed to be an affiliate of any of its LPs unless such LP has the unrestricted right to replace the PEF's managing partner under the articles of incorporation, or is the actual manager of the PEF through a side agreement with the PEF's managing partner or by other means.

Thus, the restriction on cross-holding becomes an issue only when an affiliate of a cross-holding restricted business group is a managing partner of a PEF. In such case, the PEF faces restrictions on eligible counterparties with regard to its investments.[6]

---

5 "Report on Changes in Cross-Holding Restricted Business Groups for June 2011" published by the Korean Fair Trade Commission on July 4, 2011.

6 In practice, it is quite common for subsidiaries of financial holding companies to become managing partners of PEFs. Nevertheless, this does not trigger application of the restriction specified here since the Monopoly Regulation and Fair Trade Act exempts business groups that engage in banking or insurance business from being designated as cross-holding restricted business groups.

4. Restriction on borrowing funds and giving guarantees

PEFs are permitted to borrow funds or give guarantees for investee companies (or anyone related to such company) only when (1) it is necessary to return money to a withdrawing member, (2) there is a temporary shortage in its working capital or (3) there is a temporary shortage to meet its investment commitment.

However, to structurally lower the possibility of PEFs incurring excess leverage and damaging their financial health, the aggregate amount of borrowing or guarantee that may be made by a PEF is limited to 10 percent of its assets

5. Ban on mergers of PEFs

PEFs are banned from merging with other companies, including other PEFs. This restriction is based on the fact that the role intended for PEFs under relevant legislation is participation in the management of investee companies.

6. Management of idle assets

PEFs may use idle assets that are not yet deployed for investment in (1) making short-term loans, (2) making deposits with financial institutions, (3) investing in stocks (in an amount not exceeding 5 percent of the PEF's assets), (4) acquiring certificates of deposit denominated in KRW, and (5) purchasing commercial paper issued, discounted, sold, brokered, underwritten or guaranteed by financial institutions (excluding corporate commercial paper). The restriction on equity investment in item (3) is to prevent any attempt at circumventing the limitation on the primary purpose mandated by relevant legislation for the establishment and operation of PEFs.

I. Investment Purpose Vehicles

The FSCMA explicitly allows PEFs to form special purpose vehicles to be used as conduits for executing investment strategies. Being essentially a paper company, such investment purpose vehicle does not need to have any permanent employees. Investment purpose vehicles give more flexibility to PEFs in structuring investments and allow PEFs to take advantage of limited liability status and manage risk exposure by being a shareholder or limited liability member of an investment purpose vehicle rather than a direct owner of the ultimate investee company.

As discussed above, PEFs are subject to certain restrictions on borrowing, giving guarantees and mergers, which prevent PEFs from engaging in leveraged buyouts (LBO). But, such restrictions are waived for investment purpose vehicles of PEFs, except for the borrowing cap which is increased to 200 percent of its capitalization. Thus, it becomes possible for PEFs to engage in LBOs through investment purpose vehicles.

J. Duties of the Managing Partner

The FSCMA explicitly provides that a managing partner has the obligation to carry out his/her duties faithfully in accordance with all applicable laws and the articles of incorporation of the PEF it manages. It also lists a number of prohibited activities for managing partners. A violation can be punished by an imprisonment of no longer than 1 year or a fine of KRW 30 million or less.

A managing partner may not delegate to a third party his/her duties to (1) select investee companies and form or choose investment purpose vehicles, (2) determine when and how to dispose of investments in investee companies and investment purpose vehicles, (3) determine whether and how to exercise voting rights held by the PEF, (4) determine price, timing and method when transacting in securities, derivatives, real estate and other assets and (5) select candidates to be dispatched to or be elected for the management of any portfolio company or investment purpose vehicle.

K. Filing and Approval Issues Relating to PEF Formation

1. Prior approval under the Act on the Structural Improvement of the Financial Industry (the "SIF Act")

When a financial institution (limited to those listed in the SIF Act which are mostly domestic financial institutions) and financial institution(s) that belong to the same business group as such financial institution ("Group Financial Institution") (1) holds at least 20 percent of the total issued voting shares of another company or (2) holds at least 5 percent of the total issued voting shares of another company and a Group Financial Institution or the business group that such Group Financial Institution belongs to is deemed to control such company, a prior approval from the FSC is required.

Since a PEF is a company in its legal form, the prior approval under the SIF Act was required in connection with participation in a PEF as GP and/or LP. However, there was a criticism that imposing the prior approval requirement under the SIF Act with respect to investment purpose LP participation was an excessive regulatory practice. The FSC announced a press release on September 1, 2010 in which it declared that a financial institution that invests in a PEF as an LP is exempted from the prior approval requirement under the SIF Act while a financial institution that participates in a PEF as a GP is subject to the prior approval requirement under the SIF Act regardless of the size of its interest in such PEF.

Therefore, when a newly formed PEF is to have a GP that is a financial institution, it is necessary to bear in mind that a prior approval under the SIF Act is required while a financial institution that participates as an LP is exempted from such requirement.

In practice, it takes about 3 weeks to obtain a prior approval under the SIF Act.

2. Business combination report under the Monopoly Regulation and Fair Trade Act (the "Fair Trade Act")

When a company whose total assets or revenues are at least KRW 200 billion (including assets or revenues of affiliates) participates in formation of a joint venture company with another company whose total assets or revenues are at least KRW 20 billion (including assets or revenues of affiliates) and becomes the largest contributor to such joint venture company, a business combination report should be filed with the Fair Trade Commission under Article (12)(1)(5) of the Fair Trade Act.

Since PEF is a company in its legal form, if any two members of its GP and LP include an entity with total assets or revenues equal to KRW 200 billion or more and an entity with total assets or revenues equal to KRW 20 billion or more, a business combination report under the Fair Trade Act is required. One thing to be especially noted here is that when a company whose total assets or revenues are KRW 2 trillion or more (including assets or revenues of affiliates) participates as a GP or an LP, a business combination report should be filed and accepted before the first contribution is made to the PEF.

Business combination report filing relating to a PEF is one of the simplified filing processes and takes about 2 weeks in practice.

III. STATUS OF PEFS IN KOREA[7]

A. Development of the PEF Market

Since its introduction on December 6, 2004 pursuant to the amendment of the Asset Management Act, the PEF market has grown exponentially, as

---

[7] Statistical figures in this section come from "The Evaluation of the First 6 Years of the PEF Market and Issues" published by the FSC on June 7, 2011.

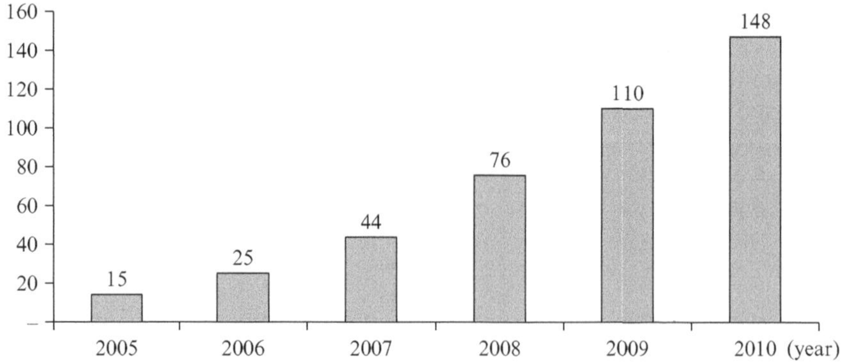

(*) Cumulative year-end figures

Figure 10.1 Number of PEFs

shown in Figure 10.1 above. As at the end of May, 2011, there were 167 PEFs with aggregate commitments of approximately KRW 28.9 trillion.

In the 3-year period following the global financial crisis, 104 PEFs have been formed by investors who view PEFs as the optimal vehicle for pursuing attractive investment opportunities in the market.

As shown in Figure 10.2 opposite, the aggregate commitment amount of all PEFs has also grown exponentially. As at the end of 2010, the aggregate commitment amount of all PEFs stood at KRW 26.6 trillion, which represents a 234 percent increase since 2007.

B. Regional Distribution of Investee Companies

As shown in Table 10.1 below, the types of investee companies selected as investment targets by PEFs have expanded beyond the traditionally favored domestic manufacturing enterprises (238 companies) to include foreign companies (25 companies). In the beginning, foreign investments were concentrated in developed countries like the US. Since 2008, they have extended their reach to include China and other developing countries. Out of 16 foreign investments made since 2008, 7 were in the US, 3 in China, 2 in Taiwan, 2 in Hong Kong and 2 in other foreign countries.

C. Performance

As shown in Table 10.2 below, by the end of 2010, KRW 2689.1 billion were recouped (the principal amount being KRW 1838.1 billion), showing

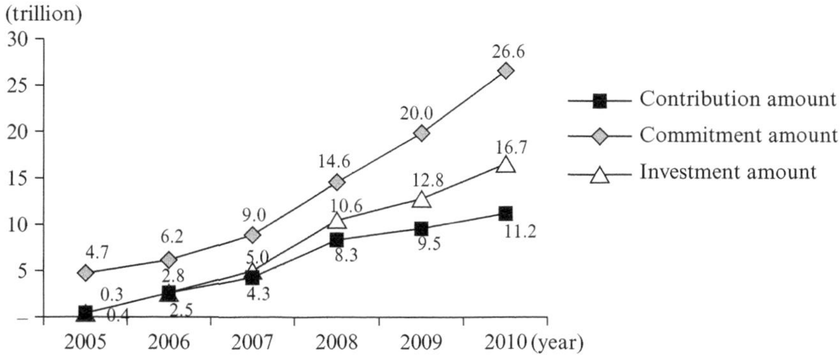

(*) Cumulative year-end figures

Notes:
Commitment Amount: Aggregate amount of commitments made by partners of PEFs at the times of PEF formation.
Contribution Amount: Aggregate amount of contributions actually made by partners of PEFs.
Investment Amount: Aggregate amount of investments, including any borrowed amounts, made by PEFs.

Figure 10.2 Trends in PEF commitments, contributions and investment amounts

a notable performance. Considering that the financial markets have been quite volatile and the number of PEFs has skyrocketed in the past 3 years, it is expected to take some time for PEFs to recoup their investments and realize their gains and/or losses.

D. Further Growth of Participation of Experienced Asset Managers and Diversification of Investor Pools

As more financial companies and their affiliates with extensive investment experience and financial expertise participate in the PEF market as managing partners, the PEF market has found them to be an essential ingredient for further growth. As shown in Figure 10.3 below, a large portion of such financial companies that act as managing partners (48 percent) are securities companies and asset management firms, while a substantial portion of ordinary companies that act as managing partners are affiliates of financial institutions or companies established by former employees of financial institutions.

As shown in Figure 10.4, in the early days of the PEF market, nearly

Table 10.1 Regional distribution of portfolio companies

	'05	'06	'07	'08	'09	'10	Total
Domestic entities	8	39	40	51	41	59	238
Foreign entities	–	2	7	5	2	9	25
US/Japan/Europe	–	2	6	2	2	5	17
Misc.	–	–	1	3	–	4	8
Total	8	41	47	56	43	68	263

Table 10.2 Status of investment returns of PEFs (Unit: KRW 100 million)

Exit year	Investment return amount	Investment principal
2005–07	5652	2799
2008	3449	2749
2009	8611	6837
2010	9179	5996
Total	26891	18381

90 percent of commitments from LPs came from financial institutions and pension funds. Now, the participation rate of non-financial companies and individual investors has grown to 41 percent. The pool of investors for PEFs is expected to diversify further.

E. Balanced Growth of PEFs of Various Sizes

PEFs can be categorized into the following categories based on their commitment amounts: Large (KRW 300 billion or more), Medium (KRW 100 billion or more and less than KRW 300 billion), and Small (Less than KRW 100 billion). As shown in Table 10.3 below, since 2007, small PEFs targeting small-cap companies, which are comparatively more stable, have shown marked growth. At the same time, large and medium PEFs have each shown stable growth. Overall the PEF market managed a balanced growth among PEFs of various sizes.

F. Growing Number of Leveraged Investments

As PEFs have built positive track records and the confidence in managing partners has increased, the number of leveraged investments has grown since 2008, as shown in Table 10.4 below. Among small PEFs, leverage is

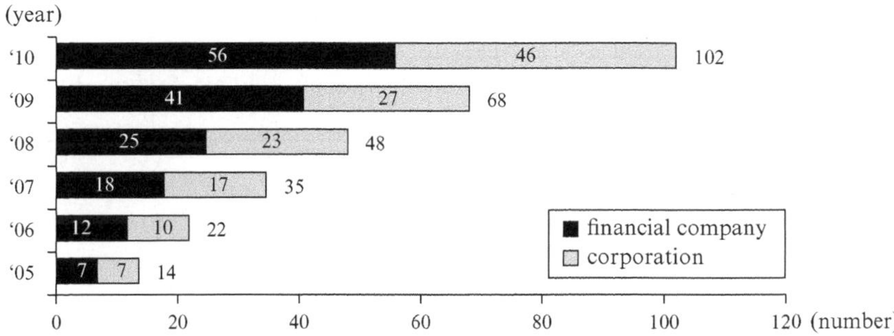

Figure 10.3 Types of managing partners

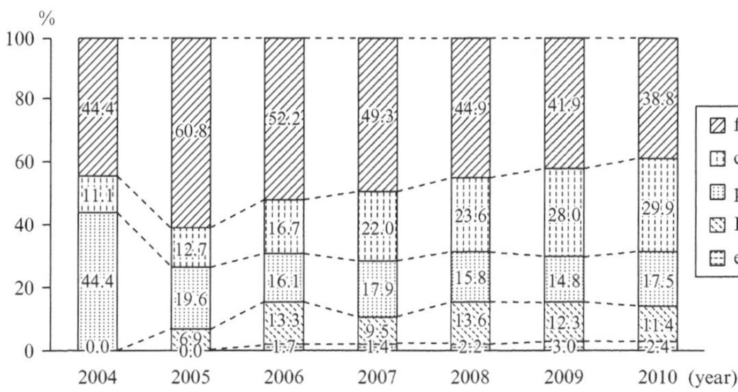

Figure 10.4 Types of LPs

used more often by deal-by-deal funds, which tend to face comparatively lower risks. Among large PEFS, blind funds have been the active users of leverage.

IV. TYPICAL PEF M&A DEAL – REPRESENTATIVE CASE (KDB VALUE PRIVATE EQUITY FUND VI'S ACQUISITION OF DAEWOO E&C)

On November 15, 2006, Kumho Industrial and its affiliates together with financial investors entered into a share purchase agreement with the creditor group led by KAMCO to purchase 244 655 611 shares (representing

Table 10.3 Number of PEFs per commitment amount category

	Commitments	End of 2005	End of 2006	End of 2007	End of 2008	End of 2009	End of 2010
Large	KRW 300 billion or more	7	9	13	20	23	31
Medium	KRW 100 billion -KRW 300 billion	4	6	13	20	23	38
Small	Less than KRW 100 billion	4	10	18	36	64	79
Total		15	25	44	76	110	148

Table 10.4 Debt ratio of PEFs' investments (Cumulative, KRW in trillions)

Year	Contribution (A)	Investment Amount (B)	Debt (C=B−A)*	Debt Ratio (C/A)
2007	4.3	5.0	0.7	16.3%
2008	8.3	10.6	2.3	27.7%
2009	9.5	12.8	3.3	34.7%
2010	11.2	16.7	5.5	49.1%

Note: * Debt amounts are estimated by subtracting the total contribution amounts from the total investment amounts.

72.1 percent) of Daewoo E&C, a listed company. At the same time, Kumho Industrial entered into a side agreement with financial investors whereby it granted a conditional put option to each financial investor with the exercise price guaranteeing 9 percent compounded annual return on the share purchase price.

Because of the global financial crisis and concurrent dip in the construction market, the share price of Daewoo E&C stayed below the purchase price and the financial investors exercised the put option, which subsequently led Kumho Industrial to sign a restructuring agreement with its primary bank creditor under the Corporate Restructuring Promotion Act.

To resolve this problem, the Korea Development Bank decided to acquire Daewoo E&C through KDB Value Private Equity Fund VI, one of the PEFs it was managing at the time, and began discussions with Kumho Industrial and the financial investors. Being creditors of Kumho Industrial, the financial investors had an interest in seeing Kumho Industrial successfully restructured to recoup their investments through the exercise of the put options. The financial investors reviewed a plan put forward by the Korea Development Bank to deal with the put options as part of the restructuring process under the Corporate Restructuring Promotion Act and had negotiations regarding the sale of their holdings in Daewoo E&C.

After a series of negotiations, KDB Value Private Equity Fund VI entered into a share purchase agreement with Kumho Industrial on December 9, 2010 and another share purchase agreement on December 13, 2010 with 17 financial investors to acquire 121 027 407 shares of Daewoo E&C. Subsequently, KDB Value Private Equity Fund VI participated solely in a designated third-party capital increase by Daewoo E&C on December 29, 2010 to acquire an additional 89 903 802 shares. KDB Value Private Equity Fund VI acquired existing shares at KRW 18 000 per share (total purchase price KRW 2 178 493 326 000) and new shares at KRW 11 123 (total subscription price KRW 999 999 989 646).

To fund these acquisitions, KDB Value Private Equity Fund VI needed to borrow money. As PEFs are not allowed to borrow money in principle, KDB Value Private Equity Fund VI formed an investment purpose vehicle named KDB Value VI Ltd., capitalized it and had it borrow KRW 1 000 000 000 000 to pay for the acquisitions.

The case above is representative of a typical approach taken by PEFs in acquiring distressed large-cap companies on a leveraged basis. It is noteworthy for its success amid the restructuring process under the Corporate Restructuring Promotion Act, which increased the necessity for engaging in sophisticated negotiations to bring together many parties with different interests.

V. REPRESENTATIVE CASES OF OVERSEAS INVESTMENT BY PEF

When Fila Korea Ltd. acquired Acushnet Company, which holds trademarks of Titleistand and Footjoy in 2011, a PEF participated as a financial investor in the consortium.

Moreover, around the end of 2011, a PEF which is managed by the Korean GP, invested as a financial investor in a Delaware company producing photovoltaic modules by acquiring its preferred stock and convertible notes.

While there have not been many cases where PEF invested overseas, more PEFs formed with funds raised domestically are expected to participate in overseas investment more actively.

VI. FUTURE OF PEFS IN KOREA

A. Industry Forecast

PEFs are engaging in buyouts, distressed investments and various other types of investment activities. Recently, a PEF has been chosen as a vehicle to manage distressed bank debts related to project financing. PEFs are expected to take a more active role in the distressed asset market.

However, PEFs in Korea have been subject to onerous investment restrictions, especially when compared to their counterparts (in the form of limited partnerships) abroad. For Korean PEFs to become true global players, it appears necessary to reduce the current level of regulation to allow PEFs to take on a greater variety of roles in the financial market.

B. Amendments to the FSCMA for the Introduction of Hedge Funds

There has been a criticism that PEFs in Korea are subject to excessively onerous regulations, especially in comparison to foreign hedge funds, and have been less competitive than they could have been. At the time of its enactment in 2009, a special provision was added to the FSCMA to provide a legal basis for allowing PEFs with qualified investors to act as hedge funds.

However, discussions took place in the US and the EU on regulating hedge funds in the aftermath of the global financial crisis triggered by subprime mortgages in 2008 – based on the view that hedge fund activities exacerbated the crisis, the financial regulatory authority has been reluctant to introduce hedge funds in Korea. Finally, on December 21, 2009, the Enforcement Decree of the FSCMA was supplemented to allow PEFs with qualified investors to be formed. The regulations adopted provided that: (1) only pension funds and qualified investors may be investors, (2) 50 percent of the fund must be invested in companies undergoing restructuring, and (3) borrowing is limited to 3 times the fund assets. No PEF with qualified investors has been registered under these restrictive regulations.

To promote alternative investment opportunities and easier funding for new growth areas, the FSC announced its plan on June 20, 2011 to enact amendments to the Enforcement Decree of the FSCMA to somewhat reduce the regulatory burden on PEFs with qualified investors (i.e. essentially an introduction of hedge funds under Korean law) and introduce a legal framework for prime brokers who would provide securities lending, credit and custody services to hedge funds.[8]

The main parts of the relevant amendments are as follows:

1. Expansion of the scope of qualified investors
The definition of "Qualified Investor" is changed to include individuals contributing KRW 500 million or more.

2. Elimination of investment guideline and increase of borrowing limit
The requirement of investing 50 percent of the fund's assets in companies under restructuring is eliminated. Ceilings on borrowing and derivative transactions are raised.

3. Addition of a license sub-category for PEFs with qualified investors
As these changes have made the regulatory framework governing PEFs with qualified investors quite different, a new license sub-category has been added for hedge funds. The existing system for collective investment schemes has been adjusted to accommodate this.

4. Addition of reporting obligations on PEFs with qualified investors
To reflect the global trend in regulating hedge funds more tightly, details of the items to be reported by hedge funds (e.g. borrowing, derivatives transactions, investment strategies and types of investment assets) are publicly disclosed.

5. Introduction of prime brokerage
Prime brokerage, i.e. furnishing securities lending, credit and custody services to hedge funds, and related regulations have been introduced in the Korean market.

6. Relaxation of prime broker credit provisions
Relevant regulations have been revised to allow prime brokers to provide credit in forms other than loans secured by securities.

7. Streamlining regulation of prime broker custody services
The regulations have been revised to allow prime brokers to provide securities lending and credit in addition to custody services and to permit prime brokers to delegate the performance of their custody services to third parties.

---

[8] FSC Public Announcement No. 2011-92.

8. Regulations concerning Chinese walls for prime brokers

Under proposed amendments, a company desiring to engage in prime brokerage activities would be allowed to have one of its divisions handle proprietary trading, brokerage and custody services, so long as there is a Chinese wall between the prime brokerage division and all the other divisions.

It should be noted that the amendments described above are still in the drafts stage and the proposed contents have been announced to elicit industry comments. Thus, they may be further amended before being adopted in final form.

VII. CONCLUSION

Since their introduction in Korea, PEFs have achieved substantial growth in both quantity and quality and are now solidly established as a preferred vehicle for investing in M&As and restructuring. Nevertheless, strict regulations not found in the western countries have prevented the PEF form gaining further popularity. Therefore, it is necessary to streamline the current regulations to further promote the growth of PEFs. At the same time, it is hoped that the proposed amendments to the regulations on hedge funds will result in further relaxation of restrictions and ultimately be adopted in a form that makes it possible to nurture domestic hedge funds to become competitive internationally.

11. The market for corporate control in Korea*

Hwa-Jin Kim

I. INTRODUCTION

Korea may be qualified as one of the "inefficient controlling shareholder systems" under the taxonomy proposed by Professor Ronald Gilson.[1] Recent research shows that the average of controlling family ownership for public firms in Korea was 29.51 percent, compared with controlling families' cash-flow rights of 8.42 percent. In the case of Samsung Group, the largest Korean conglomerate, those numbers were 13.52 percent and 1.14 percent, respectively, for public firms in the group.[2] The private benefit of control is also relatively high in Korea. The value of corporate control amounts to about 34 percent of firm market value in Korea, as compared to about 29 percent in Italy, 1 percent in Denmark, 9 percent in Germany, and 2 percent in the United States.[3] The poor corporate governance practices of some large Korean firms are responsible for the still-continuing discussions on how to abolish the "Korea discount," i.e., how to eliminate or reduce agency costs in the inefficient controlling shareholder system.

One of the solutions to the problem may be the increasing exposure of corporate control to the (global) market. This requires Korea to facilitate corporate takeovers and promote the market for corporate control. As a matter of fact, contested mergers and acquisitions emerged in the business world of Korea in the mid-1990s and have since served as a popular

---

* This chapter is a shortened version of Hwa-Jin Kim, *The Case for Market for Corporate Control in Korea*, 8 Journal of Korean Law 227 (2008).

[1] *See* Ronald J. Gilson, *Controlling Shareholders and Corporate Governance: Complicating the Comparative Taxonomy*, 119 HARV. L. REV. 1641 (2006).

[2] James Jinho Chang & Hyun-Han Shin, *Family Ownership and Performance in Korean Conglomerates*, 15 PACIFIC-BASIN FIN. J. 329 (2007).

[3] *See* Tatiana Nenova, *The Value of Corporate Voting Rights and Control: A Cross-Country Analysis*, 68 J. FIN. ECON. 325 (2003).

topic for the media. The surprising takeover of Hannong Corporation by Dongbu Group in 1994 opened the gate for such transactions in Korea. This was followed by the abolition of the statutory protection of control as of April 1, 1997. Now the largest company in Korea, Samsung Electronics, is also said to be vulnerable to potential takeover threat by foreign competitors and/or hedge funds.

This chapter describes and analyzes the market for corporate control in Korea by summarizing landmark cases together with relevant laws and regulations: SK Corporation's (SKs') fight against Sovereign Asset Management, contest for control over the Hyundai Group (Hyundai), and KT&G's fight against Carl Icahn and his allies. This chapter, in particular, focuses on the role of takeovers in the improvement of the corporate governance of Korean companies as dramatically exemplified by the cases. Active policy discussions in respect of the market for corporate control and takeover defenses, including the poison pill, and the reshaping of large corporate groups are all on-going in Korea and should lead to new legislation. As was the case in the United States and other jurisdictions, many of the important developments in Korean corporate law are emerging out of judicial decisions in the context of corporate control contest. The new institutions, once finally adopted, may lead to a significant number of litigations, and Korean corporate law will open a new era in its dynamic evolutionary process.

II. CORPORATE GOVERNANCE AND TAKEOVERS

It is well known through numerous reports and scholarly works that many efforts to improve the corporate governance system of Korean companies have been undertaken since the 1997 Asian financial crisis.[4] The Korean Securities and Exchange Act (KSEA), which stipulated rules governing public companies regarding their corporate governance, went through 16 revisions since 1997, and the Korean Banking Act, 11 revisions. The Korean Commercial Code (KCC) has also been subject to six revisions and is currently being scrutinized again for another major amendment.[5] It is also noteworthy that various sectors have continuously engaged in endeavors to improve the corporate accounting practice and capital

---

4 Hwa-Jin Kim, *Toward the "Best Practice" Model in a Globalizing Market: Recent Developments in Korean Corporate Governance*, 2 J. Corp. L. Stud. 345 (2002); Bernard Black et al., *Corporate Governance in Korea at the Millennium: Enhancing International Competitiveness*, 26 J. Corp. L. 537 (2001).

5 *See* Korean Ministry of Justice Press Release, March 30, 2012.

market structure as evidenced by the enacting of the Securities Class Action Act, *inter alia*. Legislators have also integrated the seven individual acts covering the capital market and are working on developing a new infrastructure for developing investment banks in the Korean capital markets.[6] On February 4, 2009, the new Korean Financial Investment Services and Capital Market Act (KFISCMA) went into effect, which also substitutes the KSEA.

Contested mergers and acquisitions are no longer viewed with unfavorable judgment in Korea. In fact, a number of corporate control contests and hostile takeover attempts have since taken place. Especially following the critical period in 1997, contested mergers and acquisitions have been playing a valuable function in improving corporate governance, and this led the way to amending many laws to facilitate and promote hostile takeovers. As a result, advocates for having takeover defensive tactics in place to protect incumbent management face objections. Additional restrictions are being imposed on member companies of large corporate groups instead, and the government is also considering implementing a number of regulations for the ownership structure of conglomerates in an effort to make them subject to market discipline. Two of the most noted devices are investigation of the discrepancy between the control right and cash flow right within the large conglomerates and making the ownership structures known to the public.[7]

No tender offers were attempted in Korea prior to 1994. However, beginning with Hansol Paper's attempt to acquire shares of Daesang without the consent of the company's management in October 1994, the number of hostile tender offers has since increased in Korea. Competing tender offers are not unusual. Tender offers have grown in number, but, more notably, the types of and purposes for tender offers have also become more diversified.

The Korean rule for tender offer[8] has been evolving to facilitate corporate takeovers through tender offers and promote the market for corporate control. The Korean law basically allocates the decision-making role in relation to a takeover bid to the shareholders. It is made after the U.S. rules in that directors cannot control access to the shareholders.[9] The

---

6 *See* Korean Ministry of Finance and Economy Press Release, June 29, 2006.

7 *See, e.g.,* Korea Fair Trade Commission Press Release, July 13, 2005 (showing improvements).

8 Articles 133 through 146 of the KFISCMA.

9 However, as Korea is introducing the poison pills, it moves toward the UK model which allocates a decision-making role to target management in addition to the shareholders.

KSEA had mandatory tender offer provisions that required the acquirer to offer for at least 50 percent plus one shares when the acquirer crossed the 25 percent threshold. The rule, however, was taken out of the statute during the 1997 financial crisis as it blocked acquisitions of financially distressed firms by foreign investors.

III. TAKEOVER DEFENSIVE TACTICS

Now that the business environment in Korea is no longer so favorable to the current owners/directors, they are urging new means of takeover defense such as the poison pill and dual-class common shares and at the same time, are keeping themselves busy searching for other legitimate ways to protect their management control. Amid the alert state, some yet to be legally proven tactics such as the golden parachute are quite popular for them. The court cases on the takeover defenses are not informative, and the available cases are limited to the most commonly used methods like rights offerings and selling treasury shares to friendly parties. In particular, the sale of treasury shares has been the favorite tactic of Korean corporations in their attempt to protect their corporate control.

Sale of Treasury Shares: Disposal of treasury shares must, in principle, comply with the procedure laid out in KIFSCMA. Under the KIFSCMA, listed companies would first have to obtain approval from their board of directors for the disposal of their treasury shares and then file a report on the disposal of treasury shares with the Korea Financial Services Commission (KFSC). Where the company disposes of its shares through the Korea Exchange, the order for the shares must be placed in a certain way and the asking price will have to be within a particular range. In contrast, if the disposal of the shares takes place off-the-market, there are no restrictions on the asking price and method of the order. Therefore, sale of treasury shares to a friendly party based upon an elaborate contractual arrangement, including the fair price and other terms, might be an effective defensive tactic against a takeover. Although there was a lower court decision that outlawed the disposition of treasury shares to the controlling shareholder,[10] other courts keep validating the disposition of treasury shares to friendly parties.

Issuance of New Shares: Under the KCC shareholders of stock

[10] Seoul Western District Court, Decisions of March 24, 2006 and June 29, 2006, Case Nos. 2006-Kahap-393 and 2005-Gahap-8262, respectively.

companies have preemptive rights.[11] However, the KCC provides that the board of directors has the authority to issue new shares to third parties and/or shareholders not in proportion to the current shareholding ratio when necessary to achieve the objective of the company's management, such as introduction of new technology and improvement of capital structures.[12] This also applies to the issuance of convertible bonds (CB) or bonds with warrant (BW) (equity-linked securities). The articles of incorporation for most listed companies in Korea provide that the board has, under certain circumstances, the authority to issue new shares or equity-linked securities to third parties and/or shareholders not in proportion to the current shareholding ratio. Thus, the issuance of new shares can be an effective tool that the incumbent management can use to fend off hostile bidders. However, there have been several cases where the validity of issuing new shares or equity-linked securities to defend against takeover has been put to the test and several court cases have held that such issuance is invalid (and is subject to preliminary injunction).

Strategic Alliance: Many Korean companies enter into an agreement with a potential "white knight" to mutually hold the other's shares and come to their aid if there is a hostile takeover attempt. For instance, POSCO and KB Financial Group recently agreed to cross-hold shares amounting to 300 billion Korean won.[13] Quite often, the strategic alliance partner is a customer or business partner of the company. There are no laws in Korea that prohibit companies from entering into such an alliance agreement where parties mutually agree to hold the other's shares. However, Art. 369 Paragraph 3 of the KCC provides that where a company owns 10 percent or more of shares of the other company, the other company cannot exercise the voting rights on the shares of the first company. Further, in mutually acting as a potential white knight to the other, companies sometimes enter into an agreement to exchange non-executive (or outside) directors. The KCC now contains regulations on the qualification of non-executive directors. Under these regulations, one ground for disqualifying a candidate from being a non-executive director is if the candidate serves as the current officer/employee or served, in the past two years, as an officer or employee of the company that has important business relationships or is in a competitive or cooperative relationship with the electing company.[14]

---

11 KCC, Article 418, Paragraph 1.

12 KCC, Article 418, Paragraph 2.

13 Maeil Kyungje, December 22, 2008.

14 KCC, Article 382, Paragraph 3.

Restrictions on Qualification of Directors: To defend against a hostile takeover certain restrictions on the qualification of directors can be placed in the articles of incorporation. For example, the company's articles of incorporation could provide that to become a director, the candidate must have served at least a certain period as an officer or employee of the company. This may make it difficult for a person who attempts a hostile takeover to nominate his or her own director candidates. In fact, some of the listed companies' articles of incorporation contain such provision. As long as requirement concerning the period of employment is not too advantageous for the current management, such provision in the articles of incorporation would be held valid. However, such arrangement may backfire on the board. Recently, KT, the largest telecommunications company of Korea has experienced difficulties in recruiting its new CEO.[15]

Golden Parachute: The so-called "golden parachute" provides directors or management with lucrative severance payments in case they are ousted by hostile takeover. It is intended to make the company less attractive to a potential acquirer by placing a heavy financial burden on the acquirer who seeks to acquire the company. Although there is no reported court case, it is widely believed that the golden parachute is allowed under Korean law if the company's articles of incorporation allows it and/or if the company's internal severance pay regulations allow the granting of golden parachutes and the company obtains approval from the shareholders concerning the maximum remuneration of directors at the shareholders' meeting. In fact, some of the companies in Korea currently provide golden parachutes to its directors/management. As of August 2008, 15 listed companies have adopted golden parachutes.[16] However, there is a substantial risk that directors who approve payment of severance pay, which is considered excessive, may be in breach of their fiduciary duty under the KCC or Korean Criminal Code, depending on the seriousness of their actions. Moreover, it seems that there is negative sentiment on the part of shareholders and general public in Korea regarding the granting of golden parachutes.

Staggered Board: When the term of a director under the company's articles of incorporation is three years, a way to avert hostile bidders from acquiring control of the board is by adopting the so-called "staggered" board in the articles of incorporation so that each year, for example, the terms of only 1/3 of the board members expires. This way, it would take at least two additional years for the hostile bidders to acquire a complete

---

15 Maeil Kyungje, November 25, 2008.
16 Hankuk Kyongje, September 2, 2008.

control over the board. It is understood that this device is, in the United States, one of the most popular and powerful anti-takeover arrangements when combined with the poison pill.[17] However, in Korea, it is not clear how strongly the directors can resist the successful bidder and this approach would not be effective if the hostile bidders can obtain sufficient votes to pass a special resolution and terminate the terms of all of the directors. The KCC, different from the Delaware General Corporation Law, does not confer any legal effect to the articles of incorporation that formally adopts the staggered board. Therefore, the directors can be discharged without cause,[18] and their seats will be filled by the shareholders, not the remaining directors. Also, as the KCC currently does not allow the companies to adopt the poison pills, the effectiveness of the staggered board is questionable. As of August 2008, 20 listed companies have adopted a staggered board.[19]

Supermajority Voting: Another defensive tactic would be to provide for a stronger requirement in the company's articles of incorporation than the special resolution for certain events such as merger or business transfer that the acquirer may try to effect after the acquisition.[20] However, there

---

17 Lucian Bebchuk, John Coats IV & Guhan Subramanian, *The Powerful Antitakeover Force of Staggered Boards: Theory, Evidence, and Policy*, 54 STAN. L. REV. 887 (2002).

18 KCC Article 385 (Dismissal): (1) A director may be dismissed from office at any time by a resolution at a general shareholders' meeting in accordance with Article 434: Provided, that in case where the term of office of a director was fixed and he is dismissed without cause before the expiration of such term, he may claim for damages caused thereby. (2) If the dismissal of a director is rejected at a general shareholders' meeting notwithstanding the existence of dishonest acts or any grave fact in violation of the relevant acts, subordinate statutes or the articles of incorporation in connection with his duties, any shareholder who holds no less than 3/100 of the total outstanding shares may demand the court to dismiss the director, within one month from the date on which the above resolution of the general meeting was made.

19 HANKUK KYONGJE, September 2, 2008.

20 The board of directors of a Korean corporation has broad power and wide discretion to manage all matters which are reasonably necessary to achieve the purposes of a corporation. Generally all the affairs and business of a corporation are considered and determined by the board of directors except for the matters required to be resolved at shareholders' meetings under the KCC or by the articles of incorporation of the corporation. The following matters are basically within the authority of the board, but may be reallocated to the shareholders' meeting if the articles of incorporation so provide: (1) appointment of a representative director (Article 389(1)); (2) issuance of new shares (Article 416); (3) conversion of reserves into capital (Article 461(1)); (4) issuance of convertible bonds (Article 513(2)); and (5) issuance of bonds with warrants (Article 516-2(2)). The Commercial Code

is a view that articles of incorporation that provides for stricter requirement than special resolution under the KCC is void. There was a lower court decision that outlawed the supermajority requirement for removal of directors without cause.[21] Thus, if the company provides for stronger requirements than the special resolution in relation to a hostile takeover in its articles of incorporation, it is possible that such requirement will be held void. Notwithstanding such a view, there are some listed companies in Korea that provide for stricter requirements than the special resolution in their articles of incorporation. As of August 2008, 38 listed companies have adopted supermajority voting.[22] It should also be noted that even if setting forth such stricter requirements in the articles of incorporation is held to be valid, this would result, in effect, in minority shareholders having a veto right, which could place a burden on the management.

IV. CASES

A. *SK*

The SK case uniquely provides empirical data and resources to show that first its problem-ridden corporate governance triggered a hostile takeover attempt, and then the takeover threat brought about major improvement in its corporate governance. Furthermore, it raised fierce political and economic controversies because (1) the hostile takeover threat came from a foreign investment fund, (2) energy was the core business of SK Group, and (3) SK Group's most important member company was the key telecommunication provider, SK Telecom, which was the 450th largest company based on its total market capitalization as of March 31, 2005.

---

also lists matters which require resolution at a shareholders' meeting, i.e., matters which cannot be removed from shareholders' authority even via the articles of incorporation. Certain important matters of a corporation can be adopted only by the affirmative vote of shareholders holding at least two-thirds (2/3) of the shares represented in person or by proxy at a general meeting of shareholders which represents the affirmative vote of the holders of at least one-third (1/3) of the total issued and outstanding shares. Article 434. This is called a "special resolution." All other matters, including the election of directors (Article 382(1)) can be resolved by a simple majority vote of the shareholders present or represented at a general meeting of shareholders which represents the affirmative vote of the holders of at least one-fourth (1/4) of the total issued and outstanding shares.

[21] Seoul Central District Court, Decisions of June 2, 2008, Case No. 2008-Gahap-1167.

[22] Hankuk Kyongje, September 2, 2008.

The development of the "SK Saga" arose during the period of the 1997 Asian financial crisis. SK Securities incurred a huge loss from the financial derivatives deals with JP Morgan prior to 1997, and it led to lawsuits both in Korea and the United States. In an effort to bring reconciliation between the two parties, SK Global involved its overseas subsidiary, but PSPD deemed it illegal and filed a complaint against the SK management with the Public Prosecutor's Office. SK Global was found to have committed a large scale accounting fraud, and the stock prices of all the SK Group companies plummeted. When SK Corporation's stock price fell to 6100 Korean won, Sovereign Asset Management suddenly emerged as the largest shareholder.

When Sovereign came into play, the public viewed it as a mysterious entity and scorned it as an ill-intended speculator. But Sovereign claimed to be a serious corporate governance fund. It is believed that Sovereign's actions taken in Korea not only were unpredictable and lacking consistency, but the Fund also seemed to be without any fundamental strategies. Sovereign persistently assailed SK Group's flaws in its corporate governance and eventually demanded the removal of Chey Tae-won, doubting his leadership qualifications as the head of SK Group. Sovereign further attempted to gain control of the board of SK Corporation by nominating outside director candidates. Notwithstanding the suspicion that Sovereign intended to take over SK Corporation, Sovereign kept its public announcement on the issue of corporate governance alone and expressed no plan to engage in the management and business. But the press cast doubt on Sovereign's true intentions.

Sovereign vied for the control of SK at two annual shareholder meetings. At the March 2004 meeting, it tried to remove the opt-out clause on cumulative voting from the articles of incorporation of the company and elect outside directors of their choice, but both attempts failed. With strong support from National Pension Service and minority shareholders, the 51.5 percent to 39.5 percent vote was in favor of the company.[23]

Prior to the March 2004 shareholder meeting, SK tried to increase the share of its allies by disposing of its treasury shares to friendly parties. It decided to sell 13 208 860 treasury shares (accounting for approximately 10.41 percent of the issued and outstanding shares) to certain financial institutions friendly to the existing management. Sovereign sought a preliminary injunction of the directors' decision. It claimed that the board's decision to sell its treasury shares to friendly parties would cause the dilution of Sovereign's voting rights and, therefore, it was being prevented

[23] Hankuk Kyongje, March 13, 2004, at 13.

from fairly exercising its voting rights in the 2004 general meeting of shareholders. The Seoul District Court, however, refused to grant a preliminary injunction in its decision of December 23, 2003.[24] The court opined that the disposal of any treasury shares should not be prevented even in the midst of a dispute for control of the company; provided, however, that the shares have not originally been acquired to perpetuate the existing management and the controlling shareholder(s). The decision to sell the treasury shares in the court's view was justified as business judgment. The March 2004 shareholder meeting was prevailed by the management.

Around October 2004, Sovereign demanded that SK hold an extraordinary general meeting of the shareholders to amend SK's charter to disqualify anyone with a criminal conviction from being a director of the company, and to elect certain persons designated by Sovereign as outside directors of SK. SK refused Sovereign's request to hold the meeting, stating that the proposal to amend SK's charter was, in substance, identical to the proposal that was rejected in the 2004 annual meeting, and that since the 2005 annual meeting was at close hand, there was no reason to urgently hold an extraordinary meeting to elect outside directors. In response, Sovereign filed a petition with the court seeking the court's permission to hold an extraordinary meeting. The court rejected Sovereign's petition.[25] Sovereign then made a shareholder proposal to include amendment of SK's charter and election of outside directors in the agenda of 2005 annual meeting, SK and Sovereign carried out a proxy contest in relation to the issue.[26] The March 2005 shareholder meeting began in a highly tense setting; while Sovereign had demanded Chey Tae-won's removal from the board, the meeting agenda included renewal of Chey's term as director. But again, the shareholders voted by a wide margin to allow the company to defend its corporate control and re-elected Chey Tae-won to the board. The Seoul High Court convicted Chey Tae-won in June 2005 but he was saved from imprisonment and granted to stay on probation.

Sovereign, in July 2005, disposed of its entire stake in SK and gained

---

[24] Seoul Central District Court, Decision of December 23, 2003, Case No. 2003-Kahap-4154.

[25] Seoul Central District Court, Decision of December 15, 2004, Case No. 2004-Bihap-347. However, the court viewed Sovereign's petition not abusive.

[26] Sovereign had a tough fight. SK demanded that Sovereign provide certificates of registered seal impression of the shareholders who issued proxy to Sovereign. Surprisingly, Sovereign complied with the company's demand. Therefore, the issue of the means and standards for confirming the veracity of a proxy did not arise at the shareholders' meeting of SK.

about 1 trillion Korean won in profit, which is as an outstanding performance by a corporate governance fund. The Fund thereafter invested in LG Group, putting the market on alert again, but sold its stocks after six months and left the Korean market altogether.[27]

Sovereign's withdrawal from the Korean market evoked wild speculation but Professor Sang Yong Park of Yonsei University rendered an evaluation of Sovereign's strategies from an academic perspective.[28] According to Park, unlike undervaluation due to the "Korea discount" which results from a multitude of factors, undervaluation that is triggered by a discount of subsidiary shares due to matters relating to poor corporate governance creates unique opportunities for arbitrage, and the SK case exemplifies the latter. The aggregate value of SK Corporation's listed stock fell under 40 percent of the equity (20.85 percent) value of SK Telecom owned by SK Corporation at the time when Sovereign's hostile takeover attempt was in the initial stage. During the period subject to the analysis, while the rate of increase of share price of other oil refining corporations did not even reach the rate of increase of the composite stock price index, SK's rate far exceeded it. Such phenomenon cannot be explained by anything other than hostile takeover threats.

While under the threat of Sovereign's hostile takeover, SK Group assiduously worked on improving its corporate governance. It should be noted that there are several apparent reasons for such effort. First, it was not a surprise that they saw the need to fix their corporate governance, since it triggered their public criticism and disgrace. Second, Chey Tae-won was imprisoned and was going through trials. SK needed to make public that it was striving to improve its corporate governance system in order to render the situation favorable to the convicted chairman. Lastly, Sovereign assailed the corporate governance of SK, which was lagging behind global standards.

SK Corporation's effort to restructure its board by appointing a majority of outside directors was not a nominal political move. SK Group even went as far as to reform the boards of its private-member companies into outside-director dominated boards, which was not required by law. Regardless of the motive for such drastic change, the result was building a well functioning board and earning a name as the pacesetter for high standard corporate boards in the Korean market. Professor Hasung

---

27 *See* Maeil Kyungje, August 24, 2005, at A1.

28 Sang Yong Park, *The Political Economy of Corporate Governance: Hostile Takeover and Labor's Participation in Management*, 34-2 Korean Management Review 569 (2005) (Korean).

Jang's widely quoted comment well summarizes the overall impact: "Sovereign achieved in one year what the Korean government could not in many years." SK Group also tried to transform itself as a loosely integrated entity within which the member companies shared its brand. When the current market was infested with problems caused by the complicated relationships amongst member companies of large conglomerates, SK's move was praised as a prudent strategy. Finally, in April 2007, SK Group ended up announcing its plan to transform itself into a holding company structure. The market applauded the move.

B. *Hyundai*

The Hyundai case also reflects a corporate governance issue resulting in a hostile takeover attempt, but it is much more complicated than the SK case in terms of its historical background and high level of politics involved. Both the bidder and defender in the Hyundai case vied for support from the shareholders on a platform of improving corporation governance. This case demonstrates that corporate governance issues can lead to hostile take over attempts or disputes over corporate control.

After the unexpected death of the former chairman, his widow, Hyun Jeong-eun, succeeded him, and a foreign fund began to actively purchase the stocks of Hyundai Elevator, the flagship of Hyundai Group. In November 2003, allegedly to salvage the Hyundai Group from foreigners, the brothers' uncle and the president of Kumgang, Chung Sang-yung, who disliked the officers of late chairman and was displeased with Hyun taking over Hyundai Group, made a hostile takeover acquiring, directly and indirectly, approximately 44.39 percent of the issued and outstanding shares of Hyundai Elevator.[29] Hyundai Group tried first to increase its capital by a public offering on a large scale but was enjoined by the court. The board of directors of Hyundai Elevator, in an attempt to defend against Kumgang's hostile takeover attempt, resolved to issue 10 million new shares, which was 178 percent of the then outstanding shares, at a 30 percent discount, with a condition that the number of the newly-issued shares to which any one person may subscribe cannot be more than 300 shares. Kumgang sought a preliminary injunction of the proposed issuance of new shares by Hyundai Elevator, arguing that the proposed issuance was improper as it infringed the preemptive rights of the existing shareholders and was an attempt only to perpetuate the current

[29] *See* HANKUK KYONGJE, November 5, 2003, at 1.

management. The court viewed that Hyundai's public offering did infringe the preemptive right of the shareholders.[30]

The Suwon District Court found that the proposed issuance of new shares infringed the preemptive rights of the existing shareholders, including Kumgang, and it granted a preliminary injunction. The court reasoned that, considering that any attempt to defend a takeover bid should be made within the scope allowed under the laws and regulations and the articles of incorporation of the company concerned, Hyundai Elevator's proposed issuance of new shares, which was allowed only to the extent necessary to raise funds for the business of the company under the KCC and the articles of incorporation of the company, apparently for the purpose of perpetuation of the existing controlling shareholder(s) or the management, was not proper. However, the court did not completely rule out the possibility of issuing new shares as a means of takeover defense. Specifically, the court stated that the following event may be an exception to the general rule where the company concerned may issue new shares in an attempt to avert a hostile takeover: (1) if preserving the existing controlling shareholder(s) and/or the existing management of the target company is beneficial to the company itself or the shareholders in general or there are any other specific public reasons; and (2) if the target company has taken all reasonable steps in making the decision to issue new shares, such as soliciting the opinions of the disinterested shareholders or independent experts. According to the court, if these requirements are met, the issuance of new shares may not be invalidated because it was done for proper business purposes as stipulated in the company's articles of incorporation and the KCC.

During the course of the legal battle, Hyundai emphasized that the 5 percent Rule should not be understood just as an "early warning system."[31] The purpose of the Rule was rather to protect minority shareholders who do not have the necessary resources to collect information on other (large) shareholders' intent. Certain empirical studies done by U.S. scholars[32] were heavily cited in the brief of Hyundai's counsel. The court accepted the argument and sanctioned Kumgang's violation of the

---

30 Suwon District Court Yeoju Branch, Decision of December 12, 2003, Case No. 2003-Kahap-369.

31 *See generally* WILLIAM J. CARNEY, MERGERS AND ACQUISITIONS: CASES AND MATERIALS ch.10 (Foundation Press, 2000).

32 *See* RONALD GILSON & BERNARD BLACK, THE LAW AND FINANCE OF CORPORATE ACQUISITIONS 903 (2nd ed., Foundation Press, 1995) (citing a study that shows higher abnormal rate of return in the case of compliance with the 5 percent Rule).

5 percent Rule severely.[33] The ruling of the court was perceived as extraordinary by the Korean bar partly because the Korea Financial Supervisory Service did not accept Hyundai's argument that the entire filing for over 5 percent made by Kumgang should be treated as invalid.[34]

Hyundai Group's attempt to avert the hostile takeover attempt by Kumgang succeeded in the end, because Kumgang was found to be in violation of the 5 percent Rule for material omission in reporting,[35] although Hyundai went through the fierce proxy fight. Before the crucial shareholders' meeting of March 30, 2004, Kumgang announced that it would withdraw from the contest if it would lose the proxy contest. Indeed, Kumgang sold its shares in Hyundai Group to Schindler Holding of Switzerland and withdrew from the scene in early 2006.

It is interesting to note that the incident that directly triggered Kumgang's attempt for a hostile takeover was a foreign fund's large-scale purchase of Hyundai shares. Hyundai Heavy Industries also made an equally interesting remark that the purchase of Merchant Marine shares was motivated by its concern over a potential hostile takeover by a foreign entity. Furthermore, the data and materials on the disputes over corporate control between Hyundai Group and Kumgang reveal that the main issues were not so much about creating synergies through mergers and acquisitions but calling attention to the problems affecting the corporate governance system and promise to correct the flaws therein. After the successful takeover defense, Hyundai Group's leadership did promise investors that it would focus further on the "responsibility, transparency and ethics" in managing its member companies.[36]

C. *KT&G*

KT&G is an outgrowth of the Monopoly Bureau founded in 1952 and Korea Tobacco and Ginseng Corporation founded in 1989. In 1999, the Corporation spun off its red ginseng business division and was listed in

---

[33] Seoul Central District Court, Decision of March 26, 2004, Case No. 2004-Kahap-809. The petition for the preliminary injunction was filed by Hyundai Securities.

[34] *See* HANKUK KYONGJE, March 30, 2004, at 3.

[35] *See* Korea Financial Supervisory Service Press Release, February 11, 2004; Suwon District Court Yeoju Branch, Decision of March 23, 2004, Case No. 2004-Kahap-51. Grounds for sanctions such as restraint on voting rights include not only defective reporting, but also false reporting and omission in reporting. *See* KOREA FINANCIAL SUPERVISORY SERVICE, UNDERSTANDING KOREA'S "5% RULE" (December 2005).

[36] *See* HANKUK KYONGJE, April 2, 2004, at A15 (full page advertisement).

the same year. Issuing GDRs and disposing of stock owned by the government in 2002, it was entirely privatized and renamed KT&G. As of September 30, 2005, Kiup Bank was the largest domestic shareholder with 5.75 percent. KT&G listed its GDRs on the Luxembourg Stock Exchange and its management is run by professional managers and an independent board of directors. Since 2004, KT&G has been selected as the company with the best corporate governance practice every year by the Korea Corporate Governance Service. According to the sources from the Korea Exchange, the rate of return to shareholders of KT&G during the period between 2003 and 2005 was 96.09 percent, a record rate in Korea.

Carl Icahn's attack on KT&G in early 2006[37] caught Korea by surprise.[38] It was quite shocking to see KT&G fall subject to hedge funds, belittling its past glorious records of dispersed ownership and professional management, and recognition for excellent corporate governance. This incident raised an alert for the soundness of the Korean criteria for evaluating corporate governance. Actually, during the dispute many flaws in KT&G management and corporate governance were revealed.

Carl Icahn went about his usual way in the KT&G case,[39] and due to this, the Korean capital market was able to draw lessons on the strategies and techniques of international hedge funds. His key suggestions included, *inter alia*: (1) selling down non-core assets, (2) spin-off and listing of Korean Ginseng Corporation, (3) restructuring KT&G's vast real estate portfolio, (4) increasing dividends so that the company's dividend yield would be in line with other world class tobacco companies, and (5) buying back shares, through tender offer, if necessary, and cancelling shares to the extent legally permissible.[40] On February 23, 2006, immediately after sending the "proposals for enhancing stakeholder value," the Icahn group proposed KT&G to acquire additional KT&G shares at 60000 Korean won (with 13 to 33 percent premium). They were prepared to commit an aggregate of approximately two trillion Korean won (two billion US Dollars) of their own equity capital towards the consummation of the transaction and were sure about the possibility of additional debt financing. The proposal was rejected by KT&G in a letter dated February 28, 2006.

---

37 *Icahn in South Korea Move*, FINANCIAL TIMES, January 18, 2006, at 1.

38 *See Icahn's Push in Korea Shows Rise of Raiders is Roiling New Markets*, WALL STREET JOURNAL, March 2, 2006, at A1.

39 *See* Ken Auletta, *The Raid: How Carl Icahn Came Up Short*, NEW YORKER, March 20, 2006, at 132–143.

40 Icahn group's letter to KT&G dated February 23, 2006 (on file with the author).

Despite winning the favorable stance in the proxy contest with support from Institutional Shareholder Services and Glass Lewis, due to a material blunder by one of his local counsels, who failed to file a proper shareholder proposal, Icahn had to settle for appointing one outside director of his choice to the board at the March 2006 shareholders' meeting.

There were six directorships up for election at the meeting, consisting of two slots for outside directors and four slots for outside directors who would also serve on the audit committee. While the Icahn group's three candidates appeared on the agenda as candidates for election to the board, they would be only be available to compete for the two non-audit committee directorships. By reserving four of the six directorships for directors who would also serve on the audit committee, KT&G had strategically ensured that all of its nominees would fill these positions as candidates for such positions may only be selected by the board. The Icahn group claimed that such an approach infringed their right to submit the shareholder proposals in violation of the law.[41]

However, on March 14, 2006, the Daejeon District Court rejected the petition by Carl Icahn and his allies, allowing their three nominees to vie for only two seats of KT&G's outside directorship. The Court overruled Icahn's claim, saying, "We do not find that KT&G's separate voting system for regular and audit directors encroaches upon the minority shareholders' right to a choice of directors like Carl Icahn and his partners claim . . . Both separate and collective voting for directors are consistent with the current Commercial Code and Securities Exchange Act. Which to choose between the two depends on the board as long as there is no special proposal from shareholders during a shareholder proposal period . . . The Carl Icahn consortium did not make issue with the voting method itself during a shareholder proposal period, although they argued that it was not in line with the law. All they wanted was to include three nominees they recommended as candidates for directors."[42]

The four audit committee member positions on the 12-member board were assured to go to KT&G's candidates, but one of the two outside director positions was almost certain to go to an Icahn candidate because neither side would win the 66.7 per cent support needed to take both seats. Carl Icahn and his partners succeeded in getting their candidate on the board through cumulative voting. The remaining three candidates for the two seats for which the Icahn candidates were eligible received far fewer

---

41 *See* Icahn group's letter to KT&G dated February 15, 2006 (on file with the author).

42 Case No. 2006-Kahap-242.

votes. In August 2006 KT&G accepted practically all of the suggestions made by Icahn. Carl Icahn, in December 2006, disposed of its entire stakes in KT&G and gained about 100 billion Korean won in profit (44.22 percent net return).

At the time of dispute, one commentator went as far as to say, "If Sovereign was a grade school kid, Icahn is a college student. Now a group of graduate students like KKR will flock to the Korean market. Are the Korean companies ready to defend its corporate control?"[43] As peculiar as it may sound, the statement turned out to be quite convincing. The international nature represented by the mix of the shareholders elicited participation by many international players during the KT&G and Icahn dispute. KT&G was advised by Goldman Sachs and Lehman Brothers, and Georgeson Shareholder Communications acted in the proxy solicitation at the shareholder's meeting.

KT&G triggered an explosion of debates on the merits of leaving Korean companies exposed to the possibility of hostile takeover attempts. Many economists have proved the disciplinary function of a hostile takeover attempt; a hostile takeover attempt puts a rein on directors, thereby serving as an effective external controlling mechanism. In light of the positive effect, some argue for no limitation on allowing hostile takeover attempts. According to the liberal advocates, the need for securing takeover defensive tactics as demanded by companies lacks sound judgment. Numerous companies that belong to corporate groups are already free from any hostile takeover attempts because the recourse is available for them through the means of cross and circular shareholdings and complicated ownership structure. Therefore, the government should focus more on untangling ownership structures of Korean corporations and allow hostile takeover attempts to function effectively. They further argue that KT&G could not avoid being the target of the hedge fund because its dispersed ownership was characteristic of Western corporations and because it did not belong to a conglomerate. The threat imposed on KT&G by the hedge fund in the end benefited the shareholders and other interested parties and increased the value of the company.

V. POISON PILL IN KOREA

The poison pill has been the single most controversial issue in discussions on takeover defenses in Korea over the years. This is more so because

---

43 *See* Money Today, April 13, 2006.

Japan introduced the poison pill in 2005[44] and its practical function has recently been contested before the courts in Japan.[45] According to the widely-accepted definition, "the essence of the poison pill is that the crossing by an acquirer of a relatively low threshold of ownership triggers rights for target shareholders in relation to the shares of either the target or the acquirer, from which the acquirer itself is excluded and which render the acquisition of further shares in the target fruitless or impossibly expensive."[46] Under the current laws of Korea, the poison pill that is commonly used in the United States[47] is not allowed. There are various rules and regulations that limit the company's ability to create the poison pill. Among others, as it is also the case in many European countries, under the KCC, a resolution concerning dividend payout is subject to resolution by the shareholders, not by the board of directors. Also, distribution of profit can only be made by cash or stocks, not contingent rights to purchase company's new shares. The KFISCMA also regulates the issuance price of new shares of listed companies.[48]

The poison pill, if introduced in Korea, should be used to support a better deal for the shareholders. However, as Professor Gilson did warn Japan before,[49] it may be used to simply block a bid in favor of the controlling minority, if institutions like independent directors, courts and active institutional investors do not police the uses to which the poison pill is actually put. It can also be expected that poison pills in Korea will generate lawsuits and Korean corporate law will evolve along the line developed by the Delaware takeover law as was already evidenced in the Hyundai case.[50] Large Korean law firms have been educating their young lawyers in U.S. law schools for decades, and so has the Korean judiciary. Furthermore, large Korean firms may feel safer if they retain reputable

---

44 Satoshi Kawai, *Poison Pill in Japan*, 2004 COLUM. BUS. L. REV. 11.

45 *See* Osugi, Kenichi, *What is Converging?: Rules on Hostile Takeovers in Japan and the Convergence Debate*, 9 ASIAN-PACIFIC L. & POLICY J. 143, 157–159 (2007) (Bulldog case).

46 This definition is from Lucian Bebchuk & Allen Ferrell, *Federalism and Corporate Law: The Race to Protect Managers from Takeovers*, 99 COLUM. L. REV. 1168 (1999).

47 Moran v. Household International, Inc., 500 A.2d 1346 (Del. 1985); RONALD GILSON & BERNARD BLACK, THE LAW AND FINANCE OF CORPORATE ACQUISITIONS 740–748 (2nd ed. Foundation Press, 1995).

48 Articles 118 through 132.

49 *See* Gilson, *supra* note 1, at 41–42.

50 *But see* Bernard S. Black, *The Core Fiduciary Duties of Outside Directors*, ASIA BUS. L. REV. 13, 27 (July 2001) ("[I] would not wish for another country to copy our confused case law.")

U.S. law firms when confronted with a control contest. The expert group commissioned by the Korean Ministry of Justice has been working on another draft bill to amend the KCC since early 2008. In November 2008, the expert group came up with tentative draft provisions to introduce the poison pill into the KCC as follows:

Article 432-2 (Subscription Option for New Shares).

(1) A company may grant the right to the shareholders to request the company to issue the new shares within a specified period ("Exercise Period"), at the pre-determined price ("Exercise Price") in proportion to the number and types of shares held by the shareholder ("Subscription Option")

(2) The company shall not receive any consideration in exchange for granting the Subscription Option.

(3) The company intending to issue the Subscription Option must specify the following items in the Articles of Incorporation.
   1. The statement that the Subscription Option may be granted to the shareholders.
   2. The limit on the number and types of new shares that could be issued pursuant to the exercise of Subscription Option.

(4) The Company may provide the following statements under its Articles of Incorporation incorporating the terms described under the Section 3 above. In such case, the company may grant the Subscription Option pursuant to the terms under the Articles of Incorporation only to maintain or increase the benefit of all shareholders and the value of the company.
   1. In certain cases, the Subscription Option may not be granted to some shareholders.
   2. In certain cases, some shareholders may not be able to exercise the Subscription Option, or the terms of the Subscription Option may be different for some shareholders as compared to other shareholders.
   3. In certain cases, the company may redeem all or part of the Subscription Options and in this case, the redemption terms may differ for some shareholders.

(5) Where the company grants the Subscription Option pursuant to the terms provided under the Articles of Incorporation, which incorporated the terms described under Section 4 above, the exercise price may be the fair price on the date when the Subscription Option is granted or the exercise date or the price below the par value of a share.

Article 330 (Restriction on the Issuance of the Shares at a Price below the Par Value)

The shares shall not be issued at a price below the par value except the issuance pursuant to the Article 417 and Section 5 of Article 432-2.

Article 432-3 (Granting Subscription Option)

(1) Where a company grants the Subscription Option, the following items must be specified by the resolution of board of directors thereof.
   1. The Subscription Option will be granted to the shareholders on a specified date.
   2. The number and type of shares to be newly issued pursuant to the exercise of Subscription Option or the method to calculate the number of shares thereon.
   3. Issues relating to the exercise price of the Subscription Option and the adjustment thereon.
   4. Exercise period and conditions on exercise of the Subscription Option.
   5. Where the company decided not to grant Subscription Option to some shareholders, the scope of shareholders who will not be granted with the Subscription Option.
   6. Where the exercise of the Subscription Option is restricted or the terms of the Subscription Option are different for some shareholders, the detailed information and the scope of shareholders who will be granted with a restricted Subscription Option or different terms thereon.

(2) The company must publicly notify the resolutions of the board of directors within seven days from the resolution date, approving the items under the Section 1 above.

(3) The Exercise Period under Item 4 of Section 1 shall begin after two weeks from the public notice under Section 2 above.

Article 432-4 (Redemption of the Subscription Option)

(1) Where the company decides to redeem the Subscription Option pursuant to the terms provided in the Articles of Incorporation for the purpose under item 3 of Section 4 of Article 432-2, the board of directors must decide the following items. In this case, the company must make a public notice thereon immediately.
   1. The scope of the Subscription Options that will be redeemed.
   2. If the Subscription Option will be effective under the certain circumstances, the reasons thereof.
   3. The effective date of the redemption.

4. The specifics regarding the money, assets or new shares to be paid or issued for redemption.
5. Where some shareholders will have different terms for the redemption as compared to other shareholders, the specifics of the different terms and the scope of those shareholders.

(2) With respect to the Subscription Option, which is redeemed pursuant to Section 1, the effectiveness of the Subscription Option will be extinguished on the date of the effective redemption date.

Article 432-5 (Accompaniment of Subscription Option and Retirement without Consideration)

(1) The Subscription Option cannot be transferred separately from the shares.

(2) In case when the share is transferred after the Subscription Option is granted, it shall be deemed that the Subscription Option was transferred with such transfer.

(3) The Company may retire all of the Subscription Option without a consideration through the resolution of board of directors or of the shareholders' meeting prior to the first date of the Exercise Period.

Article 432-6 (The Exercise of the Subscription Option)

(1) A person, who intends to exercise the Subscription Option, must submit two copies of applications to the Company within the Exercise Period and must fully pay the Exercise Price.

(2) For the shareholders who have exercised the Subscription Option under Section 1, Article 516-9 shall apply, *mutatis mutandis*.

VI. CONCLUDING REMARKS

The SK and Hyundai cases above show that a company's corporate governance bears a close link to hostile takeover attempts. Problems rooted in corporate governance of a company can ignite hostile takeover attempts. The KT&G case attests that Korean companies are not exempt from the international current of hedge fund activism and must promptly learn the survival and adaptation skills necessary in the market with a corporate governance paradigm shift.

The cases shown in this chapter were entangled in legal disputes. As a result, they all added great value to improving legal principles on mergers and acquisitions in the Korean market. The value is quite significant since the relatively short history of Korean market leaves a paucity of rich M&A resources. In particular, the SK and Hyundai cases called for developing various defensive tactics against takeover attempts, and a battle over the legitimacy of the new tactics unfolded at the courtrooms. All the major Korean law firms were mobilized in these cases and some U.S. law firms with long experience in the areas took part indirectly.

In view of the discussions in this chapter, it may be concluded that the market for corporate control functions as a disciplinary mechanism for poor corporate governance. The cases described in this chapter show, even empirically in the SK case, that the validity of Henry Manne's thesis may transcend national jurisdictions and cultural differences. The Korean case, in particular the SK case, also shows that the increasing exposure of control to the market could eliminate the inefficient controlling shareholder system. Hostile takeovers cannot solve all corporate governance problems of large Korean companies with controlling shareholders. However, promoting contestable control is a way forward. The new Korean Commercial Code should maintain a sophisticated balance between the active market for corporate control and effective takeover defensive tactics for the benefit of shareholders. Last, but not least, the usual emphasis on the role of judicial review in the controlling shareholder system should apply to the Korean case.

12. Issuance of new shares as a takeover defense and countermeasures

Sang Gon Kim

I. INTRODUCTION

In a hostile takeover situation, the most important issue for both the bidder and target is securing friendly shares. This is because, in order for a hostile takeover to succeed, the bidder's designees must be elected as the directors of the target and such election is decided by votes at the meeting of shareholders.

Generally speaking, there are three ways of securing friendly shares in a hostile takeover situation: (1) proxy contest, (2) sale of treasury shares to friendly shareholders and (3) issuance of new shares to friendly shareholders.

Proxy contests in listed companies are regulated by the Financial Investment Services and Capital Markets Act ("FSCMA").[1] There are numerous legal problems regarding the methods for soliciting proxies and for validating power of attorneys at meetings of shareholders. Furthermore, there still remain concerns of proxy contests being handled in favor of existing shareholders who have the power to call meetings of shareholders.[2]

Regarding the sale of treasury shares and issuance of new shares, since they are subject to approval of the target's board, in practice they are used

1 The Securities and Exchange Act ("SEA"), which was the relevant law, was abolished with the promulgation of the FSCMA on February 4, 2009. The special provisions under the SEA relating to listed companies have been incorporated in the Commercial Code and the rest have been incorporated in the FSCMA. As such, certain provisions under the abolished SEA (as referred to herein) are equally applicable under the FSCMA.

2 *See* "Problems Related to the Management of Meetings of Shareholders of Listed Companies involving Proxy Contests for a Hostile Takeover Bid," *Cholgo*, No. 52, Fall 2005, Korea Listed Companies Association.

only as defensive measures by the controlling shareholder in contrast to proxy contests which can be used as offensive tools.

We discuss below the legality of the issuance of new shares as a takeover defense, which is one of the aforementioned ways to secure friendly shares, as well as countermeasures in response thereto. We also discuss briefly the similarities and differences between the sale of treasury shares and issuance of new shares.

II. LEGAL ASSESSMENT OF TAKEOVER DEFENSE MEASURES BY DIRECTORS

The issuance of new shares is subject to board approval, thus as a general matter we first discuss whether directors' takeover defense measures are lawful.

A. The Activist Thesis

Under this view, directors must actively defend against hostile takeover efforts for a variety of reasons, including the following: hostile takeovers do not increase the overall wealth of society; the target's share value increases during a takeover defense and so serves the interests of shareholders; directors have a duty to protect not only shareholders but the target's employees, customers, creditors, etc. Directors' defensive actions must be respected under the business judgment rule.

This line of argument has been set forth by Lipton of the US and Martens Wiedrmann of Germany and is known to be the majority position of the public and the courts in the US and the minority position in Germany.[3]

B. The Passivity Thesis

Under this view, directors must remain passive in the face of hostile takeovers for a variety of reasons: hostile takeovers have the effect of increasing the overall wealth of society by transferring the target's assets to more competent management; although the target's share value may increase during

---

[3] Wook Rae Lee, "Legal Assessment of Defensive Action of Directors against a Hostile Takeover," BFL, No. 12, July, pg. 12, 2005; Jong Joon Song, "Key Defense Measures against M&A," Study on Commercial Law, Vol. 14, No. 1 (Aug. 1995), pg. 190.

the course of the takeover defense, such defense may in the long run harm shareholder interests by decreasing the motivation for the takeover bid; since directors owe a duty only to shareholders to maximize the target's interests, there is no need for directors to consider other parties' interests.

This line of argument is known to be the majority position in Germany and the minority position in the US courts.[4]

C. Compromise Thesis

Under this view, directors in general are to remain passive in the face of hostile takeovers but may engage in defensive actions such as persuading shareholders or arranging for a public offering as long as they do not preclude or impede shareholders from making decisions.[5]

D. Conclusion

Where management engages in takeover defenses, there is the issue of shareholder discrimination in that they may act friendlily towards the existing controlling shareholder while behaving antagonistically with respect to the bidder. Furthermore, considering that a takeover bid is essentially a dispute between shareholders, one may wonder if the reasonable thing for directors to do in a takeover situation is to keep neutral.

However, since a director, as an appointee of the target, owes fiduciary duties thereto, it seems reasonable to argue that a director may undertake takeover defenses if he reasonably determines that such actions are necessary to protect the target's interests.[6] For example, assuming that a certain bidder's goal is to sell off the assets of the target and dissolve it, if the director reasonably determines that the long-term business outlook is good and that the target's business will improve if operations are maintained so as to increase shareholder wealth, then it would be reasonable to engage in takeover defenses. In light of a director's fiduciary duties, it may even be argued that such actions are required by law. In a lower-court case where the directors of a company undertook a large-scale capital increase with consideration to defend against a hostile takeover bid,[7] the court

---

4 Hong Chul Lee, "Defense Measures against Hostile M&A of Listed Companies," Various Issues related to Securities Transactions, Supreme Court Library of Korea, pg. 452.

5 *Id.*

6 Wook Rae Lee, *supra* n.3, pg. 13, is in agreement.

7 Suwon District Court, Yeoju Branch Court, 2003 Kahap 369 (Dec. 12, 2003).

ruled that "the question of whether such action is permissible must take into account the totality of circumstances, including the motivation or purpose behind the defense and the reasonableness of the defense tactics, and must also consider the interests of the target and the shareholders that are being protected by such actions as well as the adequacy of the procedures by which such actions are implemented." This ruling seems to be recognizing that the determination of whether takeover defenses undertaken by a director are permissible rests on how "fiduciary duty" is interpreted.

When considering the above, the issuance of new shares by a director as a takeover defense does not appear to be forbidden for the reason that it violates a director's duty to keep neutral or loyal. However, the determination of whether such issuance is permitted does appear to require a case-by-case assessment of whether applicable provisions under relevant laws such as the Commercial Code and FSCMA have been observed. We discuss this in detail below.

III. LEGALITY OF THIRD-PARTY ALLOCATION OF NEW SHARES AS A TAKEOVER DEFENSE

Allocating new shares to shareholders in proportion to their shareholdings is called a "shareholder offering" and any other method of allocating new shares is generally referred to as a "third-party allocation." This allocation can be divided into two types: private offering to designated third parties and public offering to non-designees undertaken pursuant to applicable provisions under the FSCMA. Each of these has a different legal basis for issuance and we discuss them in turn.

A. Private offering

1. Interpretation of Article 418 Paragraph 2 of the Commercial Code

Article 418 Paragraph 2 of the Commercial Code ("Clause") states that "a company may, notwithstanding Paragraph 1, allocate shares to persons other than shareholders in accordance with the articles of incorporation; provided, however, that such allocation shall be limited to situations where it is necessary to achieve the managerial goals of the company, including introduction of new technologies or improvement of financial structure." This provision was introduced when the Commercial Code was amended on July 24, 2001. Before such amendment, the Commercial Code simply read that "unless provided for otherwise in the articles of incorporation, a shareholder shall be entitled to receive new shares in proportion to its shareholding."

However, numerous legal commentaries had argued that even before the above amendment, in addition to applicable provisions under the articles of incorporation, requirements similar to those contained in the proviso of the Clause ("Proviso") had *de facto* been applicable to third-party allocations.[8] It was in acceptance of such argument that the Clause was created at the time of the Commercial Code's amendment on July 24, 2001.

Thus, if the strengthening of control in a takeover situation does not fall within the "managerial goals" provided under the Clause, then we would have to conclude that third-party allocation of new shares as a takeover defense is not permitted.

2. Legal commentaries and court rulings

Examples of "managerial goals" that legal commentaries have propounded (other than the introduction new technology and improvement of financial structure specified under the Commercial Code) have been limited to those necessary for the business operations of a company, including: expeditious capital raising,[9] corporate restructuring, joint venture or strategic partnership with foreign companies,[10] injection of foreign capital, securing of upstream/downstream markets and any other goals in furtherance of its development and which cannot be obtained through a shareholder offering.[11] Therefore, it appears that legal commentaries do not find the "managerial goals" under the Proviso to include the defense and strengthening of control by controlling shareholders or the maintaining of existing management. In particular, some legal commentaries have expressly stated that, irrespective of "managerial goals," preemptive rights cannot be restricted for the purpose of expelling a particular shareholder or wresting control away from another party.[12]

---

8 Joo Chan Son, Dong Yoon Jung (editor), Jong Joon Song (writer), Annotated Commercial Code (Corporations III), Korea Commercial Law Administrative Society, 2003, pgs. 450–451; Ki Soo Lee, Corporate Law, Pakyoungsa, 1997, pg. 502; Tae Ro Lee, Chul Song Lee, Lectures on Corporate Law, Pakyoungsa, 1992, pgs. 632–634; Dong Seung Lee, "Study on Preemptive Rights of Shareholders – Focus on Exclusion Factors," Ph.D. Thesis for Korea University, 1998, pgs. 243–245; Joon Sub Lee, "Exclusion of Preemptive Rights of Shareholders," Study on Commercial Law, Vol. 13, 1994, pgs. 228–230, etc.

9 Dong Yoon Jeong, Corporate Law, Bubmoonsa, 2003, pg. 504.

10 Ki Bum Kwon, Modern Theory on Corporate Law, Samjiwon, 2005, pg. 801.

11 Chul Song Lee, Lectures on Corporate Law, 2006, pg. 694.

12 Dong Yoon Jeong, *supra* n. 9, pg. 504; Joo Chan Son, Dong Yoon Jung (editor), Jong Joon Song (writer), *supra* n. 1, pg. 451.

Courts in general appear to hold the same position as the above legal commentators. One Supreme Court ruling held that in the face of an imminent or actual battle for corporate control, the issuance of convertible bonds for the sole purpose of causing or impeding a change of control can constitute a cause for nullification.[13] In another case of dispute for corporate control, the court held that the third-party allocation of shares, despite the absence of any real managerial need to deprive the shareholders of their preemptive rights (and whose main purpose was to serve as a takeover defense), was null and void.[14] Another court dealing with a similar case stated that preemptive rights serve to help existing shareholders maintain their control over the company in a takeover situation, thus in order for the company to undertake a third-party allocation at the expense of preemptive rights, the purpose for raising capital thereby must coincide with the company's interests and the necessity to quickly and flexibly raise funds to meet such purpose at the exclusion of preemptive rights must be established. If a third-party allocation by a company were to result in the substantial weakening of the existing shareholders' control over it, then such allocation would be valid only if there existed a managerial need that rendered it imperative to preclude preemptive rights even before the conclusion of a corporate control dispute. This last court decision[15] appears to make it all the more clear what the general position of the courts is.

However, in the corporate control dispute case between KCC and Hyundai Group where Hyundai Elevator tried a public offering of "Kukmin" shares,[16] the court held that where "maintaining the control of the existing shareholders or the management powers of the existing management serves the interests of the target and general shareholders or is warranted by a special social necessity, and where the opinion of general shareholders and neutral experts on the issuance of new shares has been heard", then such issuance may be necessary to meet a "managerial goal" under the Clause. This ruling is different from the conclusions reached by the aforesaid courts and it almost appears as if in certain circumstances defending against a takeover may fall under the "managerial goal" of the

---

13 Supreme Court, 2000 Da 37326 (Jun. 25, 2004). Although this decision is in regards to the issuance of convertible shares of Samsung Electronics, since Article 513 Paragraph 3 of the Commercial Code provides for the application of the Proviso for the issuance of convertible bonds, it can be argued that the logic behind issuing convertible bonds applies equally to the issuance of new shares.

14 Seoul Central District Court, 2005 Gahap 71241 (Jul. 7, 2006).

15 Seoul Central District Court, 2005 Kahap 744 (May 13, 2005).

16 Suwon District Court, Yeoju Branch Court, 2003 Kahap 369 (Dec. 12, 2003).

Clause. However, this judicial position is very uncommon, and considering that the Supreme Court ruling and lower court opinions in the above paragraph have all been issued after this rare decision, it seems safe to say that the court's stance is that defending against takeover bids does not fall under the "managerial goal" of the Clause.

3. Subconclusion

As seen above, it appears that legal commentators and the courts are in agreement that, in a hostile takeover situation, issuing new shares to the controlling shareholder or a white knight friendly thereto violates the Clause and is thus not permitted.

In particular, considering the ruling in case no. 2005 Kahap 744, Seoul Central District Court (May 13, 2005) which held that even where the managerial need to undertake a third-party allocation is recognized, such issuance is illegal unless it can be established that there existed circumstances that made it impossible to delay such issuance until after the conclusion of the dispute for corporate control, the position of the courts on this matter seems very clear. In practice, the courts seem to prohibit third-party allocation of shares in hostile takeover cases without exception.

B. Public Offering

1. Issue

A public offering differs from a private offering in two major ways.

First, in contrast to a private offering, in a public offering it is not determined in advance who will participate in the capital increase to become a shareholder and so the issuance of new shares by itself does not immediately render to a particular third party the effect of a change in control.

Secondly, Article 165-6 of the FSCMA (Article 189-3 of the abolished SEA), which permits a listed company to undertake a public offering, does not provide for compliance with the Clause and so it is unclear whether the "managerial goal" requirement for third-party allocation as discussed above is applicable to a public offering.

Should a large-scale public offering take place, the equity of the existing shareholders would be substantially diluted and although this would not lead to a particular third party acquiring control over the company, it would have the effect of causing loss of control by the controlling shareholder. As such, in the case where the shares acquired by the bidders already exceed the equity interest of the controlling shareholder, the existing management would try for share dilution through a public offering instead of a private offering (which would most likely be forbidden), and if the public offering succeeds, then control over the company will ultimately be decided through a proxy contest. This renders a public offering a meaningful takeover defense.

2. Legal commentaries and court rulings

Legal commentators agree that the Proviso applies to public offerings[17] and there do not appear to be any opposing views in this regard.

The basis for this position is that the nature of preemptive rights is such that they cannot be arbitrarily restricted by majority vote, and only where the interests of the company or all of the shareholders are served should they be limited.[18]

The only case precedent on this issue seems to be the court decision in the aforesaid dispute between KCC and Hyundai Group (Suwon District Court, Yeoju Branch Court, case no. 2003 Kahap 369, December 12, 2003). In this case, the court stated that the legislative history behind the FSCMA's providing for public offerings by listed companies, indicated the goal to achieve the division of ownership and management by encouraging and inducing the widespread ownership of shares. Also, public offerings were made available to listed and registered companies to enable expeditious and efficient capital raising. Considering the above, the court held that it was difficult to find the Clause as being more than a standard by which to determine whether the issuance of new shares was abused and to find that it was directly applicable. Thus, the court ruled that the Clause does not apply to public offerings.[19]

---

[17] Hyun Tae Kim, Yong Joon Yoon, "Study on Practical Issues Regarding Preliminary Injunctions against the Issuance of New Shares," Hwa Jin Kim, Ok Ryeol Song (editors), Hostile Takeovers and Defenses, 2007, pgs. 109–110; "Study on the Propriety of Issuing Securities as a Defense in a Hostile Takeover," Masters Thesis for Seoul National University, 1998, pgs. 51–53; Ki Bum Kwon, *supra* n.10, pg. 800; Choong Myung Jeong, "Legal Study on Hostile Takeover Defenses – Focus on Third Party Allocation of Shares," Study Materials on Administration of Justice, Vol. 25, 1999, Supreme Court Library of Korea, pgs 433–434; Eung Jin Kim, "Study on Restrictions on Shareholder Preemptive Rights," Masters Thesis for University of Seoul, 2004, pgs. 42–43.

[18] Tae Ro Lee, Chul Song Lee, *supra* n.8, pg. 633.

[19] Article 9 Paragraph 2 of the articles of incorporation of Hyundai Elevator provided that "new shares may be allocated to non-shareholders by a board resolution under the following subparagraphs where it is necessary to achieve the managerial goals of the company, including introduction of new technologies or improvement of financial structure," and Subparagraph 2 of the same Paragraph specified "issuance of new shares through a public offering in accordance with the provisions of the SEA." The court interpreted the above to mean that the necessity to achieve managerial such as the introduction of new technologies or

3. Subconclusion

Although the rationale behind the above ruling is unclear, it appears that the court took into account the fact that Article 84-5 Paragraph 1 of the Enforcement Decree of the SEA (currently Article 176-8 Paragraph 1 of the FSCMA) defines "public offerings" as excluding preemptive rights and as having unspecified masses subscribe to new shares and that the SEA (currently FSCMA) is considered a special law of the Commercial Code.

However, considering the factors listed below, the Proviso should apply to public offerings as legal commentaries argue.

First, public offerings were introduced on January 13, 1997 when the SEA was amended (the same provisions are incorporated in the FSCMA) and the Clause was newly created when the Commercial Code was amended on July 24, 2001. As discussed in Section III.A.1 above, most legal commentators recognized that even before such amendment of the Commercial Code certain requirements needed to be met in order to preclude preemptive rights, and such views were incorporated to create the Clause. To the extent that public offerings are a way of increasing capital at the exclusion of preemptive rights, considering the purpose of the Commercial Code amendment, it appears reasonable to conclude that public offerings should also meet the requirements under the Commercial Code.[20]

Also, the reason that the FSCMA (now-abolished SEA) is generally seen as a special law of the Commercial Code is because it provides for special provisions regarding listed companies, and where restrictions in addition to those under the Commercial Code are to be applied to listed companies, such special provisions are then applicable. It is in this sense that the FSCMA (now-abolished SEA) takes on the form of a special law, and it is not the case that whenever a matter is addressed by both the FSCMA (now-abolished SEA) and the Commercial Code, the former prevails.[21] Therefore, arguing that the FSCMA (now abolished SEA), which

---

improvement of financial structure applied to public offerings and prohibited the issuance of new shares.

20 Hyun Tae Kim, Yong Joon Yoon, *supra* n.17, pg. 112.

21 For example, with respect to the relationship between Article 366 of the Commercial Code, which requires minority shareholders to hold 3 percent or more shares in order to demand the convocation of a meeting of shareholders, and Article 191-13 Paragraph 5 of the SEA (currently Article 542-6 Paragraph 1 of the FSCMA), which requires a 3 percent or 1.5 percent shareholding (depending on the size of the company) for the same, the Supreme Court (2003 Da 41715, Dec. 10, 2004) has ruled that since the above SEA provision cannot be seen as a special law of the Commercial Code, a shareholder that meets either of the above requirements may demand the convocation of a meeting of shareholders.

provides for public offerings, is a special law and thus the Clause should not be applicable, seems to be a logical leap.

Finally, the reasonable conclusion from a practical perspective also seems to be that the Proviso is applicable to public offerings. For public offerings, all that is prescribed by law is the minimum issuing price and the board is free to decide the issuance price, number of shares and disposal of forfeited stocks. Therefore, if the board sets a high issuing price and undertakes a massive public offering so as to induce a large number of forfeited shares, the board would be able to dispose of such shares at its discretion. The effect would be to allow the new shares to be allocated to specified third parties in circumvention of the Clause, which clearly contravenes the legislative purpose behind promulgating it.

As such, it seems reasonable to conclude that the Proviso is applicable to public offerings, thus they should be treated the same way as private offerings. Some legal commentaries argue that the Clause embodies requirements recognized under German law, i.e. principles of equal treatment of shareholders and benefit to the company, and that the former does not have any significant implications in a public offering which involves numerous unspecified persons. Similarly, with respect to the latter, in the absence of any special purpose of the public offering such as a change in or maintenance of control, its scale is not large and issuance is at near-market price, it is recognized not to pose a problem.[22] Based on this rationale, these legal commentaries argue the Proviso requirements are presumed to be met in public offerings.[23]

However, as discussed earlier, the fact that there is a high risk of a public offering circumventing the Clause appears to render it dangerous to presume that the Proviso requirements are satisfied in public offerings. It seems that even in this case a strict assessment should be made as to whether the Proviso requirements are actually met.[24]

C. Third-party Allocation through Contribution in Kind

1. Legal commentaries and case rulings

Two opposing views are held on this matter. One view argues that since a contribution in kind is a means of receiving a third-party allocation, there must be a basis therefore provided under the articles of incorporation in accordance with the Clause or a special shareholder resolution (which

---

22 Dong Seung Lee, *supra* n.8, pg. 222.
23 Choong Myung Jeong, *supra* n.17, pg. 434.
24 Hyun Tae Kim, Yong Joon Yoon, *supra* n.17, pg. 114.

has the same effect).[25] The other view argues that a contribution in kind is an exception to preemptive rights, thus it is permitted through a board resolution pursuant to Article 416 Paragraph 4 of the Commercial Code without any basis in the articles of incorporation.[26] These two views are pitted against each other.

In a Supreme Court case, although the main issue was tax-related, the court held that preemptive rights are not applicable to contributions in kind, thus new shares for a contribution in kind can be issued solely based on a board resolution.[27]

Logically speaking, it would be reasonable to state that those who view contributions in kind as a means of a third party allocation, will argue that the Clause applies and those that say contributions in kind are an exception to preemptive rights, will argue that it does not. In reality, it appears that contributions in kind are seen as an exception to preemptive rights but nonetheless are found to be subject to the Proviso requirements.[28] This position seems reasonable when considering that the nature of preemptive rights is such that they cannot be arbitrarily restricted even by majority vote.[29]

2. Restrictions on contributions in kind as a takeover defense

As seen above, even where the Proviso requirements are recognized as being applicable to contributions in kind, since such contributions by nature would most likely be necessary for the company's business operations, it appears that the Proviso requirements would be easily met. If so, when defending against a takeover, would there be any way for a controlling shareholder to prevent the bidder from increasing its equity stake by contributing assets necessary for the operations of the target?

The case that sheds light on this point is the aforementioned 2005 Kahap 744 case. Here, the court held that even if the issuance of new shares is in line with the managerial goals of the company, issuance thereof at the preclusion of preemptive rights before the conclusion of the corporate control dispute would be justified only if there existed

---

25 Chul Song Lee, *supra* n.11, pgs 690–692; Gun Shik Kim, "Contribution in kind and Preemptive Rights," Jurisprudence Vol. 31, Nos. 1–2, 1990, Seoul National University.

26 Gi Won Choi, New Principles of Corporate Law, Pakyoungsa, 2005, pgs 730–731; Ki Bum Kwon, *supra* n.10, pgs. 798–799; Dong Yoon Jeong, *supra* n.20, pgs. 504–505.

27 Supreme Court, 88 Nu 889 (March 14, 1989).

28 Dong Yoon Jeong, *supra* n.9, pgs. 504–505.

29 Hyun Tae Kim, Yong Joon Yoon, *supra* n.17, pg. 127.

managerial needs that made it compelling to do so. The court's point was that, even if the issuance met the Proviso requirements, considering that a corporate control dispute was ongoing, the main purpose of the issuance can be said to have been to defend against the takeover. Thus, unless there is no other justification for the timing of the issuance, then such issuance is unlawful. It appears that this reasoning can be equally applied to issuance of new shares for contributions in kind.[30]

D. Shareholder Offerings

1. Issue

Shareholder offerings grant preemptive rights to shareholders in proportion to their respective shareholdings, thus in principle they do not infringe upon their rights. Also, even if a shareholder waives its preemptive rights, such waiver is of a right already bestowed, thus it can be argued that the disposition thereof by the board is not problematic. However, in reality, in the context of a takeover situation, where a significant number of shareholders waive their preemptive rights and if the board allocates the forfeited shares to a particular third party, then the result would be the same as if a third party allocation occurred. Therefore, even with shareholder offerings, if the board has the power to dispose of forfeited shares and where no restriction is placed thereupon, there is a risk that through the setting of certain prices and number of shares to be issued, the board will be able to induce forfeited shares and thus bring about the same result as a third party allocation. As such, the issue of whether a shareholder offering whose purpose is to bring about a large number of forfeited shares is unfair (and thus should be outlawed) is a very important issue for discussion.

2. Legal commentaries and case rulings

In cases involving shareholder offerings, those seeking a preliminary injunction to prevent such issuance have argued that (1) a large-scale capital increase with consideration is being undertaken in the absence of

---

[30] A same decision was reached by the court in a Seoul Central District Court case (2005 Gahap 71241, July 7, 2006). In this case, the court held that where a third party allocation is undertaken in the special situation of a corporate control dispute in order to bring about a change in control or to impede such change, then even if such issuance conforms in some way with the company's managerial goals, the need to attain such goal will need to be negated and ultimately such issuance of shares will need to be seen as invalid.

any dire and immediate need for funds, (2) the issuing price[31] is high as the discount rate[32] is lower than usual and (3) the share offering aims to induce a large number of forfeited shares by forbidding the transfer of preemptive rights and allowing the board to dispose of forfeited shares, the result being an infringement of shareholder rights.

In response, the courts have rejected most of the above claims, stating that (1) the need for a capital increase is a matter that requires a high degree of business judgment and (2) since shareholders' preemptive rights are recognized, the board resolutions themselves cannot be seen as bringing about a change in shareholdings.[33] In particular, in response to the argument that forfeited shares were induced, one ruling stated that "even if the exceedingly high issuance price rendered a large number of forfeited shares, and the disposal thereof was delegated to the board so as to give rise to the possibility that the current management of the debtor will increase the number of friendly shares, if such disposal and the discount rate are determined in accordance with the law and articles of incorporation, it cannot be found that such disposal method is materially unfair."[34] On the other hand, no cases were found in which the court forbade shareholder offerings in the context of a takeover situation.

By contrast, although not a preliminary injunction case to prevent the issuance of new shares, one lower case court[35] held that "an issuance of new shares found to be materially unfair by both legal commentators and the courts is . . . where new shares are intentionally issued at high prices by the board in order to induce a large number of forfeited shares . . . so as to discriminate among shareholders and harm the interests of certain shareholders." This is in direct contrast to the above ruling.

---

31 According to Article 5-18 of the Regulation on Securities Issuance and Disclosure, the base share price for the issuance of new shares is calculated using the higher of (1) the arithmetic average of 1-month average closing price, 1-week average closing price and base date closing price (the base date for third-party allocation being 3 days prior to the subscription date and for a public offering, 5 days prior to the subscription date. The issuing price for a shareholder offering can be freely determined) and (2) the base date closing price.

32 Article 5-18 of the Regulation on Securities Issuance and Disclosure states that base price shall be discounted up to 30 percent for public offerings and up to 10 percent for third-party allocations to set the issuing price.

33 Busan District Court, 2004 Kahap 2046 (Oct. 5, 2004); Seoul Central District Court, 2005 Kahap 2904 (Aug. 25, 2005); Suwon District Court, 2007 Kahap 247 (Jun. 25, 2007); Seoul Central District Court, 2008 Kahap 138 (Jan. 24, 2008); Cheju District Court, 2005 Gahap 1588 (Feb. 16, 2006).

34 Suwon High Court, 2005 Kahap 823 (Nov. 17, 2005).

35 Seoul High Court, 2005 Noh 2371 (May 29, 2007). This is the case sometimes referred to as the "Everland Convertible Bond Issuance Case."

There is also a view among legal commentaries that where share prices are below par value, if new shares are issued at par value or at a price substantially higher than market value so as to induce a large number of forfeited shares, such issuance is materially unfair.[36] No views in opposition to the above were found.

Thus, it appears reasonable to conclude that "the issuance of new shares at exceedingly high prices so as to induce large numbers of forfeited shares" can become the target for a claim to prevent the issuance of new shares.

On the other hand, even if new shares are issued at an adequate price, what happens where too many shares are issued? In this regard, lower courts have held, without exception, that in a shareholder offering the timing and scale of the capital increase requires a high degree of business judgment and so they have denied relief to the plaintiffs. In a case where a shareholder offering was undertaken in the course of a corporate control dispute, one lower court even held that "the argument that there is a problem with the capital procurement for the reason that the capital increase is on a massive scale and there is a short time interval between the disclosure date and record date cannot be a factor in the consideration of whether the issuance of new shares is materially unfair as long as the determination of the scale and timing of the capital increase is in compliance with the provisions of the Commercial Code and articles of incorporation."[37]

3. Subconclusion

As seen above, the position of the courts is to permit shareholder offerings in takeover situations, and they are reluctant to forbid them even in situations where a large number of forfeited shares are induced so as to have an effect similar to a private offering and thus render the result unfair.

However, in some of the aforesaid cases where a claim for a preliminary injunction to prevent the issuance of new shares was denied, the court stated that "there was insufficient evidence to support a finding of inducement of large-scale forfeiture . . .", which also means that if sufficient support had been provided, the court may have granted the injunction.[38] Also, in the aforementioned Everland convertible bond case, the Seoul High Court held that the issuance of new shares by directors with the aim of inducing large-scale forfeiture was materially unfair. Taking these into

---

36 Chul Song Lee, *supra* n.11, pg. 710.
37 Seoul District Court, 99 Kahap 1747 (Jul. 7, 1999).
38 Busan District Court, 2004 Kahap 2046 (Oct. 5, 2004).

account, it would be reasonable to conclude that issuance of new shares at a high price so as to induce forfeited shares and to allocate such shares to particular shareholders is unlawful.

In practice, it is very difficult to establish that shares were issued at a high price for the purpose of inducing forfeiture for the following reason: A listed company conducting a shareholder offering determines the issuing price pursuant to Article 57 of the Regulation on Securities Issuance and Disclosure (a subordinate law under the SEA prior to the promulgation of the FSCMA), whereby it uses the third trading day prior to the subscription date as the base date and takes the arithmetic average of (1) 1-month average closing price, (2) 1-week average closing price and (3) base date closing price. It then compares this calculated number against the base date closing price, takes the lower of the two and applies a 30 percent discount to determine the issuing price.[39] The problem here is that the share price at this point in time is several times higher than usual as it has increased in a short interval due to the takeover bid, so acquiring new shares at the issuing price calculated using the increased share price, is not easy for minority shareholders. This means that even if the issuing price was calculated in accordance with the law, it is likely that a large number of forfeited shares will result.[40] Nonetheless, as discussed above, the courts have held that if the disposition of forfeited shares and discount rate are determined in accordance with the law and articles of incorporation, it is difficult to find that the share issuance is materially unfair.

In addition, in cases where shares are issued at a 30 percent market-price discount (i.e. at a low price) but issuance is on a massive scale so as to induce share forfeitures, the courts have even held that the fact that a massive issuance occurred cannot be considered in the determination of whether the issuance was materially unfair.

Therefore, where a shareholder offering is undertaken in the face of a share price bubble caused by a corporate control dispute, there is the problem that share forfeiture can be induced with relative ease and they can then be allocated to friendly shareholders.

---

[39] Under the FSCMA, the Regulation on Securities Issuance and Disclosure has been amended to do away with the issuing price restrictions in a shareholder offering. This means that now a company undertaking a shareholder offering can set the issuing price at its discretion as long as it is at least equal to par value.

[40] Even if there are no restrictions on the issuing price of shares in a shareholder offering, it appears that listed companies will continue to issue shares either at market price or with a certain percent discount in order to minimize the effect on share price. Therefore, the possibility of mass forfeited shares seems to continue to be significant and so this discussion appears to remain pertinent.

Taking into account the position of the courts, the issuance of new shares as a takeover defense is generally thought to be difficult. However, this is due to the fact that the courts have almost completely forbidden the issuance of new shares to specified third parties, i.e. controlling shareholder or white knight. In fact, with respect to the inducement of forfeited shares through a shareholder offering, the courts have almost always permitted this for the convenient reason that insufficient evidence has been provided. As such, the issuance of new shares as a takeover defense still seems to remain as a viable takeover defense. Personally, my hope is that further study will be conducted regarding the takeover defense of using forfeited shares arising out of a shareholder offering, and also that continuous challenges will be made to the court's prevailing attitude in this regard so as to bring about changes thereto.

IV. COUNTERMEASURES AGAINST THE ISSUANCE OF NEW SHARES AS A TAKEOVER DEFENSE

A. Overview

As discussed in Section III above, issuing new shares to defend against a takeover may be found illegal. So how would the bidder prevent such issuance?

The first countermeasure that can be considered is a preliminary injunction to prevent the issuance ("Preliminary Injunction"). However, if the subscription payment is made and the new shares are issued before filing for such injunction or before the court grants the injunction after the motion is filed, then this would no longer be a viable countermeasure. In this case, one would need to file a motion to provisionally suspend the validity of the issuance ("Provisional Suspension"). These measures are provisional in nature so ultimately the main action would need to be instituted to obtain a final resolution. However, in practice, considering that offensive and defensive measures are quickly instituted in these situations and that the party filing for the above provisional dispositions is usually satisfied with the result thereof, most of the time the main action is not instituted and the dispute typically ends at the provisional stage of litigation. This is the reason why most cases involving a battle for corporate control do not end up at the Supreme Court level and are mostly concluded at the lower courts. In consideration of the above, we limit our discussion below to the legal practice of filing for Preliminary Injunctions and Provisional Suspensions.

B. Preliminary Injunctions

The typical order granting a Preliminary Injunction reads "The issuance of [ ] common stock with par value of [ ], which the debtor is preparing to issue pursuant to the board resolution adopted on [ ], shall be prohibited."[41]

As can be seen above, a Preliminary Injunction case involves several issues.

1. Rights protected by a Preliminary Injunction

Article 424 of the Commercial Code states that where shares are issued (1) in violation of law or the articles of incorporation or (2) in a severely unfair manner so as to harm shareholder interests, shareholders may demand the issuing company to desist from such issuance ("Share Injunctive Right").

Therefore, generally speaking, the Share Injunctive Right is the right being protected by the Preliminary Injunction. Looking at each type of issuance of new shares discussed above, it could be argued that (1) a private offering infringes upon shareholders' preemptive rights and is thus in violation of law and the articles of incorporation, (2) a public offering and contribution in kind can either constitute an issuance in violation of law or a materially unfair issuance and (3) a shareholder offering is a materially unfair issuance.

On the other hand, there is a question of whether, in addition to the Share Injunctive Right, the right of shareholders to demand a director to desist from engaging in unlawful acts ("Director Injunctive Right") can constitute a right eligible for protection by a Preliminary Injunction.

The difference between the Director Injunctive Right and Share Injunctive Right is that (1) the former is available only for minority shareholders with an equity stake of 1 percent or more whereas the latter is available for all shareholders, (2) the former deals only with acts in violation of law or the articles of incorporation whereas the latter can, in addition to such violations, be exercised where there is a material unfairness and (3) the former is a public-interest right exercised in the face of irreparable damage to the company whereas the latter is exercised where a shareholder faces the threat of sustaining injury.

There is a view among legal commentaries that rights protected by Preliminary Injunctions include both of the above Injunctive Rights,[42] and

---

[41] Court Practice Manual, Execution of Civil Affairs IV, pg. 359.

[42] Gi Won Choi, *supra* n.26, pg. 780; Dong Yoon Jeong, *supra* n.9, pg. 528; Joo Chan Son, Dong Yoon Jung (editor), Jong Joon Song (writer), *supra* n.1, pg. 503, etc.

there do not appear to be any opinions that expressly oppose it. However, my personal view is that, to the extent that the issuance of new shares causes an increase of capital in a company, the issue concerned is the infringement of shareholder rights and it cannot be said that a company sustains irreparable damage. Therefore, I have doubts as to whether Director Injunctive Rights should be something that can be protected by a Preliminary Injunction.

2. Timing of filing for the Preliminary Injunction and duration of prohibition

Where payment for subscription of the new shares has occurred before a motion is filed for a Preliminary Injunction or before the court renders its decision in response thereto,[43] then a subsequent grant of the Preliminary Injunction has no effect upon the share acquirer.[44] Thus, it is common sense that the filing should be made prior to the issuance of new shares. The problem is that with unlisted companies often shareholders do not know whether a board meeting is convened. With listed companies, although the general rule for a third-party allocation is that the subscription payment can be made only after a securities notification is filed and the mandatory waiting period lapses, there is an exception where if the new shares are deposited with the Korea Securities Depository ("KSD") for 1 year, then it is possible to make the subscription payment on the date of the board meeting. Thus, it is very difficult to file for the Preliminary Injunction and obtain a judgment before the new shares are issued.

The above problem would be solved if it is possible to obtain the Preliminary Injunction prior to the convocation of the board meeting, and this seems to be related to the issue of whether there is need for protection under a Preliminary Injunction and whether there exists a right that is eligible for protection by a Preliminary Injunction, i.e. whether there is something against which a Share Injunctive Right can be exercised.

One lower court ruling denied a motion for a Preliminary Injunction, holding that in the absence of a board resolution to issue new shares (which is what was being asked to be prohibited), there is nothing against which to exercise a Share Injunctive Right.[45]

---

43 In the event a claim for a Preliminary Injunction is filed, the FSC restrains the issuance of new shares by not giving effect to the securities report until the court issues its decision. Thus, in contrast to an immediate issuance of shares through deposit, where issuance is sought through the filing of a securities report, actual issuance is difficult while the claim is pending.

44 Court Practice Manual, *supra* n. 41, pg. 358.

45 Busan High Court, 2002 Ra 96 (Jul. 21, 2003).

However, if theoretically there is a probability that an unlawful issuance of new shares will occur, then there should not be any reason not to prohibit it. Further, considering the practical need to ensure the actual efficacy of the Share Injunctive Right, the above ruling seems unfair.

In contrast to the above decision, there has been a lower court ruling prohibiting the issuance of new shares before a scheduled board meeting took place (at which a resolution was to be adopted to that effect)[46] and another court prohibited such issuance for a set period of time even though there was no scheduled board meeting.[47] This decision held that "Until the date that a decision is issued in case no. 2006 Kahap 685, Daejon District Court, Chunahn Branch, (i) debtor [ ] corporation shall not issue any new shares to a third party and (ii) debtors [ ] shall not engage in any acts in furtherance of the issuance of new shares, including voting at the board meeting of debtor [ ] corporation for the third-party offering of new shares."

Considering that in a battle for corporate control, the target may continuously try to issue new shares without any managerial reason, and once new shares are issued it is difficult to deny their validity,[48] it appears reasonable to argue that the law should permit provisional rulings that prohibit the issuance of shares for a set period of time as above. In particular, considering that (1) both Share Injunctive Rights under Article 424 of the Commercial Code and Director Injunctive Rights under Article 402 of the same are generally recognized to be eligible for protection under a Preliminary Injunction, and (2) it is typical for a court granting a Preliminary Injunction to prevent directors from engaging in unlawful acts to set the duration of the prohibition until the date the court ruling is handed down in the main

---

46 In a Daejon District Court case (Chunan Branch Court, 2006 Kahap 671, Oct. 31, 2006), the court ruled that "the issuance of new shares that the respondent is preparing to undertake through a resolution of the meeting of the board scheduled for Nov. 3, 2006 shall be prohibited."

47 Daejon District Court, Chunan Branch Court, 2006 Kahap 696 (Dec. 4, 2006).

48 In a Seoul Central District Court case (2008 Kahap 2561, Aug. 11, 2008) involving a claim for Provisional Suspension, the court held that "in cases such as the present one where the provisional disposition affects the validity of shares already issued by the respondent, the plaintiff obtains relief tantamount to a final relief at the conclusion of the main action whereas the respondent, without having the opportunity to fight the main action, has its issuance of new shares invalidated and so may subsequently face difficulty raising capital. Thus, the Provisional Suspension will be allowed only if the reason to nullify the issuance and the need to suspend its validity without delay through a Provisional Suspension is established at a higher degree than in typical provisional disposition cases."

action,[49] it appears reasonable to argue that a similar period of prohibition should be set in a Preliminary Injunction case.[50]

Before its amendment on December 31, 2004, Article 23 Paragraph 4 of the FSCMA contained a provision forbidding a target to issue new shares during a tender offer. In one case, the bidder, in order to prevent the target from issuing new shares, made an offer for an insignificant amount of shares and set the offer period at 60 days, which was the legal maximum. However, this provision has now been removed from the FSCMA, and so it appears to be even more necessary to permit a provisional disposition to set a fixed period during which to prohibit the issuance of new shares.

C. Provisional Suspension

As seen above, once new shares are issued, a Preliminary Injunction is no longer an adequate defense. In such case, one must file for a Provisional Suspension.

Typically, a court decision granting a Provisional Suspension reads "The validity of the issuance of [ ] new shares with par value of [ ], which the respondent [ ] corporation issued to respondent [ ] pursuant to a resolution adopted at the board meeting on [ ], shall be suspended." The court sometimes adds language prohibiting the exercise of voting rights.

The problem here is that Provisional Suspensions are hardly granted by the courts. In case no. 2008 Kahap 2561, Seoul Central District Court held as follows: "In cases such as the present one where the provisional disposition affects the validity of shares already issued by the respondent, the plaintiff obtains relief tantamount to a final relief at the conclusion of the main action whereas the respondent, without having the opportunity to fight the main action, has its issuance of new shares invalidated and so may subsequently face difficulty raising capital. Thus, the Provisional Suspension will be allowed only if the reason to nullify the issuance and the need to suspend its validity without delay through a Provisional Suspension is established at a higher degree than in typical provisional disposition cases." Also, this ruling seems to have been influenced by a Supreme Court decision[51] that held that, once shares are issued, even if there is no board resolution or there is a defect therein, board resolutions are merely internal decision-making procedures and so do not affect the validity of the new shares.

---

49 Court Practice Manual, *supra* n. 41, pg. 349.

50 Hyun Tae Kim, Yong Joon Yoon, *supra* n. 17, pg. 134.

51 Supreme Court, 2005 Da 77077 (Feb. 22, 2007).

This attitude of the courts seems to be taking into consideration the safety of share transactions as shares, once issued, may have passed through several hands. This is all the more so when considering one ruling by a lower court[52] that granted a Provisional Suspension, which held that "shares issued to the respondent are currently deposited with the Korea Securities Depository, thus temporary invalidation thereof will not affect the safety of transactions."

As mentioned above, in order for a listed company to issue new shares, it must either file a securities report with the Financial Services Commission and wait for a prescribed period to lapse or deposit the shares with the KSD for 1 year (which would enable immediate payment of the subscription price and hence the issuance of the shares). In case of subscribing for shares under the former method, an opponent may file for a Preliminary Injunction during the waiting period for the securities report to become effective, and once such filing is made the FSC will not give effect to the securities report until the court's ruling is handed down. Therefore, the opponent would be able to obtain a court judgment. In the case of subscribing for shares under the latter method, it would be difficult to file for a Preliminary Injunction if the subscription payment is immediately made through the KSD-deposit method, but the likelihood of obtaining a Provisional Suspension in this case seems higher compared to where the same relief is sought with respect to new shares that are not deposited with the KSD.

V. CONCLUSION

Previously, takeover defenses were undertaken in the form of issuing new shares (or convertible bonds) to the controlling shareholder or a white knight. In response, the courts prohibited such issuance almost without exception for the reason that it infringed upon shareholders' preemptive rights.

Attempts have been made to change the way the takeover defense of issuing new shares is used so it is not conspicuous but at least from the outside it appears not to infringe upon shareholder rights. The first of such attempts was the public offering of Hyundai Elevator in the takeover dispute between KCC and Hyundai Group. Although the court ultimately forbade this attempt, the reason therefore was not because of infringement upon shareholder rights but rather due to the interpretation of provisions

52 Seoul Central District Court, 2005 Kahap 744 (May 13, 2005).

in Hyundai Elevator's articles of incorporation regarding the requirements for a public offering. Considering that most listed companies, unlike the articles of incorporation of Hyundai Elevator, do not restrict public offerings to be conducted only to meet managerial goals, this issue continues to be open to interpretation.

Recently, more drastic attempts have been made in the form of shareholder offerings. In the situation where there is a share price bubble caused by the takeover dispute, the target issues a massive number of shares at a price calculated using the inflated share price as the base, the aim being to induce a large number of forfeited shares. In theory, legal commentators and the courts seem to agree to some extent that this type of issuance is materially unfair. In practice, however, if a motion is filed for a Preliminary Injunction, the courts have almost always denied it, stating that there was insufficient evidence to support a finding that the forfeited shares were induced.

This is currently a problem with the practice of the courts. Considering that there have been cases of abuse where shareholder offerings are used to induce forfeited shares so as to enable their allocation to specified shareholders, the hope is that further study will be conducted on this issue and that the courts' practice will change in this regard.

Index